Create
Your Own
Blog

TRIS HUSSEY

SAMS   800 East 96th Street, Indianapolis, Indiana 46240

Create Your Own Blog: 6 Easy Projects to Start Blogging Like a Pro

ISBN-13: 978-0-672-33065-0
ISBN-10: 0-672-33065-2

Library of Congress Cataloging-in-Publication Data is on file.

Printed in the United States of America

Second Printing July 2011

Trademarks

All terms mentioned in this book that are known to be trademarks or service marks have been appropriately capitalized. Sams Publishing cannot attest to the accuracy of this information. Use of a term in this book should not be regarded as affecting the validity of any trademark or service mark.

Warning and Disclaimer

Every effort has been made to make this book as complete and as accurate as possible, but no warranty or fitness is implied. The information provided is on an "as is" basis. The author and the publisher shall have neither liability nor responsibility to any person or entity with respect to any loss or damages arising from the information contained in this book.

Bulk Sales

Sams Publishing offers excellent discounts on this book when ordered in quantity for bulk purchases or special sales. For more information, please contact

U.S. Corporate and Government Sales
1-800-382-3419
corpsales@pearsontechgroup.com

For sales outside of the U.S., please contact

International Sales
international@pearson.com

Associate Publisher
Greg Wiegand

Acquisitions Editor
Michelle Newcomb

Development Editor
Todd Brakke

Managing Editor
Kristy Hart

Project Editor
Andy Beaster

Copy Editor
Kelly Maish

Indexer
Cheryl Lenser

Proofreader
Dan Knott

Technical Editor
Paul Chaney

Publishing Coordinator
Cindy Teeters

Designer
Gary Adair

Compositor
Gloria Schurick

Contents at a Glance

Table of Contents

About the Author

This is the first book from **Tris Hussey**, a long-time technologist, blogger, and writer, who started off as an academic and found tech support much more to his liking. After picking up blogging on a whim in 2004, he quickly became both a professional blogger and a leading expert in business blogging. He has been a part of several Web 2.0 startups from blogging software to blogging agencies and continues to write, blog, teach, and consult.

In addition to providing workshops and speaking at conferences, Tris also teaches social media, blogging, podcasting, and WordPress at the University of British Columbia, British Columbia Institute of Technology, and Capilano University.

Tris lives and works in beautiful Vancouver, British Columbia.

Dedication

For my Dad who always told me to read the manuals.

Acknowledgments

This book couldn't have happened without the help, direction, and prodding of many, many people. Thanks to Paul Chaney for believing in me that I could do this book and letting the publisher know this. The whole editorial team at Pearson, especially my editors Michelle Newcomb and Todd Brakke, for being so patient with a new author. Rob Cottingham of Social Signals for the cartoon at the beginning of Chapter 5. My friends and family for inspiring and supporting me while I've been writing this book. Most importantly, my beloved Sheila for supporting me and believing in me through this whole process.

We Want to Hear from You!

As the reader of this book, *you* are our most important critic and commentator. We value your opinion and want to know what we're doing right, what we could do better, what areas you'd like to see us publish in, and any other words of wisdom you're willing to pass our way.

You can email or write me directly to let me know what you did or didn't like about this book—as well as what we can do to make our books stronger.

Please note that I cannot help you with technical problems related to the topic of this book, and that due to the high volume of mail I receive, I might not be able to reply to every message.

When you write, please be sure to include this book's title and author as well as your name and phone or email address. I will carefully review your comments and share them with the author and editors who worked on the book.

E-mail: consumer@samspublishing.com

Mail: Greg Wiegand
            Associate Publisher
            Sams Publishing
            800 East 96th Street
            Indianapolis, IN 46240 USA

Reader Services

Visit our website and register this book at informit.com/register for convenient access to any updates, downloads, or errata that might be available for this book.

It's All about Storytelling

Welcome to my book, pull up a chair, get a drink, and let me tell you some stories. Now, before you put this book down, shaking your head, let me explain what I mean. Blogging is about storytelling. Regardless of the technology, the topic, the style, or any of that, it's about telling a great story. Blogging is about having a platform to express yourself. It's a place to let your expertise and passion show through. I've written this book to help you do just that.

Over the past four years, I've taught hundreds of people how to blog. I've led blogging 101 classes in person and online. I've guest lectured on the future of blogging and taught continuing education courses on multimedia and creating their own websites using blogs. If there is one thing that people figure out as soon as I start talking—*I love what I do*. Everyday I sit back, think, and read what the news of the day is, and then my job is to tell the world what I think. Dream job? Yeah, I'd say so.

So I wrote this book to help everyone I can to use technology to make his or her own soapbox on the Internet. While reading this book, I want you to laugh, cry, smile, and get excited. I write like I blog—I feel so sorry for my editors—and I blog like I talk. I hope you enjoy this book and, if you don't, I hope you leave me a comment on the book's blog: www.sixbloggingprojects.com.

Wait, You're a Professional Blogger?

Well, I wasn't a professional at *first*, but I became one eventually. However, like many of you reading this book, I started blogging on a whim. I said to myself one afternoon, feeling rather dissatisfied with my job as a market researcher, that if I wanted to revive my Internet consulting practice, I should "learn about this blogging thing." Yep, that's pretty much exactly what I thought—a whim, a "gee this could be fun" idea that turned into something that I love *and* I get paid to do.

I wasn't always a blogger, of course. After finishing graduate school, I started out in the working world running a lab at Duke University. Yep, I'm a science geek. I've always been interested in computers (a rather handy skill when pretty much all the instruments and even microscopes were computer controlled) and worked in the campus computer lab in college helping people with their computer questions. (No, I never managed to get a date helping all those cute girls with their questions.)

After a short while as a lab geek, and realizing that at 25 I had maxed out my career potential, I left academia to go back to the front lines of tech support. This might not have been glamorous, but I was good at it, and it had lots of fun moments. This was also a watershed job because it was at that job where I learned HTML and how to develop websites. That was about twelve years ago.

When I started blogging in 2004, I did it to learn about this new medium and have a place to express myself. As it happens, that's pretty much why and how blogging started in the first place—more on that later. Back in 2004, most people had their blogs on Blogger, so that's where I started out, too.

Because the blogosphere was a smaller place back then, it didn't take too long to get noticed, and by the end of the year I was being paid to write posts on other people's blogs. In

2004 this was a daring thing. There were a good number of people very much against the idea of people getting paid to blog, much less post on other people's blogs. I was one of the first people in Canada to do this and one of only a handful doing it in *the world*.

If I thought 2004 was a whirlwind in blogging, 2005 blew it away. That year professional blogging took off—like a rocket. Businesses started blogging with blogging conferences. I started to make a name for myself with "live blogging" sessions at conferences. I had some of my first sponsorships and was regularly speaking and teaching about blogging. It was nothing short of mind boggling (or maybe mind "blogging").

Now in 2009, we speak more about "social media" than blogging. Social networking sites like Facebook and Twitter have exploded onto the scene and now we're "tweeting" what we're doing and creating "lifestreams." Am I still blogging? You bet. I might consider it more "writing" or being a new media journalist, but I'm still blogging and helping more and more people and companies blog.

I'm writing this book to share my experiences, tips, tricks, and even spin a yarn or two with you. By the end of this book, I hope that you will be starting off blogging. Yes. Really. By the time you've put this book down, you will know enough to start your own blog and how to structure it to suit your niche.

How to Use This Book

I've written this book so that chapters 1–3 give you the tools to start blogging, but the rest of the book is tailored to what kind of blog you want to write. For example, if you want to start a blog for your business you might want to

skip from Chapter 3, "Writing and Creating a Conversation," to Chapter 6, "Creating a Business Blog," because Chapter 6 is all about setting up a blog for your business. I've taken the basics from the first three chapters and tailored them and expanded on them to make them relevant to a business blogger. What about the rest of the book? Well I have a secret for you, it's really hard to draw a line in the sand between a "business" blog and a "personal" blog or a portfolio blog. They are all very closely related, so although you may only want to create a personal blog, flipping to the chapter on podcasting or lifestreaming will give you a deeper knowledge of blogging overall.

Think of this book like a blog cookbook. I'm going to give you a tour of the blog kitchen in the first three chapters, which show you everything. I might not delve into all the details about some things, but I'll introduce them. Each chapter then is like a recipe for a specific kind of blog. You want a portfolio blog for your paintings? Great, start with these basic components, add some things, remove others, and viola! You have a portfolio blog!

Somewhere along this journey together you're going to wonder what my favorite blogging engine is and whether I have a bias towards it. I'm going to answer simply and openly (like a good blogger should, by the way)—yes and yes. My blog engine of choice is WordPress, and yes because it's my preferred engine I have a bias towards it. That said, I've tried and used many different engines and know one thing for certain, all of them do at least one thing well: create content.

As I take you through the various types of blogs covered in this cookbook, I'll note whether one engine is better than another for one type of blog. Even though I really like WordPress and know the people who developed it, this doesn't mean I don't see its flaws and ignore the strengths of the other engines. In fact, it's because I've used all the engines that I am friends with the developers—I give them the straight deal and honest feedback.

Throughout the book, I include various informative elements, like Sidebars and Idea Galleries, that elaborate on or complement the current topic. There are also the following types of helpful asides:

TIP

Tips with valuable information I've gleaned from years of being a pro blogger. Essentially the stuff I wish I knew when I started.

NOTE

Notes that might be a little "Did you know..." or something to watch for when you're working on something. Like, did you know the creator of WordPress, Matt Mullenweg, wasn't even 20 years old when he released the first version?

CAUTION

This is code for "a mistake I've made in the past, so don't do it!" Things like: When someone says "backup your database files like this before proceeding..." It's a good idea to listen.

NEW TERM

Sometimes in the text you'll see a new piece of jargon that is bolded. When you see that, you'll see an accompanying New Term element like this one that explains what it means.

If I were teaching this book as a class, I'd answer questions as I go along. Unfortunately this isn't a live class so the best I'm going to be able to do is direct you to the book's blog where you can post questions in the forum. Also, because the Internet is a fluid place, check the blog—www.sixbloggingprojects.com— for updates since this book was published. By the time this book hits the shelves, there will be several updates to plug-ins and even blog engines themselves. Although these updates won't change the mechanics of how you blog or set up a blog, they are helpful pieces of information (and will explain if a screenshot doesn't match 100% what you're seeing on screen).

Ready? Let's get down to brass tacks in Chapter 1, "Welcome to the Blogosphere: Planning Your First Blog."

CHAPTER 1

Welcome to the Blogosphere: Planning Your First Blog

A Brief History of Blogging

Believe it or not, blogging has been around for over ten years—this is an eternity in the tech world. Remember that the computer mouse and the Internet are only 40 years old, which makes them ancient technologies in comparison. Yes, contrary to what the mainstream media (MSM) says, this *isn't* a new fad from the geek set. In fact, if you think in terms of people writing in journals and recording their thoughts, the spirit of blogging is centuries old. The difference now is that you can publish these works not only on *paper*, but also *electronically*. Instead of only a few people reading your missives, the world can read them.

When you get right down to it, a blog is simply a website.

Blogging started out with people making public lists of bookmarks and links, mostly for themselves, and putting up a page on their website to display them. New items on the website were added at the top of the screen, which gave us the accepted blogging style of items presented on the page in reverse chronological order. This style helped website visitors easily view new items instead of having to scroll down the page.

In those days, however, blogging *was* the word of geeks. Individuals created their own "blogging engines" to publish their content—certainly not a task for the faint of heart or faint of code. It wasn't until 1999, when the folks at Pyra Labs created the first easy-to-use blogging tool called Blogger, that the world of blogging was able to leave the geek set and start to be used by "normal" people.

FIGURE 1.1

Tanya Davis' blog NetChick.net, Vancouver's longest-running blog.

In 2001, soon after the emergence of Blogger, Ben and Mena Trott started working with something that would become Movable Type. (Later, in 2003, they introduced the Typepad blogging service.) Movable Type was one of the first blog engines you could install yourself. This was necessary to the birth of blogging because now people could not only sign up for a service but also install a stable and extensible blog engine on their own servers. Because there were folks, like me, who quickly outgrew a hosted service (or who wanted to integrate a blog into their existing sites), being able to manually install a blogging engine on any basic blog host was a giant leap forward.

By 2006, you could, in a short amount of time, buy a domain name, get website hosting from the same company, and install a blog. It became so easy that everyone was expected to be blogging. Blogging would be the next great thing in commerce, communication, and technology, saving everyone time and energy. Like nearly all tech pronouncements (like flying cars by the year 2000), blogging hasn't come to pass as it was expected; however, some pretty amazing things have happened along the way, which were not predicted.

FROM A GUESTBOOK TO A BLOG: ONE GAL'S JOURNEY IN BLOGGING

Tanya Davis (also known as NetChick) of the blog, This Chick's Life, has been blogging longer than anyone I know (about ten years) and is Vancouver's longest-publishing blogger. When she started out, she used a guestbook on her website to jot down notes about her day and respond to people's comments on her posts. Like many of the "early bloggers," she didn't think about it as blogging then. That was a term that came later (1999, to be exact).

BLOGOSPHERE TIMELINE

December 1997: Weblog coined as term for online journal "web log"

April–May 1999: Shortened to "blog"

April 1999: LiveJournal born

August 1999: Blogger launched by Pyra Labs

October 2001: Movable Type launched

2001: Drupal to open source

February 2003: Google acquires Blogger

May 2003: WordPress 0.7 released

October 2003: TypePad launched

November 2002: Technorati launched

April–May 2004: Tris starts his first blog

January 2005: LiveJournal purchased by Six Apart

January 2005: *Fortune* names "Eight Bloggers You Shouldn't Ignore"

January 2005: First "Business Blogging Summit"

August 2005: WordPress.com opened to private testing

December 2006: *Time* names "You" person of the year because of rise of blogs

December 2007: Six Apart sells LiveJournal to SUP

December 2007: Movable Type released as open source

The Blog Heard Round the World: Blogging Gets Mainstream Attention

In 2005, Canada hosted its first blogging conference (Northern Voice), and two Blog Business Summits were held in Seattle and San Francisco. Back then, I would sit down at a conference session, fire up my blog editor, and start typing to beat the band. When the session was over, I would take lots of pictures. These were uploaded to the photo-sharing site **Flickr** for all to see. All my posts and pictures were "tagged" with the agreed upon **Technorati** tag for the event. I wasn't the only one doing this either. At any given conference, there might be 10 or more people all doing the same thing at the same time.

NEW TERM

Technorati was launched in November 2002 as an index of the blogosphere. It added identifiers called tags as a way to categorize posts and group them together.

NEW TERM

The Flickr photo-sharing site, born in Vancouver originally as a game, was later purchased by Yahoo and is now the preferred site for bloggers to share their photos.

> **NOTE**
>
> It was important that people all used the same Technorati tag for an event so everyone's content could be searched and found together. Asking "What's the tag for this event?" was like asking where the coffee is at a conference. It was just one of those important things to know.

During this time, people were starting to think there was something to this blogging thing and that money could be made from it. Uh, oh. Blogging "purists" started to get more than a tad antsy at this point. Could you have blogs written by a business? Could people blog for companies they didn't work for? Could a fictional character blog? These were the hot topics of 2005–2006, which caused some heated debates, but in the end, well, we've pretty much all settled down.

Throughout 2005 and into 2006, businesses were told they had to start blogging or they would be left behind. The anecdotal story of Kryptonite locks being picked with a disposable ball-point pen and resulting public relations disasters were proof that social media and blogs were going to be the be all and end all of the marketing world.

In 2006, *Time* magazine declared "You" the people of the year, saying on the cover, "Yes, you. You control the Information Age. Welcome to your world." Bloggers were clamoring for attention and their rightful place as "new media" or "citizen journalists." Also in 2006, CES realized that bloggers couldn't be ignored and started giving them passes. Podtech christened the "Bloghaus" as the hip-cool place to be during CES and now no conference was complete without a "blogger room."

> *With blogs, blogging, and Web 2.0, a lot of technologies were invented, but what individuals were really doing was creating better and better ways for people to connect and communicate.*

In 2007, people started talking about the "blog bubble" and Web 2.0 getting overinflated. There were serious discussions that "blogging was dead" and several a-list bloggers publically gave up blogging (a few "gave up blogging" several times). The blog bubble, if there ever was one, passed but the pragmatists won in the end. Blogging matured into a stable form of online writing and expression. Today not having a blog is like not having a website, which, of course, a blog is anyway.

The Blogosphere's Giant Dysfunctional Family

> *"Social Media is nothing more than what you'd do at a cocktail party...but online. And in your pj's."*
> —*Erin Koteki Vest (Queen of Spain)*

When you talk to a long-time blogger, eventually you'll hear him or her say something like "well that's just the culture of the blogosphere" or "people expect me to tell it like it is…" If there are any hallmarks or uniting principles of the blogosphere, it's openness, honesty, and transparency. There is an expectation, almost demand, that you lay it all out there. Being open, telling it like it is, baring your soul to the world to peer in and judge is what bloggers *expect* a blog post to be like. I honestly don't know how it all started to be like that, but the informal, rapid fire posts that people were writing struck a chord with people. The expectation is a gritty, real, exciting, powerful, emotional post made for great reading, maybe not great analysis, but great reading. Often the grammar and spelling are incorrect, but the stories are so moving or infuriating that you just *have* to comment or write a post of your own.

> ### It is important to read other people's blogs, be inspired by them, link to them, and give them credit.

The culture of the blogosphere is about telling stories, being open and honest, and giving credit where credit is due. Whoa a tech Utopia! Yeah, not so much all of the time. Bloggers have their petty fights and turf wars. It is important to read other people's blogs, be inspired by them, link to them, and give them credit.

Blogs, the Mainstream Media, and Journalism—World Turned Upside Down

I can think of no other field or industry that has been changed more since the advent of blogging than how people create, consume, and disseminate the news. The news had been "revolutionized" when publications started to put articles online, but when bloggers were scooping newspapers, TV, and all other forms of media on breaking stories, the real change began. Suddenly CNN was catching up to bloggers, and they weren't amused. Newspapers were getting railed on for not reporting fast enough and that they were becoming irrelevant in the era of instant news. Bloggers were the new "investigative journalists," except they often only investigated what Google brought to them in search results. They were breaking new ground. They were, well, just mucking things up all over the place and having fun doing it.

The debate isn't over either. Bloggers are often quoted in the news as expert sources. Some bloggers have made the transition to mainstream media and many great journalists are blogging—some very well I must add. Newspapers have blogs for columnists so they can report on news in their area of expertise on the days they don't have a column in print. What's the future then?

In the waning days of 2008, major newspaper and media chains have filed for bankruptcy protection (Tribune Media Group) and reduced home delivery (*Detroit Free Press*). CNN sourced whole shows from bloggers and social media and during the elections of 2008 (not just in the U.S.), blogs and social media played a tremendous role in all facets of the campaigns. It is plain to see that what has happened since 2005 has completely changed how people think about news and information, even if you don't know about blogs or blogging.

The lines aren't getting blurry, they were buffed out and bloggers are drawing new ones. People are going to see some amazing things as print media, online media, and video start to converge from desktops.

Are you excited to get writing yet?

Blogging: Pet Rock or New Foundation?

If you step back and look at what blogging is all about, it's really just a set of technologies that make communicating easier. These technologies have allowed individuals to publish information rapidly. Text, images, video, and audio are so quickly available online that the world can know about an earthquake, tsunami, or disaster within minutes of it happening. That isn't going to change. People expressing themselves online with words, images, and audio, enriching our lives with their stories, knowledge, and opinion won't change either. Neither will how politics and protest are now organized online. That has been changed forever.

NOWPUBLIC TURNS JOURNALISM ON ITS HEAD—WE'RE ALL JOURNALISTS

What about reporting? A few years ago a "citizen journalist" was a nosey person who wrote a lot of letters to the editor. Today, they are bloggers. Once it became apparent that bloggers were just as agile and deft at reporting the news, as any news outlet on the planet, people wanted to leverage that. NowPublic was born in Vancouver to do just that.

Built on an open-source blogging engine, NowPublic made anyone a journalist. A member of the NowPublic site could post text, audio, video, and images of anything he or she thought was news. This is when things started to get hairy. People who have spent their lives being journalists bristled at bloggers calling themselves "online journalists" or "news media journalists." Bloggers didn't generally follow the rules of journalism. They were biased and freely gave their opinion and spin on the news. Bloggers accepted free things from companies to try. Some people were better at disclaiming these potential conflicts of interest than others. But then, as in all things, some bloggers are better citizen journalists than others.

If you step back and look at what blogging is all about, it's really just a set of technologies that make communicating easier.

Blogging, however? Blogging like how I started in 2004, with the blog shown in Figure 1.3, is changing. So I want you to think about self expression and technology as you read this book. If you're writing a personal blog, what do want to tell the world? As a business, what do you want people to know about you? What do you want to know from or about your customers?

I'm going to talk and write about blogging throughout this book, but while I am doing that, I'm also going to paint you a bigger picture. I'm going to show you why, when I

started this book, I started a new blog. I'm going to show you why I have my photography portfolio online and why I encourage professionals like lawyers and writers to have blogs. I'm going to show you how to build and design a blog now that is based not on jargon or the latest thing, but on the essential human fact that individuals like to communicate and share with each other.

Starting Your First Blog

Now that you know a bit about me, the history of blogging, and a touch on where blogging is headed, let's dig into the meat of things and get going. There are only four things that you need to think about when you're starting a blog and once you've set up one blog; the last step becomes second nature.

FIGURE 1.3

My blog circa August, 2004. Stop laughing it was state-of-the-art for the time.

► What are you going to write about?

► What are you going to call your blog?

► Which blog engine will you choose?

► Who are you going to write as?

I'm going to introduce you to thinking about your blog's topic here, but will cover that and writing good blog posts, in Chapter 3, "Writing and Creating a Conversation." We'll wrap up this chapter with what to name your blog, and then Chapter 2, "Installing and Setting Up Your First Blog," is dedicated to getting your blog up and running.

Choosing a Topic for Your Blog

This is one of the most important steps for starting your blog. If your answer is "I don't know, I just want to blog," stop now and think it through for a minute. What do you do for a living? What are your hobbies? What are your passions in life? No matter what you might be thinking, all of those are interesting and great topics for blogs. I've started blogs on cooking, fountain pens, coffee, technology, photography, business blogging, and even men's grooming. I haven't kept all of them up and some have died slow and painful deaths, but they were fun and, yes, people did read them. No matter what you might think, there is an audience for almost any topic you can write about. I'll add a note of caution here: Don't write for readers. Don't write for traffic. Write for you. I didn't start writing to be famous or get a book deal. I wrote because I had opinions I wanted to share and nowhere else to do it.

If you want to write about knitting beanies for baby bunnies, more power to you. Just do it.

When my friends have told me they wanted to blog, I always start with that question: What

are you going to write about? Actually, often I start with saying "you should have a blog about that…" because I can see the passion in their eyes when they talk about it. I see how excited it makes them to delve into the minutia of a topic. Those people always make great bloggers. Blogging is about passion and storytelling. You can learn storytelling, but passion? You either have it or you don't.

Another great way to find a good topic for your blog is finding a gap in the information you can find online about that topic. Say you have a particular medical condition, writing about your trials and tribulations can be very therapeutic, but you also have an opportunity to education others about the condition. A friend of mine's husband contracted MRSA (Methicillin-resistant Staphylococcus aureus) and started a blog talking about it, how to prevent it, and current treatments. That blog and her other blogs on health and beauty became a career for her. Just like I found that few men were writing about men's grooming (like shaving, hair products, and skin care) so I started a blog about it, and it became very successful very quickly. I took advantage of an opportunity to write about something I liked and that no one else was really talking about.

NOTE

This isn't to say that writing about your life or technology or crafts isn't a good topic. Those are, in fact, *fantastic* topics because while other people might be writing about them, none of them are writing with *your unique perspective*. No matter what anyone else might say or tell you, everyone has a story to be told and, frankly, having a blog is the best way I know to tell your story—to the whole world.

What's in a Name: Picking a Name for Your Blog

Picking a name for your blog sometimes just comes to you. Mine has always been "A View from the Isle" in some fashion or another. When I started blogging, I lived on Salt Spring *Island*, BC, followed by Pender *Island*, and Victoria, BC. Luckily Victoria is on Vancouver *Island*, which while huge, is still an island. Now I live in Vancouver and that's not an island at all. I'm stuck with the name, so oh well.

Lots of people use their online moniker like "QueenofSpain" from earlier in this chapter (see Figure 1.4). Other people have a fun name, but use their name for the domain name of the blog. Regardless of what you choose, put some thought into it.

NOTE

Try to think long term with the name of your blog. My blog makes a specific geographic reference (being on an island), which doesn't fit with where I live any longer. Something that specific might not be the best choice for the long term.

First, is the name long or hard to spell? If you put it all together as a domain name, does it spell something you'd rather it didn't? (Don't laugh. Several companies have made this mistake.)

FIGURE 1.4
Queen of Spain Blog by Erin Koteki Vest.

Here's my history (and this is *not* the best way to pick a name, by the way). My consulting company's name was Larix Consulting, so I had larixconsulting.com. This makes sense because a company should try to own a domain as close as it can to its real-world name. As you can figure out, my website's URL was www.larixconsulting.com and my blog became blog.larixconsulting.com. So, people typed blog.larixconsulting.com into their browser to get to my blog, which I called "A View from the Isle." I soon realized that my blog was becoming my calling card because it hosted the best examples of my work. I ditched my old website and went forward with just the blog alone.

Eventually, I dropped larixconsulting.com as my primary URL in 2008 because I found that, regardless of what my business name was, it was *my* name that had become paramount. This wasn't ego as much as branding, not to mention I was tired of spelling "larix" for people. (You get bonus points if you know what "Larix" refers to.) As you can see, you can have a domain that people will recognize (trishussey.com) and a blog that maintains a sense of branding. I could have also bought aviewfromtheisle.com and used that all along (it would have been smart to do that), or do both.

Here is what I'd suggest that you do. Start with a clever name for your blog. Got it? Awesome. Go to a domain registrar like NameCheap.com and see whether it is available as a domain name (see Figure 1.5). Yes? Super, buy it. No? What about your own name? This is a bit of a long shot for most people, but try it. Keep working at it.

TOP 10 WORST DOMAIN NAMES FOUND BY INDEPENDENT SOURCES

Who Represents—www.whorepresents.com

Experts Exchange—www.expertsexchange.com

Pen Island—www.penisland.net

Therapist Finder—www.therapistfinder.com

Italian Power Generator—www.powergenitalia.com

Mole Station Native Nursery—www.molestationnursery.com

www.ipanywhere.com

www.speedofart.com

Lake Tahoe—www.gotahoe.com

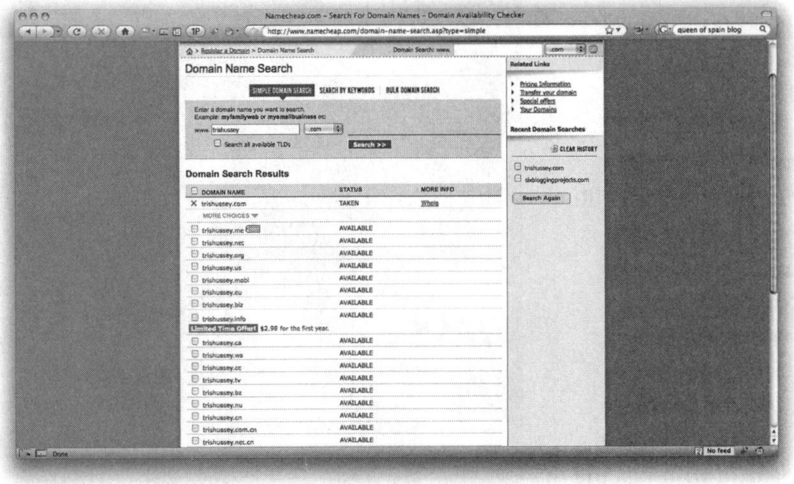

FIGURE 1.5
Basic domain name
search at
NameCheap.com.

NEW TERM

A domain registrar is the site/service where you "buy" your domain name. Buy is in quotes because when you register a domain name you, typically, have to renew the registration in a year. So maybe "rent" or "lease" is a better term.

Here are some of the blogs who I think have great names and URLs:

- ► Lifehacker.com
- ► AskDaveTaylor.com
- ► Technosailor.com (Technosailor is the author's nickname, sailing the seas of technology)
- ► DrinksAfterDark.com (I came up with the name)
- ► Miss604.com
- ► GlobalNerdy.com
- ► DoItMyselfBlog.com
- ► Copyblogger.com
- ► Digital-Photography-School.com

TIP

You're probably wondering why I'm suggesting you buy a domain name when you might start out with a service like Blogger or WordPress.com, which give you a domain name without a fee. Well, while not free, for just $10 a year, you can reserve that namespace for yourself. More to the point, this plans ahead so that if you start with myreallycoolblog.wordpress.com you can switch to myreallycoolblog.com if you want to later. This is just insurance. You don't have to buy the domain, but I think it's a really good idea.

Notice the domains and blog names I've listed previously. You can probably guess what the blog is about, can't you? This isn't an accident. Another important consideration in choosing a name is search engine optimization (SEO). The previous domains use the keywords I want the search engines to index. Keyword rich names don't have to be long, and they can be clever; it just takes a little more effort to get just the right name.

If you're talking about knitting, writing, painting, or collecting action figures, the name should reflect that. Hold on, you're saying, I don't really *care* about SEO, I'm just doing this for fun. I know, but it's just like buying a domain name ahead of time. It's about planning ahead. Many of my friends started blogging for fun or just to test it out or someone said "here, start a blog" and then found themselves suddenly popular. They're people who are now sought out as consultants and speakers. However, their blogs have some goofy, off-the-cuff name, or they didn't buy the domain when they should have. The blog is now "stuck" at .blogspot.com or .wordpress.com, and they can't move it now because of the links to that URL. Moving to a domain of their own would break all the links to the old blog, or at least you'd have to keep redirecting people from your "old" blog to your "new" blog.

Yes, redirecting people is technically easy, but it's like riding a bike uphill—once you have momentum, you want to keep it. Stopping in the middle of the hill to change to a "better bike" might be a good idea, but you are going to lose all the momentum you built up with the previous one. That momentum is all the SEO value you've built up, all the links, and all the branding.

At least by buying the domain and thinking about SEO early, you're just being prudent. You're planning ahead.

How are you doing on that name?

Remember:

- Think about what you are going to blog about
- Think catchy
- Think about branding
- Think about if it spells something you don't intend.

I'm going to get a little more into the choosing of a domain name now by dispelling a couple of myths first. One, all the good domain names aren't gone. There are lots of great names, you just might need to be a little more clever about it. Two, the TLD (top level domain like .com, .net, and .org) does matter, but you don't need to buy all the variations of your domain name unless you are a business or organization. Personally I try to buy a .com domain first. If I can't get my first choice of .com, I might explore variations of the name before I try adding a "-" to the name (like manscaping-101.com). If all else fails, I'll look for a .ca (I'm Canadian after all, so I can do that) or a .net. I'm not a fan of the .org, .me, or .info. Avoid .info like the plague. Yes, it makes a lot of sense to have knittingpatterns.info, but the problem is that (at the time I'm writing this book) the majority of .info domains are spam sites and the search engines are blocking them from their indices. Getting indexed by Google with a .info domain isn't worth the hassle when you can opt for a good .com, .org, or .net in the first place.

Getting indexed by Google with a .info domain isn't worth the hassle when you can opt for a good .com, .org, or .net in the first place.

What about the other domains like .tv? If you are doing a video blog, sure grab it, but .tv domains are *much* more expensive than a regular domain (it is the country code for Tuvalu like .us is for the U.S. or .ca for Canada). Unless you're reading this and really planning to make a go of it online, hold off for now. Buy an inexpensive domain, maybe two, and leave it at that.

Summary

By now you are well on your way to having a blog. I know it still seems early, but just that first idea of "I could write about…" is all it usually takes to get someone going down the blogging path.

With a short history of blogging in your head, I hope you understand how *rapidly* everything changed for blogs and bloggers. Blogging went from a niche thing that geeks did to something every company had to have almost overnight. While it is safe to call blogs mainstream now, the sense of what a blog is has changed and matured to a point where I think most people surfing the Internet don't realize or think they are looking at a blog; it just looks like a website to them. Honestly, I'm pretty happy about that because the days of considering blogs as some strange and unique part of the Internet was getting tiresome.

We're ready now to make the next jump setting up your first blog. Chapter 2 is probably the most techie and geeky chapter in the whole book. Don't worry though, you can take it slow, nothing is all that complicated. If you get stuck, well help is only just a few clicks away on the book's blog: www.sixbloggingprojects. com.

CHAPTER 2

Installing and Setting Up Your First Blog

Choosing a Blog Engine

This is the geekiest section of the book. Don't be scared. While I am fluent in geek, I also speak regular human as well. I'm going to make this as jargon free as possible. No, there won't be a quiz at the end. I begin with the decisions about which blog platform to use and where your blog will "live" and then get into the tweaking and tuning part. Think of this as first choosing between Ford, Toyota, or GM, then picking what kind of car, and then adding the options. Start with the big picture and work down.

First, decide whether to start a hosted blog or do it yourself (self hosted). What this boils down to is who is responsible for setting up, installing, and maintaining the "backend" of your blog. The backend of your blog is not where all your bad ideas go, it's the files, settings, and databases that make it work. When your blog is hosted, making sure stuff works and generally keeping the lights on is someone else's problem. If you can't get into your blog to post, you have someone else to scream at. When you have a self hosted blog, it's *mostly* just the opposite. While you'll probably have to do the installation and database setup yourself, making sure the server (the big computer) is running and working is the responsibility of the web host.

I've done both hosted and self-hosted blogs, and I prefer to host the blogs myself. I have more control and I can play around with new technologies as they come out. That said, if you don't like having to mess around with FTP, updates, and so on, then hosted is what's right for you.

TIP

Don't rule out a self-hosted blog because you don't think you're "techie" enough. Many web hosts automate the most technical aspects of hosting for you!

Hosted

There are three kinds of hosted blog solutions: free, paid, and "freemium." Freemium is a bit of an odd duck in the Internet world, but I'll get to that in a moment. Remember, with the hosted model you're trading flexibility for having less to worry about. This is not a bad thing. I used hosted systems for years and only made the switch to self-hosted/DIY recently. The following are some of the hosted platforms of which you might have heard:

- ► Blogger
- ► TypePad
- ► Livejournal
- ► MySpace
- ► WordPress.com (the .com is important here)

There are certainly more than these few, but these are also the "big players" in the market. These are the blog hosts that have the best infrastructure and would be least likely to have problems with uptime (that is to say, working). Will they give you the best support? That is a completely different question and one that often depends on the individual.

Let's get into the three types of hosted blog solutions. Free solutions are, as you might guess, free. Because nothing is ever really free in this world, your blog is generally supported by ads around your content that the blog host owns and runs. Running the ads helps them recoup the cost of the servers, people, and such that keep the proverbial lights on and the blogs running. Yes, if you have an incredibly popular blog, you are potentially making a lot of money for the host. Consider this as the cost of having a free blog. MySpace and Livejournal are the two solutions that have the most ads around the content. Blogger, owned by Google, generally doesn't put ads around your blog, just a navigation bar to guide you to the next related blog. On Blogger you can put your own ads on your blog to earn money from it. On MySpace and Livejournal, you are much more restricted as to what you can do.

CAUTION

Read the terms of service (TOS) carefully when you sign up for any free service! Sometimes you are restricted to the kinds of topics or things you can do with your blog.

Generally, free solutions don't let you have or use your own domain name for your blog. If you use your own domain with Blogger, you honestly might as well go self-hosted. With free services, your domain name is something like myawesomeblog.blogspot.com (if you are using Blogger). Is not controlling the domain *really* a bad thing? Yes and no. Having your own domain name gives you more legitimacy and a professional touch. It looks like you're taking your site seriously. There is some debate about the search engine benefits of having your own domain versus .blogspot.com, but I think that can be overcome with simple **search engine optimization** (SEO) techniques. So why go free?

NEW TERM

SEO is a process by which you attempt to improve your site's traffic by optimizing its content so that it's more likely to appear higher in the results a search engine generates.

Frankly, free is a great way to start out. There is no monetary risk to it. You can practice and experiment, getting a good feel for blogging, before committing to something larger. I have free blogs set up for teaching or when I want to have an anonymous blog to experiment with different writing styles. Before you stop reading and go sign up, I have to give you the "but…" part of having a free blog: You don't own the URL.

If you'd like to just learn and experiment a bit or even do some anonymous blogging, go with free. Just keep in mind that if your "experiment" starts getting some attention, you should think about switching to something else. In the free category, I suggest Blogger over Livejournal or MySpace, unless you're a teenager or band. Livejournal and MySpace aren't considered very professional nor are they taken seriously within the blogging crowd. From Blogger, shown in Figure 2.1, you can "easily" move to another blog platform or even have a hybrid solution where you have a blog on your own domain, but run by Blogger.

TIP

If this blog is for your band, then you should have a MySpace page. MySpace is still the leading blogging platform within the music world.

FIGURE 2.1
Many aspiring bloggers find that Blogger.com offers the best balance of free and freedom.

There is a step between free and paid that I do recommend and that is "freemium." Freemium means that you can sign up for a service, in this case a blog with no fee, but if you pay a fee (generally reasonable) you get more features. In the blog world, the stand-out leader is WordPress.com (see Figure 2.2). I'll let you know right now that I know and am friends with the key people at WordPress.com/Automattic (in other words, "yes, I might be biased") and think that not only is the service awesome, but the people are, too.

FIGURE 2.2
Wordpress.com home-page where you can sign up and can explore other wordpress.com-based blogs.

With WordPress.com you can sign up for a blog and have myawesomeblog.wordpress.com. Later, if you decide that you want to have myawesomeblog.com, just pay a small fee to map that domain to that blog. Done like dinner. All the links to the old blog work, but they just point to the new location. This is the best of both worlds. If you decide that you'd like to have more control over your blog or if you have already used domain mapping for WordPress.com, you can switch to your own host without worry or penalty.

Although WordPress.com is better than a purely free host, they do have some of the same limitations. You have a limited number of theme choices on WordPress.com, though the number of choices is extensive as far as hosted services go. You also cannot put advertising of your own on your blog or use all of the widgets that people add to their blogs (more on this later).

Moving on to the "paid" group, the leader of the pack is TypePad (see Figure 2.3). (Again, I know the people there at TypePad/MovableType.) TypePad is purely paid (after a free trial) with differing cost levels related to the number of features you want to access. The basic service gives you myawsomeblog.typepad.com moving up to using your own domain, adding more blogs, more authors, and more design control. Some pay services give you a one-price-fits-all model where you get everything for one price. I think that is a good choice if you are pretty sure about what you want and what you're willing to pay, but if you're not, the flexibility of a service like TypePad is invaluable.

Which should you choose? My recommendation is the freemium model as used by WordPress.com. You can start out free and move up as you're reading. If you want to go self-hosted in the future, then you have a clear upgrade path. I don't see the pure free hosts being worth your time, and I am hard-pressed to recommend TypePad for the first timer. TypePad is a great blogging engine and one of the most popular online. It is stable, secure,

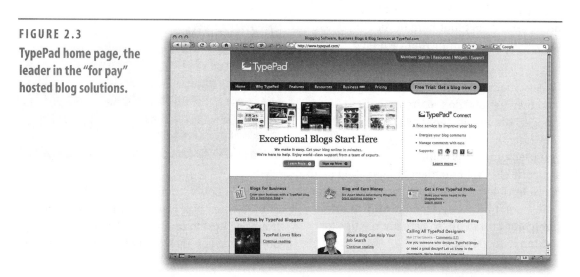

FIGURE 2.3

TypePad home page, the leader in the "for pay" hosted blog solutions.

and efficient. Personally, though, the configuration and system for changing templates drives me crazy. Yes, it's a personal thing, but because I've tried just about all the blogging engines around, I have a basis for comparison. If you want to go free, go WordPress.com.

> **TIP**
>
> Don't take my word for it! Try all the engines in this section and see which you like the best. Even with TypePad you get 30 days for free.

Self-Hosted

Self-hosted is the way to go if you want to have control over all aspects of your blog or if you already have a website (and therefore a host).

When you host your own blog, the hosting provider is responsible for making sure the server is running, configured, and secure. You are responsible for installing, configuring, and maintaining your website or blog. It can be challenging at first, if this is an entirely new experience for you. After you get your feet under you, it isn't that hard or that big a deal to install and maintain your own blog,

Picking a good web host; you'd think it would be easy, right? Just ask your geekiest friends who they use and do the same. Yeah, except bloggers all use different hosts, and overall they hate them all. No matter which web host you use, someone is going to love them and someone else will hate them. I have used great hosts, terrible hosts, and mediocre hosts in the past. I don't have any brand loyalty to any particular host at all, so here are my tips for picking a good host:

▶ Ask your geek friends who their preferred hosts are. Just don't be surprised if you get conflicting answers about the same host. Geeks are like that. Sorry.

▶ It's not always about money. Yes, I try to get the best deal I can when I pick a new host, but cheapest isn't always best. Look for the features you need (more on features later in this chapter).

▶ Look for discounts for paying for months or a year at once.

▶ Look at their support area (if it's open to the public). See whether the forums and FAQs (Frequently Asked Questions) seem helpful. These are your first line of support when you have a question, so they need to be good.

▶ Make sure you'll have room to grow. You'll start off with a "shared hosting account," which means lots of sites are going to be running off the same physical server. If your blog starts to get bigger, make sure you can upgrade to more storage space, bandwidth, or even a **dedicated server** without hassle.

> **NEW TERM**
>
> A dedicated server is where you have an entire server (the whole computer) to yourself. This gives you more flexibility if you want to run specialized software for your site, but also more responsibility if something goes wrong (often you have to fix the problem yourself).

Without a doubt, there is always a bit of a leap of faith when you pick a web host. Moving from one host to another isn't a fun thing to do. What if you pick a bad host? How will you know?

Ultimately you'll know good hosts from bad because your blog will be unavailable often or your host does charming things like shutting down your blog with no warning because it is "using too many server resources." Yeah, that one is no fun. If you run into problems, don't jump ship right away. Give the host (and your trusty geeky friends) a chance to fix it. If it happens once, cool, stick with it, but if it happens a couple more times, start shopping around for a new host.

Moving to a new host is beyond the scope of this book, so I'll give you the best piece of tech advice you'll ever get: Geeks love baked goods, chocolate, and coffee. Yes, geeks can be bribed. Asking a geek friend for help and bringing a treat for him or her with you... yeah you're in good hands. This is why you'll never see a "please don't feed the geeks" sign in a tech company. Oh and for the record: Chocolate chip cookies, dark chocolate, and strong coffee with cream.

TIP

Finding helpful geeks is as easy as going where they are! Search the Internet for blogging and tech meet ups or groups in your area. Events like Barcamps, Democamps, and local conferences are great places to meet all kinds of helpful, friendly, neighborhood geeks.

FEATURES TO LOOK FOR WHEN SHOPPING FOR A HOST

When I'm looking for a web host these are the things I look for:

- 1–2 gigabytes (GB) of disk space (often listed as 1000-2000 megabytes or MB)
- 500–1000 GB transfer limit (how much data is transferred from the host over the Internet)
- Unlimited Add-on domains and sub-domains
- Unlimited MySQL databases
- Cpanel with Fantastico De Lux support

My preference is also to choose a UNIX or Linux based host over a Windows-based host. I've found that WordPress and other blog engines work better on UNIX hosts than Windows hosts. UNIX hosts are also most likely to have all the prerequisites for installing WordPress by default.

Getting Started

By now you should have a good idea of whether you're going to use a hosted blog solution or self-hosted. Let's crank that geek-o-meter up a couple notches and get you set up with your blogging platform.

In the interests of keeping this simple, I've decided to take you through the setup of both a hosted WordPress.com blog and a self-hosted WordPress blog (via WordPress.org). For simplicity's sake, I need to pick just one platform to use for this book and I've gone with WordPress because I think it's the best overall choice if you're learning all this from square one. I've used almost all of the blog engines out there, and WordPress (WP) is the one I always come back to.

> **NOTE**
>
> If you've already decided to use one of the other options, don't worry. In terms of getting your blog set up, some of the details and visuals will differ from what I show here, but you should find enough parallels here to guide you.

In the end, all the major blogging engines do the same basic things. The content is stored in a database, and the layout is in a template. The differences come in with how easy the administration part (aka the backend) is to navigate, how flexible it is, and how easy it is to grow with you. Posting is very easy in all the platforms, so that I'm taking out of the mix right now.

Signing Up for a Hosted Blog

Signing up for a blog on WordPress.com is fast and easy. From the time you get to the WordPress.com homepage to when you can put up your first post should be less than five minutes. When you sign up for a blog you can pick just a username or a username with a blog. The key here is that for most people the username they choose and the blog name/URL are the same. Something like billswoodshop would be billswoodshop.wordpress.com. You can get just a username (like trishussey) and then set up a blog to go with that name that is different than your username.

> **NOTE**
>
> WordPress.com and WordPress.org are related but very different sites. WordPress.com is where you sign up for a free, hosted blog. WordPress.org is where you download all the files to install WordPress on your own server.

Confused yet? I know it seems rather odd doesn't it? Let's look at the process step by step.

First, go to WordPress.com (this is different than WordPress.org) and follow the link to sign up. You'll get a screen to pick a username and URL for your blog. This is a relatively important decision. You might go with something like kristieskurtains.wordpress.com or autobodycentral.wordpress.com both are good and both are descriptive. As a business blogger, you will want to tie your business name to the blog. Regardless of everything else, it's only this choice (username/blog URL) that's set in stone during this process. The blog name and administrator email address can be changed later, so don't stress over these. Do make sure that the

FIGURE 2.4

Signing up for a
WordPress.com blog.

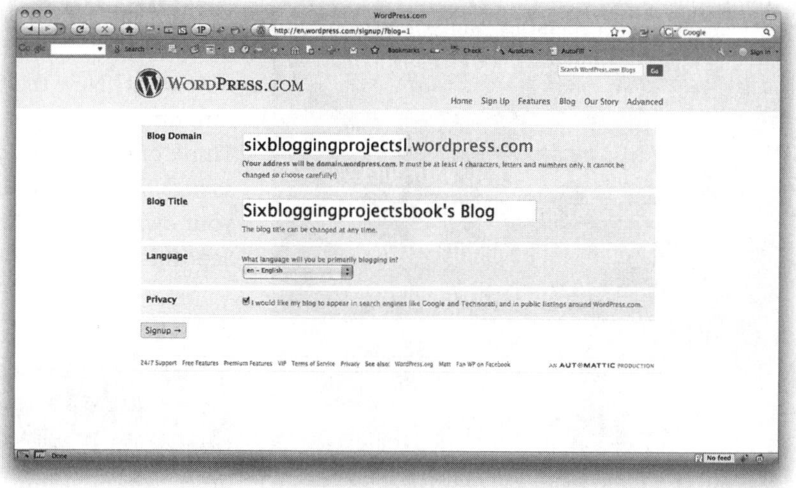

email address you enter works, because your blog won't be activated until you click a link in a confirmation email.

Second, oh wait there really isn't a second step because after you've clicked the activation link you're ready to start posting.

This is the great thing about using a hosted blog service like WordPress.com. Once you've gone through the set up process, which is usually just one form, you're done. Yes, you should do some tweaking, pick a spiffy theme, and maybe add some nice widgets, but as far as posting, you're done. We'll walk through the major sections of WordPress.com to get you familiar with them in Tweaking Your Blog's Setup later in the chapter.

Remember, if you choose to go the hosted route make sure that you can move or upgrade to be able to use your own domain in the future. I would venture that you own the domain name for your business already. I would also venture that you might want to pay the small additional amount to use your own domain with your WordPress.com blog. Strategically using your own domain name ensures that you own your "name space" online and would have the greatest influence on searches for your business name.

Several times a month, a high-profile blog is hacked by someone and the results are predictably catastrophic. What can you do to protect your own blog?

- ▶ Besides keeping your install up to date (which is much easier now with automatic upgrades and Fantastico installs)
- ▶ Change your default admin password
- ▶ Create a *new* account with administration privileges, then disable the default admin account (in WordPress you set its role to "none").
- ▶ Create a good, strong password that is not a word or name and contains a couple of numbers or characters in it (for example, ! or @).

Just the step of creating a new administrator account can foil basic hacking attempts, but if creating a new account seems daunting, changing the admin password, especially if you were emailed a default one, is essential.

Setting Up a Self-Hosted Blog

Okay you have a domain, you have a host, now what? Now the fun stuff begins. Yes, this is fun, and yes I do get out often, thank you. Think of it this way, you are about to *create something all your own*. You are carving out your own piece of the Internet. Yours, all yours. See? It is fun.

NOTE

Because of the sheer number of hosting options and flavors out there, I'm going to try to keep this as general as I can, but still give you a decent roadmap to follow.

Setting Up Your Domain Name to Work with Your Web Host

Before you can get your blog up and running, make sure that your host and your domain are matched up to work together. This is about a 6 on the geek-o-meter; don't worry, it's not bad. When you signed up for your new host, you probably were asked whether you have a domain to use with it. Hopefully your answer is yes. Often web hosts include "one free domain registration" with a hosting package. This is good, except after the first year, sometimes their renewal fees can be steep. A domain should cost you about $10 a year. If the host is going to charge you $15 in your second year, don't bother with the "free" domain.

After you tell the host in the sign-up process that myawesomeblog.com is what you'll be using, they start the wheels in motion for that to work. Now here is the geeky part—you're going to have to update the **domain name server (DNS)** address for your domain to point to your web host.

NEW TERM

Think of the DNS as a phone book. It matches each name (domain) to a unique number, called an internet protocol (IP) address. For every domain you need a "master" DNS record. This is the place that says "no matter what anyone else says, I'm right and know where this domain lives."

Your host gives you DNS addresses (like ns1.areallyawesomehost.com and ns2.areallyawesomehost.com), and "all" you have to do is go to the website where you registered your domain (your domain registrar), find in your account where you can update the name servers for your domain, and do it. Really the hardest part is finding where your registrar has hidden that function. I almost

always have to hit the help file to find it on a host I'm not familiar with, so don't feel bad if you have to look at the help section or email the registrar's support team. The support team at your registrar will be able to help you make sure that your domain is updated with the right settings.

When you're changing your DNS settings, what you're doing is telling the Internet that your domain's master record can be found at this (new) location. Your host has already edited their DNS server to add your domain and the address of the server where it will be "living." Figure 2.5 shows what it looks like when I update the DNS settings at NameCheap.com. I'm just putting the name server addresses in the boxes and clicking Save. The arcane Internet magic all happens in the background.

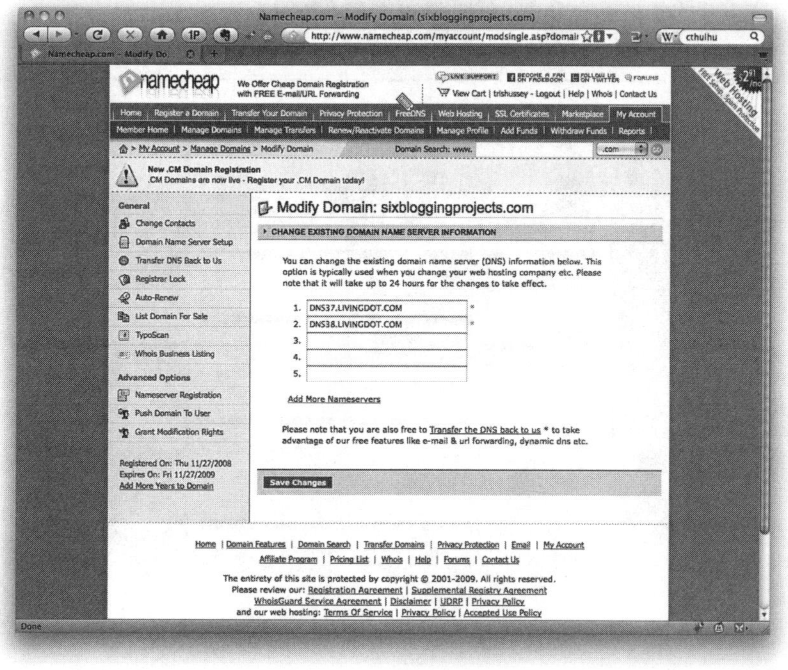

FIGURE 2.5

NameCheap.com's panel for updating my DNS settings for sixbloggingprojects.com.

Once the name servers are updated on your registrar, it takes about a day before that information has propagated around the Internet and you'll be able to get your blog set up. Sometimes I've been lucky and had it all up and working in a few hours, but don't bet on it. Typically the change should be made in about 24 hours. The best way to test if the change has been made throughout the Internet (propagate), is to type your domain name into your browser and see what comes up. If the page is something still from your registrar, it hasn't. If it's the default holding page for your web host, it has. Don't worry, there's plenty to keep you busy in the meantime.

NOTE

DNS records on servers actually look like large spreadsheets. They aren't even very interesting or arcane or even very geeky.

Remember that if your blog is hosted (for example, TypePad, Blogger, and WordPress.com), you don't have anything to install. If you're using your own domain, they help you with the previous DNS steps. Now if you're rockin' it geek style and doing the self-install, let's get to it.

Installing the Blog Software

First, log into your hosting account's cpanel, which is geek parlance for control panel (see Figure 2.6).

Scroll around a bit and look for something called "Fantastico" or "Fantastico De Luxe" (the icon might be a smiley face, as shown in Figure 2.7), and click it. Fantastico is an application that web hosts run on their servers to give you "one-click installs" of popular blog packages, wikis, and other Web 2.0 tools.

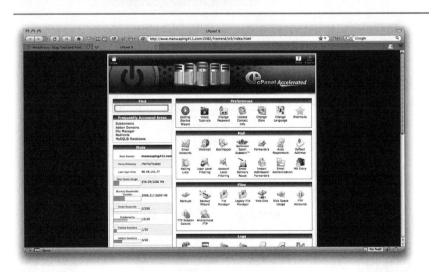

FIGURE 2.6

The Cpanel for the web host where the book's website lives. Cpanel is actually the name of the control panel software, which geeks have always called a cpanel (go figure).

FIGURE 2.7

FIGURE 2.7
**Fantastico De Luxe icon
in my Cpanel window.**

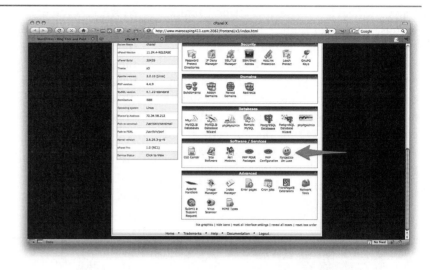

First, click the icon. A new window opens up with the main Fantastico menu. WordPress is listed under "Blogs" in the column on the left slide. Click WordPress, then you will see a link for a "New Installation." Got it? Great, you're almost done. There is one more step and you're done. Fill in the form fields and click "Install WordPress" as shown in Figure 2.8.

FIGURE 2.8
**Typical Fantastico
WordPress install screen
and form fields.**

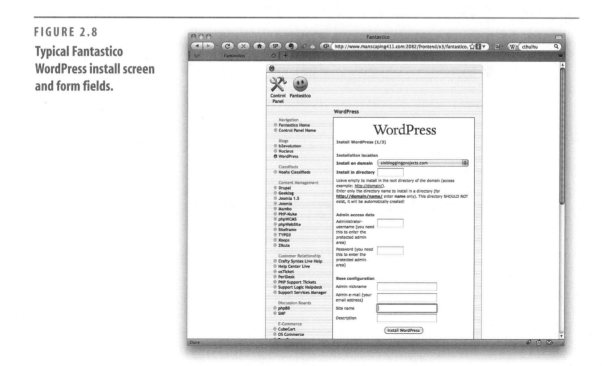

Leave the field for "Install in directory" blank because the default is fine for 95% of people. For the Administrator username I like "Administrator" instead of the standard "admin." By making that username non-standard you're making it just that little bit harder for someone to hack into your website. For the email address, make sure that it is correct; you will need the information that is emailed to you when the install is completed (it will be a backup of the final instructions). While the screen says you are just one-third complete, the next step is just clicking Finish Installation. On the final screen, see Figure 2.9, you will have the login address for your WordPress dashboard, the username (which you filled in already), and password (which, again, you already set).

Congratulations, you have now installed WordPress and have a blog!

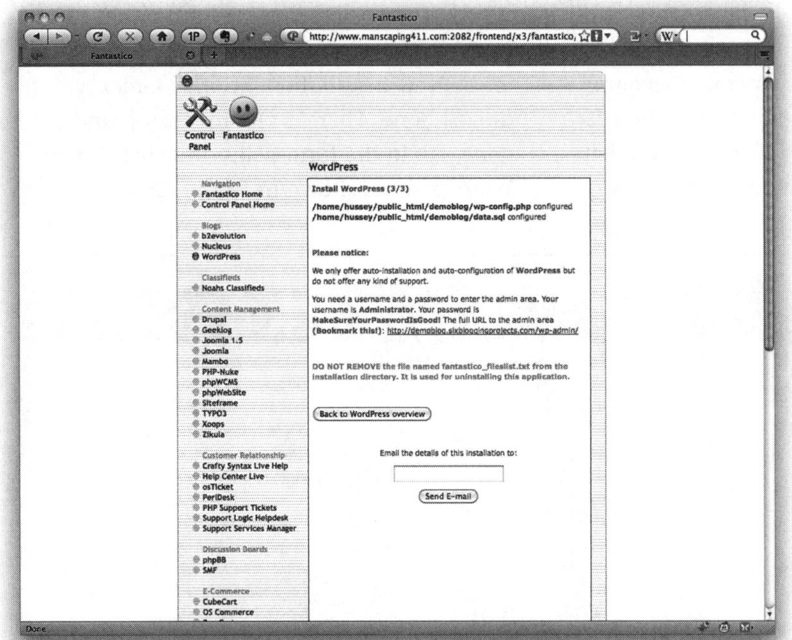

FIGURE 2.9
Final Fantastico screen with the link to your dashboard, username, and password.

That wasn't so bad, was it? Right now you have WordPress installed and ready to go. Sure it's all running default settings and the default theme isn't the most attractive site in the world, but it's *running* (see Figure 2.10). You *could* stop now and blog away, but there's a lot more fun to be had. Let's tweak and tune this baby now. There is going to be a little geekiness, but you can handle it.

FIGURE 2.10

A freshly installed, default WordPress blog ready for blogging.

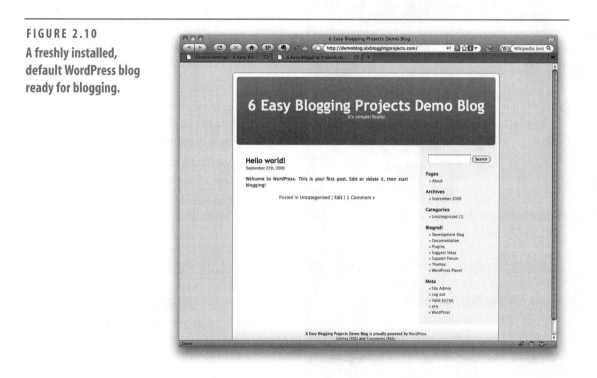

If you didn't want to go with WordPress, another engine, one that isn't listed in Fantastico, or even do a WordPress install completely from scratch, the following are the basic steps to install any blogging engine:

- ▶ Visit the main site for the blogging engine.
- ▶ Download the install package (usually a .zip file).
- ▶ Unzip and read the instructions for installing.
- ▶ Using an FTP program or your host's web-based file manager, upload the files to your hosting account.
- ▶ Set up the database as suggested.
- ▶ Install the engine and test.

What Fantastico does for you is automate this process. The files are already on the server and unpacked when you need them. The databases and configuration files are created and edited as needed. All you have to do is fill in the form: setting the username, password, and administrator's email address (that would be you). Another benefit of Fantastico is that when you need to update/upgrade the install, Fantastico backs up and upgrades everything for you.

Touring Your Blog's Dashboard

The Dashboard is the central hub where you adjust the settings for your blog, write posts, and do other administrative tasks. I'm going to use the dashboard for WordPress 2.8.4 as the example. For other blog engines, or even later versions of WordPress, things might be named differently, but you should be able to follow along.

In Figure 2.11, we have the basic, standard WordPress dashboard. I haven't added anything to it or made changes to it.

Since I will be showing you the various sections of the WordPress administration area as we tweak and tune the blog, I'm not going to show you every screen in the administration section, but I will tell you what each of them do. For the sake of consistency, I'm going to call the sections "blocks" and subsections "tabs." I know they don't look like tabs, but sections doesn't sound right either (and they *used to be* tabs in previous versions of WordPress!).

Content block: Posts, Media, Links, Pages, and Comments

This block deals with all the content on your blog, the posts, static pages, images, links, and comments. All the tabs function very similarly in that when you click the tab you see the most recent items in a table. As you pass your mouse pointer over the title of the post or other content, you see options to edit, delete, view, or in some other way manage that content.

FIGURE 2.11
Standard WordPress
dashboard as you'd see in
almost any WordPress or
WordPress.com blog.

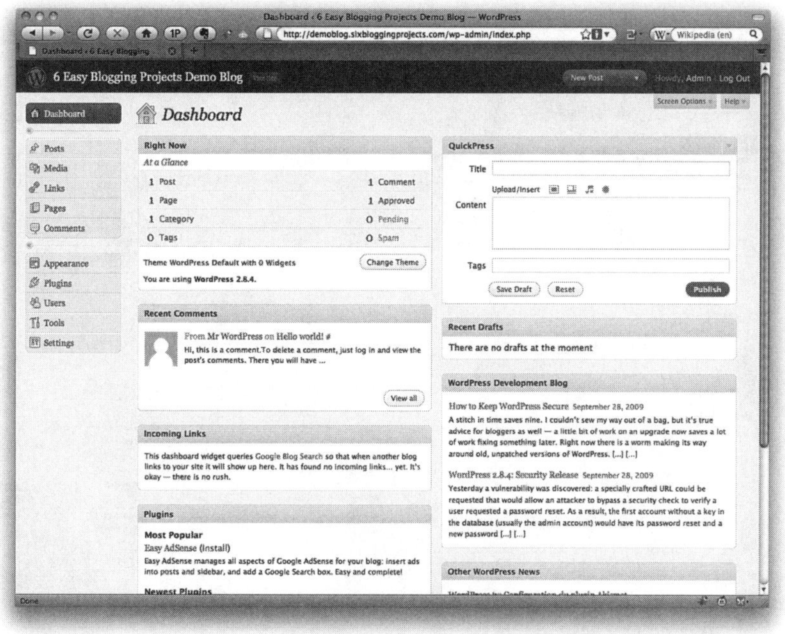

The Posts tab is where you manage the posts on the blog, as well as tags and categories. As you can see from Figure 2.12, when you click posts you see a list of the latest posts, newest first, and can manage these posts (edit, delete view) or create a new one (clicking the "Add New" link).

Clicking "Add New" brings up the post editor, all set to start writing your next brilliant post. Clicking Post Tags or Categories allows you to set the site-wide post tags and categories. I'll talk about tags and categories a little more later in this chapter.

Under the Media tab you have access to all the files you have uploaded through WordPress as well as the ability to upload additional files. This area is handy because as you start to build a library of graphics, you can review the images you have stored and see what might fit into a new post (for example a picture of a person or product).

Under the Links tab you manage your Blogroll. You have a list of current links to other blogs and websites, a link to add more links, and a link to create groups of link categories (for example if you wanted to have a group of writing links and group of graphic design links that you could display separately).

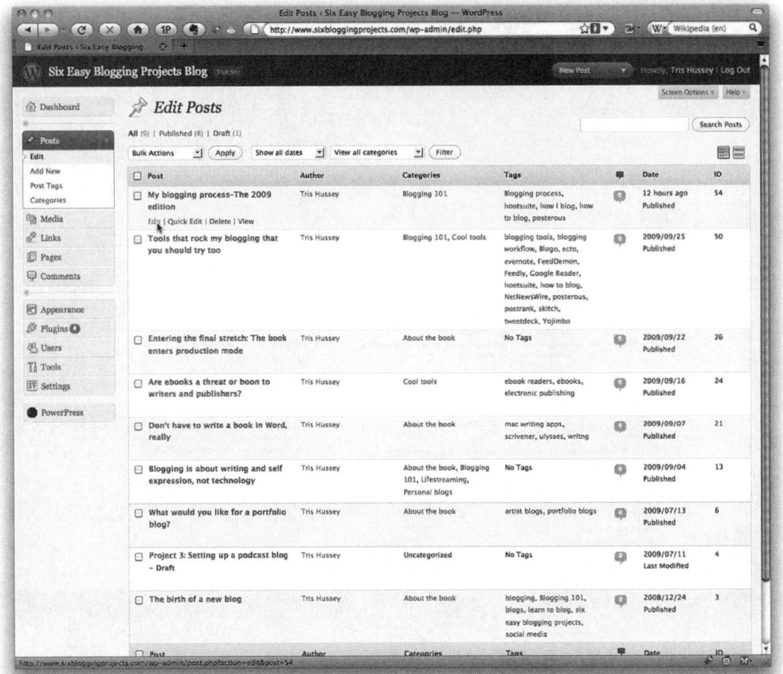

FIGURE 2.12

Posts tab showing the latest posts as well as links to add site-wide tags, categories, and create new posts.

The Pages tab is just like the Posts tab except you only have links to Edit and Add New. I'll be covering the difference between posts and pages in greater detail in Chapter 3, "Writing and Creating a Conversation."

Finally, the Comments tab allows you to edit the comments that come into your blog. You can approve, delete, mark as spam, or even edit the content of the comments here.

Administration Block: Appearance, Plugins, Users, Tools, and Settings

This is the section of the administration part of the blog where you change how it looks, behaves, and who can do what on the blog. The Appearance tab is where you change themes, add new themes, manage your blog widgets, and adjust any settings specific to your theme.

NOTE

Newer themes under WordPress 2.8 and higher have the ability to have their own easy to manage settings. These settings take the place of having to edit the code in the theme itself.

Chances are that once you pick the theme for your blog, get the basic widgets in place, and adjust any theme settings you need you won't be coming back to this tab very often; unless you're like me and like to change your blog template every few weeks just because you can.

Next is the Plugins tab where you manage the various plugins for your blog. Plugins are little add-ons you install (upload to the web host) and activate here. In Figure 2.13, you can see a list of all the plugins I have installed for the book blog. My mouse is hovering over the link to activate an inactive plugin.

As you can see under this tab you can add new plugins and *occasionally* there will be plugins that are configured here (like the anti-spam

plugin Akismet). Editing plugins through the Editor link isn't something I recommend unless you have been given specific instructions to do so. I've only edited a plugin once or twice in the three years plus I've been using WordPress, so I doubt you'll have need to edit one ever.

The Users tab, as you can guess, is where you manage the users, or accounts, on the blog. If this is just your blog there will be one or two users. One is the admin user and the other is an account for day to day use of your blog. I'll talk about why you should have two accounts on the blog when we get to tweaking this blog later in the chapter.

The tools tab is one that you'll probably only ever visit when there is an update to WordPress.

FIGURE 2.13

Plugin management area under the plugins tab, administration block.

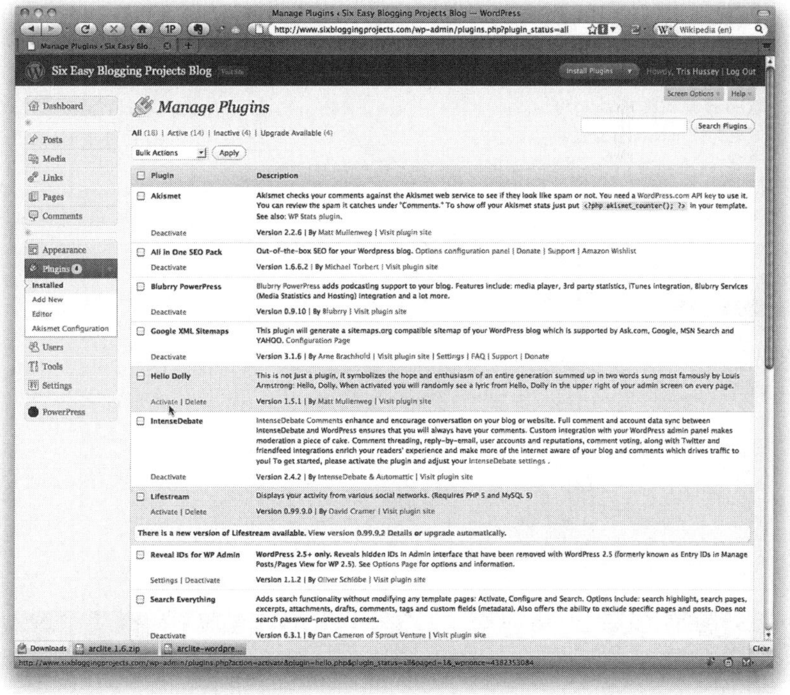

On the main section of the Tools tab (see Figure 2.14) you'll see a button to "Enable Gears," this refers to using **Google Gears** to download and store these administration screens and information to your computer. As you can see from the warning, do not enable Gears if you share the computer or it is a public computer.

NEW TERM

Google Gears is a set of technologies for the web browsers Internet Explorer, Firefox, and Safari to allow sites to store or "cache" parts of the site on your computer. Google developed Gears so services like Gmail could be used while you aren't connected to the Internet. You can learn more about Google Gears at http://gears.google.com/.

The "Press This" bookmarklet is something you can drag to the Bookmarks toolbar of your browser to make blogging faster and easier. This is a cool tool, and I'll talk about it in Chapter 3.

The Import link is if you need to Import content from another blog into this one. Conversely, Export is when you need to back up your content or save it locally to then import into another blog. Chances are you aren't going to do either of these things very often.

The Settings tab is where most of the tweaking, tuning, and configuring is done on your blog. As you can see in Figure 2.15, the settings list for this book's blog is pretty long. When you're starting out, with only a few plugins installed, it will probably be half as long.

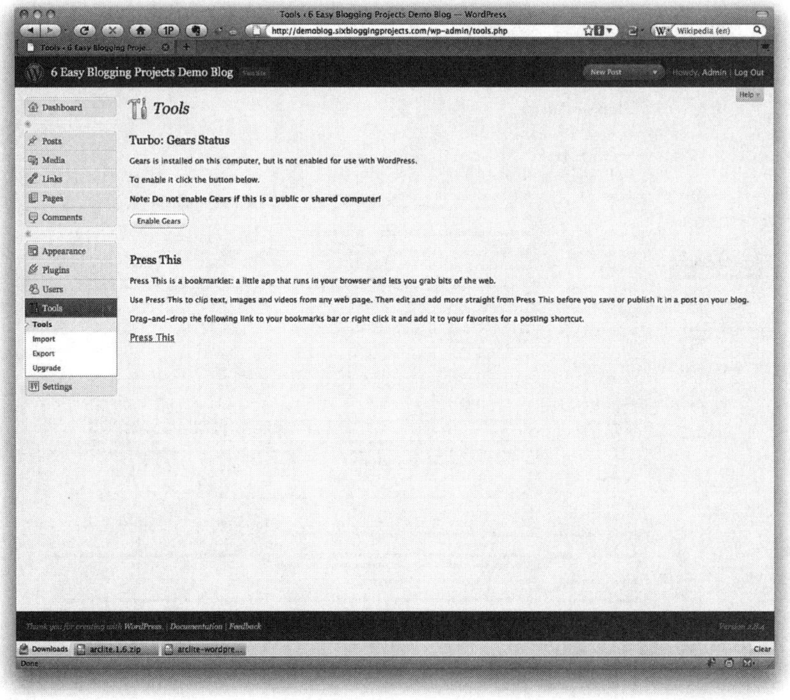

FIGURE 2.14
Tools tab showing button to enable Google Gears and Press This bookmarklet.

FIGURE 2.15
List of settings and options under my Settings tab for the blog for this book.

Tweaking Your Blog Setup

It's taken a long time to get here, but we're at the part of the chapter where we're ready to start making your blog sing; now is the time for tweaking and tuning. What we're doing here is going through and setting up things on your blog so it will look great, work fantastically, be found by search engines, and protected from the dark side of the Internet. While this *sounds* like a tremendously geeky undertaking, it isn't. All of these steps are simple, straightforward,

and make sense even to non-geeks. You have my permission, however, to brag to all your friends how difficult and technical the whole process is when you're showing off your blog.

Rather than get into the minutiae of how to tweak WordPress or Movable Type or Blogger specifically, I'm going to hit them all in broad strokes. Just as before, screenshots and examples will be from WordPress-based blogs, but the concepts are, generally, applicable to all blogs.

You probably noticed in all these screenshots that there was a little blueberry looking icon and the word "PowerPress" next to it. Well, yes that *is* actually a blueberry and it is for the podcasting plugin I like to use called, "PowerPress" from a site called Blubrry. Recent versions of WordPress allow plugins to create their own blocks in the administration area. Usually plugin developers do this because they would like to offer a more effective layout of the plugin's settings than they'd be able to if they had just the single link under Settings. PowerPress, in advanced mode, has quite a large number of options, which if you are a podcaster, you will soon appreciate.

Tweaking and Tuning a WordPress.com Blog

The entryway into the administration of your WordPress.com blog is the Dashboard (see Figure 2.16). This is the place where you can get a bird's eye view of your blog. I know you're dying to start posting, but let's configure a few of your blog's settings, choose a theme, look at widgets, and edit your "About" page first.

When you click the "Settings" button in the left-hand column, the first screen you come to is "General Settings" where you will give your blog a name and set your time zone (see Figure 2.17). When you're done, click Save Changes.

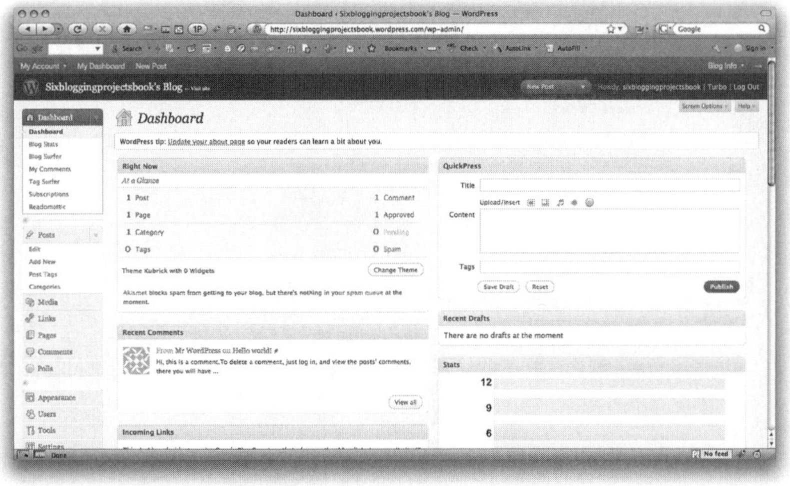

FIGURE 2.16
The WordPress.com Dashboard.

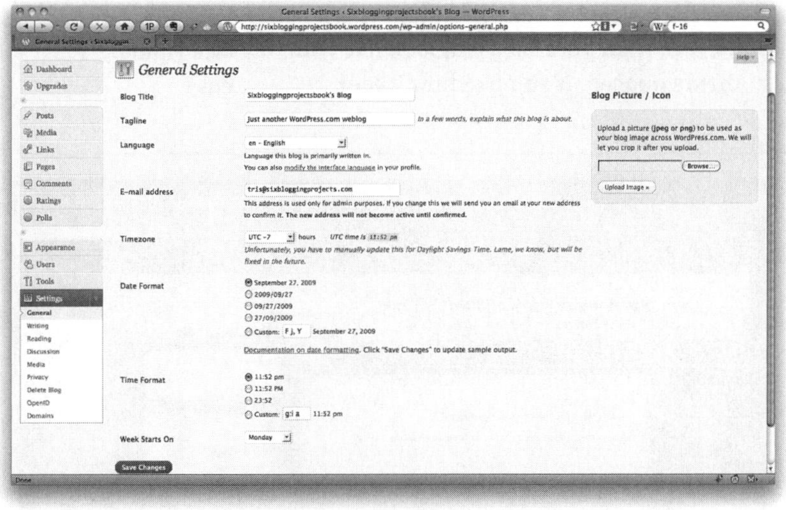

FIGURE 2.17
WordPress.com General Settings page where you give your blog its name.

Now that your blog has a name, let's make it look cool with a nice theme. As I'm writing this, there are 76 themes available on WordPress.com with a huge range of colors, styles, and special features. To change your theme, click Appearance on the left-hand side and you'll come to the Manage Themes section (see Figure 2.18).

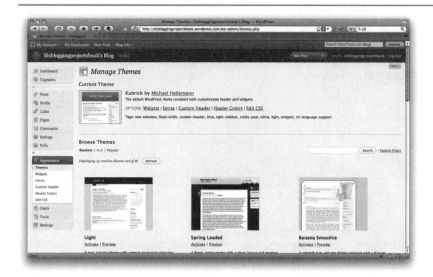

FIGURE 2.18
WordPress.com theme manager and a few of the 76 available themes.

Browse through the themes and when you find one you like, click the thumbnail and you'll see a preview of what your blog will look like with that theme applied. If you like how it looks, click "Activate [name of the theme]" and that's it; the new theme has been applied to your blog (see Figure 2.19). I told you this was going to be easy!

FIGURE 2.19
Choosing the "Spring Loaded" theme for a WordPress.com blog.

Now that your blog has a name and a spiffy new look, let's add some nice touches to the sidebar of the blog. When you visit websites and blogs these days you see all sorts of things off to the sides (left and right). These sidebar widgets are just things to either add some cool function to your blog (like showing the latest pictures you've uploaded) or a way to see the most recent article you've posted. Adding sidebar widgets on a WordPress.com blog is just a simple matter of dragging and dropping (see Figure 2.20). There are an impressive number of widgets available to you by default and I usually add Recent Posts, Recent Comments,

Tag Cloud, Categories, and Pages to my sidebar. Because you can add and remove sidebar widgets easily, I recommend trying them out and seeing which you like best. This is your blog after all, not mine.

The last thing to do is to edit your About page. This is just a short page telling readers about the blog and you as the author. You can provide as little or as much information as you like, just edit the default content of the page (and not with coming soon). To edit the page, first click "Pages" on the left side, then mouse over below the title About and click edit (Figure 2.21).

FIGURE 2.20

Dragging a sidebar widget to the sidebar space on WordPress.com.

FIGURE 2.21
Edit Pages screen on WordPress.com.

The next screen, shown in Figure 2.22, is the standard WordPress editing area (the editing areas for Pages and Posts look almost identical and work in the same way) where you can edit the content of your About page (remember "coming soon" doesn't count!). When you're done, click Update Page, and that's it!

TIP

Some things you can do right off the bat that show that you're serious about blogging are: changing the tagline "Just Another WordPress blog," editing your About page, and deleting the first "Hello World" post.

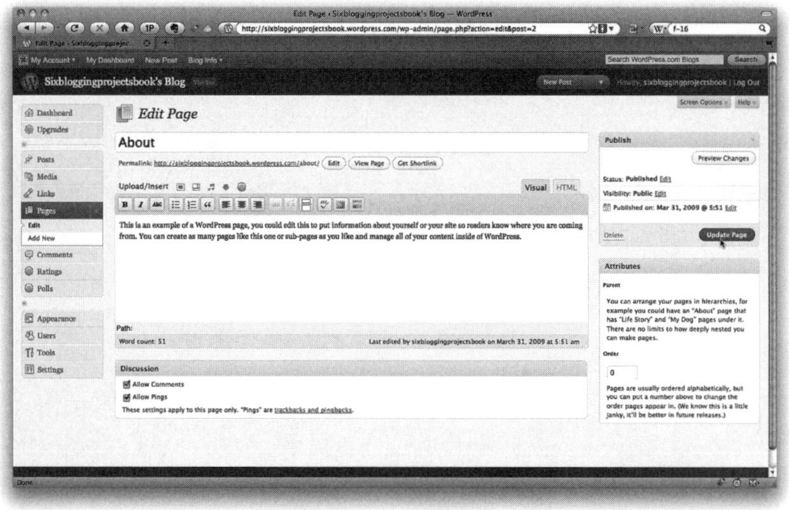

FIGURE 2.22
WordPress.com web-based Page editor where you can make changes to your About page.

I'll get into writing posts in Chapter 3, but at this point your WordPress.com blog is ready to go! In the next chapter I'll talk about adding categories, working with tags, editing your blogroll and other details. These things can all come later, but right now it's time to start thinking about those first posts. You can think while you read the rest of this chapter.

These steps I've outlined for WordPress.com can be followed, in general, for all hosted blog systems. TypePad follows a lot of the same logic to their blogging system as WordPress does. Blogger is a bit of an odd duck when it comes to themes and widgets, but it's not hard to figure out. Again, I choose WordPress.com for a hosted blog solution because I believe that it is the best and most flexible blog engine available. There are certainly more powerful blog engines, and maybe engines that are even simpler to use than WordPress.com, but I feel WordPress.com has the right balance between power and ease of use.

> **CAUTION**
>
> For the remainder of this chapter I'm going to cover various important settings and tweaks for blogs in general. Some of them don't apply to all blogs, especially WordPress.com and Blogger blogs. I will make a note of this in each section.

Setting Good Permalinks

When websites first started to use databases to store content (as blogs do), the URLs for each page were generated when someone clicked the link to go to the page. After the person left, that URL was discarded. You might remember this when you would bookmark a page on a site, but when you went back to the site using that bookmark, you either got a different page or an error. This wreaked havoc on how those sites were indexed and ranked by search engines (they weren't at all). So, as the first blog engines were being developed the idea of the **permalink** came about.

> **NEW TERM**
>
> A permalink is short for "permanent link" which means the address or URL to a post or page on a blog that can be bookmarked in a browser.

The idea of a permalink is that every page, post, category, and tag on a blog has a corresponding, permanent link that can be bookmarked *and* indexed by search engines. While this is great, the problem is that often the default permalink for many blog engines doesn't give readers or search engines much of an idea what that page will be about. Some blog setups, like Blogger and WordPress.com, do an adequate job of this by default, while others need some coaxing. For example, the default permalink for a post in a self-hosted WordPress install is something like www.myawesomeblog.com/?p=102. Not very illustrative, is it? From looking at the URL, there isn't an indication of the post title (or also no indication of what the post might be about). Yes, the post title is in the title portion of the page and would show up in a bookmark, however *search engines* pay attention to the permalink URL as well. A good permalink is a good thing for everyone.

My personal preference is something like www.myawesomeblog.com/2009/01/mypostrocks/ or /2009/01/10/mypostrocks/. The "mypostrocks" part is the title of the post that gives search engines an idea of the content (if you are writing good titles, which I'll get to) and if someone mouses over the link to the post on another site, they can get an idea of what it's about as well. In these two examples, I include the year and month with the title, in the second I include the day as well. Using the post date in the permalink helps to make sure there is no confusion around the links. You could, for example, write a birthday post to yourself every year. If the title is always "Happy Birthday to Me!" then having the year lets you and your readers know right off the bat which year you are talking about. For WordPress folks (not WordPress.com, you can't change your permalink structure), you change your permalinks under the Settings tab, then click on Permalinks.

NOTE

One last note about permalinks, to make permalinks work, the server needed to edit a file named .htaccess. If when you change your permalink structure you see a message like "You should update your htaccess now," it means you will have to edit the file yourself. This is very easy and in WordPress the code you need to copy and paste into the file is provided for you at the bottom of the permalinks settings page.

Anti-Spam

Just like email, blogs are susceptible to spam as well, and, interestingly enough, the same kinds of things you see in email spam you see in blog spam. Blog spam comes in the form of comments and links back to your blog (trackbacks), the comments and links, as you might expect, often contain links to online pharmacies, pornography, scams, and the other dregs of the Internet. To combat this scourge, anti-spam plugins were developed to block these comments and trackbacks from appearing on your blog at all.

So, the next step is to make sure the anti-spam plug-in is turned on and working. Because WordPress is my engine of choice, I use Automattic's Akismet. Matt Mullenweg wrote the first version of Akismet, and it is now maintained by Automattic, the company he helped found. Akismet is free for personal use and the license fees for commercial sites are reasonable. There is a version of Akismet for Movable Type as well, and it's one of the platform's most popular plugins. Akismet works by using a database of known spammers and common spam keywords to proactively block spam as it comes in. Akismet also "learns" how to identify new spam as people like you and me mark comments and trackbacks that are spam that Akismet missed. The details of exactly how Akismet works is a closely guarded secret for obvious reasons.

SEO Tuning

Next, tune the blog for SEO using plug-ins designed to make life easy in that respect. The first and foremost thing that needs to be changed is how many blog engines write the titles of posts and pages. By default, WordPress, for example, makes the title of the page (what would show up in a bookmark) as [Blog name] | [Post name] so for this book's blog it would look like: Six Easy Blogging Projects Blog | My blogging process-The 2009 edition. This *isn't* what you really want. You don't need Google and the other search engines continually indexing with your blog name first when that never changes!

What you want is this: My blogging process-The 2009 edition | Six Easy Blogging Projects Blog. This is exactly what you'll see when you visit the blog for this book: [Post name] | [Blog name]. This way Google indexes the *new* thing *first* (the post title or page title) and the static thing (the blog's name) last. This simple switch turns out to make a *huge* difference to Google.

There are lots of ways to achieve this result, we used to edit our theme headers to make the switch manually, but now either themes come with the tweak already done or bloggers use a plugin designed to tune and manage your SEO for you. My favorite for WordPress is All in One SEO, a great plugin that does 90% of the work for you. It also comes with a couple side benefits like being able to have a title, keywords, and description that are unique to the blog's homepage, but not subpages. For subpages the keywords and description data are automatically generated from your post. All in all, it's a slick plugin that I highly recommend.

WHAT ARE PLUGINS?

Plugins are like little programs that you add and install into your blog engine to allow it to do something new (like serve audio files) or better (like create pages that are more search engine friendly).

Think of plugins like this: you buy a car and it didn't come with a sunroof. You really *wanted* a sunroof, but for whatever reason, your new car doesn't have one. So you go down the street to a place that sells and installs sunroofs in cars and have one put in later. That sunroof in your car is like a plugin for your blog. And just like sunroofs in cars, there are plugins that work well and plugins that don't (e.g sunroofs that leak in the rain).

Categories and Tags

Next up are categories. I'll get into the differences between categories and tags in Chapter 3, but for now think of a category as your silverware drawer (it's a big bucket to describe something) and tags as the utensils themselves (knife, fork, and spoon). When setting up categories, and this isn't something that you do once, think about the big topics you might be writing about, say, Product Reviews, Social Media, Press Releases, or Thought of the Day. These are large containers that hold lots of different posts, but all generally about the same thing. Yes, a post can have more than one category, and I encourage that kind of broad thinking.

Categories are about classification. They help you and your readers place posts into some kind of context that they can relate to *and* be able to use to find similar posts. If you visit my blog, you will quickly see that I usually categorize a post several ways. As your blog evolves over time, you might add or remove categories. Categories are intended to be fluid and organic, adapting to your blog as *you* need them to. I find if after about six months, a category only has one or two posts in it, I delete it and make sure those posts are filed in other categories. In that case the category deleted probably should have been a tag, but at the time you might have thought it would be a larger bin. No problem, just deal with it now. As a rule of thumb, try to keep to about ten or fifteen categories max. Remember that you're thinking large bins here; top level stuff.

Blogrolls

Your blogroll is a list of links to other blogs that you read, like, or want to help promote. WordPress blogs have a small default blogroll to a few key WordPress sites, and most themes will display this blogroll unless you change the theme widgets. The blogroll used to be *the* way to find other blogs. Getting listed on a major blog's blogroll was a *huge* thing and it could vault a blog into a whole new level of traffic. Now, however, my opinion is that the blogroll has become superfluous. I find most new blogs through microblogging-micromessaging services like Twitter, RSS feeds, or links within posts. That said, I do still maintain a small blogroll on each blog. I link to my other blogs, my current job, my photography portfolio, and a couple of friends.

At one point there was a whole social etiquette around blogrolls and reciprocal linking. Sometimes not getting on a friend's blogroll led to hurt feelings and even minor feuds—seriously, I know as strange as it might seem. Given the needless politics involved, I eventually decided to cull mine. I link to my friends in my posts, meet them in person (gasp, I know a shocker), and chat via IM to show them I like their work.

Comments and Trackbacks

Two of the essential connectors in the blogosphere are comments and trackbacks. Make sure these are turned on by default for all your posts. Sounds strange, but sometimes people turn comments off or make people jump through hoops to comment. I moderate comments, but only if it's your first comment on my blog or it has a lot of links in it (lots of links in a comment is a red flag for a spam comment).

Trackbacks-pingbacks are on by default and you're not likely to ever have to worry about them. A trackback-pingback is when someone links back to your post. The link shows up in your post like a comment a person would make, but often above or below the "human" comments. Trackbacks-pingbacks also suffer from the scourge of spam. Spam blogs are pretty easy to pick out, so if you're unsure, follow the link to the post and check it out. If the blog and post look funny, it's probably spam and you can safely mark it as spam in your moderation section.

Security

As I mentioned in the tip earlier in the chapter, it is very important to at the very least change the default password for the admin account, and better disable it entirely and use a new account with administrator privileges. When you take this step, you deny potential hackers the first step to trying to break in—the username of the administrator account.

The next essential part of security is keeping up on security updates for plugins and your blog engine. If you're using TypePad, Blogger, or WordPress.com you don't have to worry about this, but if you have a self hosted install of WordPress or Movable Type, you need to stay on top of when updates come up and update your blog as soon as a security patch is released. When updates and patches are released the blogging community is very good about helping each other out in making sure people who are less comfortable with tech get the update in place. As you become more a part of a community of bloggers, you'll know who the generous souls are who are happy to lend a hand now and then.

About Page

Create or update your blog's "About" page to tell people about yourself and the blog. One of the most important parts of your blog isn't the posts, but the About page. Really. Your About page gives your readers insight into who you are and what the blog will be about. You can go into as much detail as you want. You can add contact information if you want—I highly recommend you do add some kind of contact info especially if you are a business—but a little about yourself is essential. One of the signs of a "real" blog is a "real" About page—something that sounds like a real person is behind the blog, not a computer program automatically generating the content. Figure 2.23 shows a look at my About page from this book's blog.

FIGURE 2.23

My about page on
SixBloggingProjects.com.

RSS Feeds

Of all the parts of a blog, your RSS feed is probably the most geeky and the most misunder-
stood. In a nutshell, your RSS feed is a
computer-readable version of the latest ten to
fifteen posts from your blog. Okay, sure you
can read your feed, too, but it isn't *meant* for
you; it's meant to be read by search engines
and RSS feed readers (which I explain later in
this chapter).

There are two types of RSS feeds, full and
partial. A full feed includes the entire post in
the feed. It gives both search engines and
people who read your posts exclusively in a
feed reader the whole post. A partial feed, as
you'd expect, gives you just a portion of the

post. Believe it or not, the argument of full or
partial feeds comes up often within blogging
circles. People who prefer partial feeds want to
bring more visitors to their blog or site so
people will see and click on ads. Additionally,
partial feeds give content scrapers (people who
steal content from blogs to republish it for their
own monetary gain) less to work with. On the
other side, full feed supporters feel that your
readers should have the whole post to read and
many readers prefer it. Search engines also
index and rank you better, and scrapers scrape
no matter what.

I have tried both full and partial feeds and feel
the benefits of full feeds outweigh the benefits
of partial feeds. Some people avoid subscribing
to partial feeds because you have to visit the

site to finish reading the post. I don't go that far, but I certainly prefer being able to read the entire article when I'm in the groove of reading. I subscribe to nearly 1,000 feeds. My advice, and the default for WordPress, is to have your blog publish a full feed.

Themes and Colors

One of my favorite things about blog engines is the capability to change the look and feel of a blog in a click or two of the mouse. Because the content is divorced from the design, you can change the design and not have to worry about "breaking" anything you've written. I've shown people who have paid thousands of dollars on a website redesign how I can "redesign" my blog for no cost in a few seconds... let's say I shouldn't repeat what they said.

Regardless, picking a theme is like having carte blanche to wander through a store and just pull awesome clothes off the racks and walk out. Most of my favorite themes are free, just requiring keeping a link to the designer's website in the footer. There are some amazing premium themes that do cost some money, but usually they're less than $100. I've purchased these themes before, and yes, they *are* worth the money.

I've shown people who have paid thousands of dollars on a website redesign how I can "redesign" my blog for no cost in a few seconds... let's say I shouldn't repeat what they said.

For hosted blogs, you'll often be given a set choice of themes or limitations on how you can edit them. Blogger is somewhat of an exception to this rule, but I'm no fan of trying to edit Blogger templates. I still have coding nightmares about it. If your blog is self-hosted, then you'll be able to download and install/load most any theme available for your blog engine. Themes are engine specific, so a Movable Type theme doesn't work for WordPress or a WordPress theme for Blogger. Picking a theme, its layout, and color scheme is up to you, but the following are what I look for when picking a new theme:

▶ Is the text easy to read? Too small, too crowded, maybe not enough contrast? Remember that you want people to be able to *read and enjoy* your blog, not have to pull out a magnifying glass.

▶ Are the colors nice and pleasant or do they make you want to claw your eyes out? One of the most criticized things about MySpace are the eye-jarring layouts. Do us all a favor and pick something that looks nice.

▶ Is there good use of white space? You know when you see a simple, clean layout and things just seem to fit and flow? Look for that.

▶ Can you tweak and edit the theme easily? How hard is it to have an image in the header of your choosing? For WordPress blogs, make sure it's "**widget** ready."

NEW TERM

A **widget** is the generic term for something you add to the sidebar of your blog. Today it also means a theme where these elements can just be dragged and dropped into place without coding.

These are just a few suggestions, but look at the free template sites for the blog engine of your choosing—this assumes your blog is self-hosted—and pick several that you like, load them all up, and try them out.

TIP

Some of my favorite places to find themes are www.wordpress.org/extend/themes (for WordPress themes) and www.smashing-magazine.com (mostly WordPress, but some for other blog engines as well). If you don't find something you like there, well I suggest giving Google a try. Search for your blog engine with theme and maybe something like a color or style. For example, "wordpress themes blue magazine style" should yield some good results to start with on your hunt for the perfect blog theme.

Tracking Your Blog's Stats

I love to look at the general traffic statistics for my blog. I like to know what posts are popular, what search terms are used to get to my site (the number one or two is "yam fries recipe"), and all the other tidbits I get from great web stats. Yes, I am a web stats junkie. Truth be told, web stats have been my bread and butter for about a dozen years. I used to spend a whole morning processing log files through arcane programs (with manually configured settings files that were oh so easy to mess up) just to see what the last day or two had been like. Because it often took so long to process all the data, I often didn't do stats runs more than once a week, unless there was a big event I needed to keep track of. Today I glance at my stats whenever I feel like it. I have real-time live stats and stats that update once a day. And I don't have to lift a finger to make it all happen.

My stats are gathered, tabulated, and reported (and even emailed to me!) automatically using two great stats services: Google Analytics and Woopra. Google Analytics gives me great info and details from the previous day, and if I put Google Adwords on my blog, they can be tied to it as well (see Figure 2.24). Woopra gives me an amazing amount of live data as it happens, plus a lot of historical data. Why two sets of data? Because I like redundancy and each service is a great complement to the other. Google Analytics gives me easy ways to slice and dice the data so I can really understand my traffic. Woopra gives me quick, easy access to high levels of data that I can use to make quick decisions.

The best part of these tools is that to use them all you need is to set up your account at www.woopra.com or analytics.google.com, enter the basic information about your site, and get a piece of code to paste into your template. Plus there are even plugins for Movable Type and WordPress that enable you to add these services without having to mess around with pasting code.

Another alternative to these two services for self-hosted WordPress blogs is WordPress Stats. Personally I don't like the level of (or lack of) detail I get from it.

CAUTION

If you have a WordPress.com blog, you get WordPress stats automatically and adding Google Analytics or Woopra isn't an option (at the time of writing). Self-hosted Movable Type and TypePad blogs have more flexibility and can use Google Analytics and Woopra.

FIGURE 2.24
My Google Analytics Dashboard for my personal blog.

Certainly, you don't have to go to the extremes I do, but setting up one or two services is a good idea. Personally, I'd set up Google Analytics and Woopra (if you can) and decide which you like better. It's easy enough to do, and because they are free, you don't have anything to lose.

Improving Your Blog's Search Capabilities

So when you get to a site and don't find what you're looking for, but you *know* it has to be on the site somewhere, what do you do? You use the handy search box.

TIP

This assumes you can *find* the handy search box. No matter what kind of theme or design you pick for your blog, make sure the search box is painfully obvious to locate.

The basic search on blog engines is pretty good. Because all the content is in a nice database, it darn well should be good. Nevertheless, pretty good isn't always good enough, which is why I like to soup up my search with a little service called Lijit (see Figure 2.25).

Lijit augments, or completely replaces, your blog search with a search engine that includes all of your online presence. For example, I have several blogs that I contribute to or author and because my readers might not remember *which* blog they read a post on,

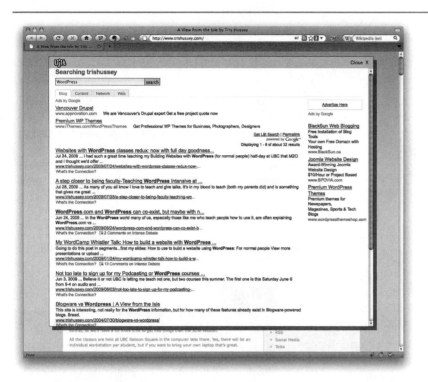

FIGURE 2.25
An example of the expanded results from Lijit on my personal blog.

when they search on one blog they might get a wee frustrated with the results (or lack thereof). Lijit solves that by including results from *all* of the places you create content. When you search my site, you get results from my blogs, from Twitter, pictures from Flickr, professional information from LinkedIn, and myriad other places. Not only that, Lijit figures out who is in your "network" of friends, and your visitors can find related content from them as well. Oh yeah, they also toss in some great web stats, too.

Summary

By now you've gone from just having an idea about a blog to actually having one. Even if you decided to just dip your toe in the water with a WordPress.com blog, you're off to a great start. If you've jumped in with both feet and have your domain, a web host, and a freshly installed WordPress blog, I hope you're well on the way to getting it set up, tuned, and tweaked.

Next up is the section that most people tend to be the *most* afraid of—writing. Chapter 3 is all about writing and creating a conversation. My goal in the next chapter is to inspire you to start writing, maybe even before you have decided if you want a personal blog, a business blog, or even a portfolio blog. I hope that you finish Chapter 3 dying to have your say, so let's get down to business.

A WORD ABOUT SIDEBAR WIDGETS

Lijit is just one of many sidebar widgets you can add to your blog. You can have tag clouds, MyBlogLog panels that show the visitors to your blog, polls, rotating pictures from Flickr, or even movies from YouTube. The sky is the limit. Well, almost. Instead of highlighting my favorite widgets, I'm going to let you find what you think is cool on your own, with one word of warning: Don't overdo it.

Okay, you twisted my arm, most of my favorite widgets come from the services I already use, like Flickr, Twitter, and Lijit. When you sign up for these services, they will often point you in the direction of their latest widget. If all else fails, a quick Google search for "blog widgets" will get you started well on your way to widget bliss (or overload).

Widgets can add great features, color, and interactivity to your blog, but they can also slow down how quickly it loads and sometimes cause the blog to not load at all for some browsers. The add-on widgets I'm talking about here shouldn't be confused with WordPress sidebar widgets that come as part of the core install. These widgets like Recent Posts, Pages, Recent Comments, and Categories run straight from the WordPress core and are just fine to add. The same goes for similar widgets on Movable Type/TypePad. These widgets won't slow your blog down very much, but they can lead to eyeball clutter, so just see how things look before you go nuts.

CHAPTER 3

Writing and Creating a Conversation

Chapters 1 and 2 focused on "the easy stuff." As much as it can confound and frustrate, technology is actually pretty easy to grasp. There are always those who can help you with that part if you feel lost. Writing, however, is completely up to you. It's your voice, your words, and your story. I can't tell your story for you, but I *can* tell you what I've learned about writing and writing for the Web.

What is great, and potentially scary, is that your blog is your own platform to say and write what you want. It's your soapbox in the vast online world. Blogs started off as personal journals, but when comments were added to posts they became *conversations*. You tell your story, people read it, and sometimes they will add to it, maybe with their own experiences. The result is that you have something more than what you started with.

In this chapter, you explore all the aspects of writing a blog: finding your voice, remaining anonymous, and making your life public or keeping it private. Although there aren't hard and fast rules about how to write a great blog post, there are some things you can do to make your writing more engaging to an online audience.

Let's get into the whole mechanics of writing a blog post.

You tell your story, people read it, and sometimes they will add to it, maybe with their own experiences. The result is that you have something more than what you started with.

Turning an Idea for a Blog into Blog Posts

After reading Chapter 1, "Welcome to the Blogosphere: Plannng Your First Blog," you should have the general topic for your blog. After reading Chapter 2, "Installing and Setting Up Your First Blog," you should have a blog to start posting content, but you might be stumped for how to get some posts going. This is fine; don't worry because *everyone*, including me, has moments of "Okay, what am I going to post about today?" This section is going to help you get the post ideas flowing.

No, I'm not going to suggest strange creativity exercises or rituals. I have tried so many of them that I forgot one very important fact— inspiration is like a flock of birds. Sometimes it's a lovely thing to watch and marvel at, and sometimes it's an Alfred Hitchcock movie. You just don't know until you stop and look at it for a while. That's a mixed metaphorical way of saying: Inspiration often just hits you and often at inconvenient times, so the trick is being ready to take advantage of it when it hits you.

Capture Inspiration Whenever and Wherever It Strikes

I get most of my news and information online through RSS feeds and social networks like Twitter. I am extremely lucky to know a lot of gifted, brilliant, off-kilter, funny, silly, and generally nice people. I try to read as much of what they write and produce as I can. Their creativity fuels my creativity, and I hope my creativity doesn't make them run screaming down the street. Because I don't really know when one of my friends is going to say something brilliant online, I have a couple tools to capture those nuggets of brilliance when they come up.

As I've gone through the process of writing this book, I've been testing and trying new software, helpful hints, and other things that fall under the heading of "Research." (They could also fall under "Making Surfing the Net Look Like Work," but I'm not going to talk about that.) Research is something that in the Internet age is a lot different than it was even just a couple of years ago. The scale of

information you can have at your fingertips with just a Google search is nothing short of mind blowing. For this reason, some very brilliant folks created note-taking apps or as Shawn Blanc calls them "anything buckets." I use two programs for anything buckets to keep track of quotes, links, pictures, and any other interesting online piece for review later.

The first app that I've been using for about a year to gather notes and track projects is called Evernote (free and paid versions, Mac/Windows/iPhone/BlackBerry/Web). (See Figure 3.1).

FIGURE 3.1

A clipped reference page of Evernote for the Mac.

The second app is called Yojimbo (paid, Mac only) and is one I've come across more recently (see Figure 3.2).

How do these apps work for capturing inspiration? Simple, whatever I'm doing on my computer, I can quickly capture in one of these programs. If I see a great website I'd like to note for later, I don't bookmark it in my browser, I put it in a "post fodder" or "book research" folder in one of these programs. When I'm looking for something to post or for that site when I get to a section of the book, it's right where I can find it: right alongside any other related items I've previously found. For example, in Safari (my browser of choice, not where I'm going on vacation) I can click the Evernote button or the "Archive in Yojimbo" bookmarklet and that page is stored in the appropriate place.

The idea here is that when you see a site, get an email, or whatever else you might come across, you can quickly just jot a note to yourself to save it for later. Evernote wins hands down in the "whenever and wherever" department because there are versions of Evernote for Macs, PCs, phones (the iPhone and BlackBerry versions are quite nice), and the Web; and best of all, they all sync up.

Regardless of the electronic tool, or even pen and paper (I always have a pen and small pad in my pocket), you should be ready to note it because you don't know when an idea or inspiration will strike. I've lost count of the number of potentially great posts that never came to be because I forgot them before I could note them.

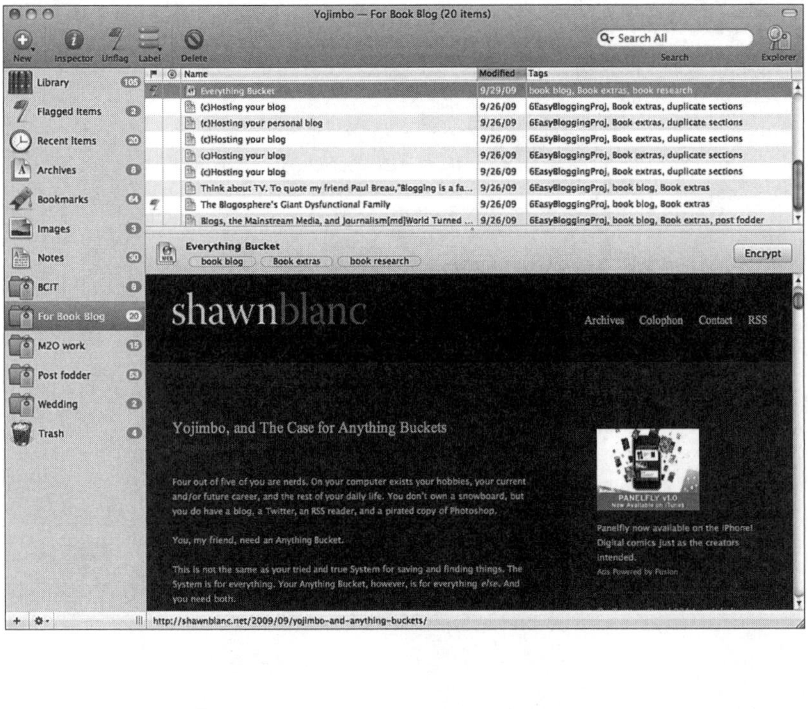

FIGURE 3.2
Yojimbo and Shawn Blanc's anything bucket post.

Finding Your "Voice"

The hardest, and the most fun, aspect of starting a blog is finding a tone and style that expresses "you" in written form. How do you find your voice? You just have to write and work at it until your comfortable style comes out.

No, this is not English class all over again (write a two-page essay on the role of Google in today's info-centric society…). Just write like you're chatting to a friend or a favorite professor or teacher.

Let me give you a couple of examples from my own writing (not that you don't have a really good idea of what my "voice" is like). The following is a section from my own blog:

You combined the persistence of a solid RSS reader with the immediacy of a dashboard or ticker? Have your ginormous list of feeds, but mark a select few as HUD feeds? Feeds that maybe could be pushed to Twitter or tapped into by Hootsuite or Tweetdeck. Like your top 20 "I don't want to miss a single thing" feeds, while in the background the "reader" part is building a relevancy-linked reading list? Find a way to consolidate articles on a topic, meme, headline, or concept into streams of articles. Sure be able to read your feeds like we do now (an interface like FeedDemon or NetNewsWire is good I think), but also have this information stream pulled together.

Looking for the day's posts on RSS or Facebook or social media or H1N1? Then they are already consolidated for you. Yes, you can build "smart folders," but you have to know the topic first to do that. Sure you can have a folder with big concepts that you're interested in, but when news breaks, wouldn't it be good to have something like your own Techmeme based on the sources you follow?

The following is from the Media2o Productions blog:

Is social media a fad? Yes, using the term social media is a fad. Just like "internet marketing", "new media", "business blogging" were all "fads." The terms fade away, thankfully, but the ideas remain. We still have websites (more and more actually), write (aka blog), and continue to find more and more ways to interact with each other, our customers, clients, and business partners.

So while none of these 15 best mindsets are magic bullets to success, if you don't employ them your chances of success are greatly reduced.

Neither of these sections are all that different, but the tone is more corporate or professional in the second, and the first is more informal. My voice is the tone that I use to write with when I write a post (or a document). It's my choice of words (informal or formal), it's my tone (serious, funny, ironic, or sarcastic), and it's my phrasing. All put together, these give you a mental picture, or a feeling, on the post you're reading.

I don't have one voice I use in writing. I change and adapt it to the writing task at hand. You wouldn't write a business proposal like you write an email to your best friend. That said, regardless of the target audience, the best voices I read are all natural; they aren't forced, and that takes practice. Switching voices isn't always easy. You might even notice subtle changes in how I've been writing this book. Each chapter was written (and rewritten and edited) at different times. Maybe one day, I was feeling very serious and philosophical while another day more funny, which *will* and *does* come out in your writing. As you're reading the book, keep an "ear" out for how my writing voice changes. Sometimes it was accidental, and sometimes it was on purpose (like when addressing a serious topic), but it's always there.

The only way to develop your voice is to write—*a lot*. It might help to try to write as another person (say one of your parents). What would your dad sound like if you were trying to portray him in words? Or create a character, maybe your alter ego, someone you want to *pretend* to be and see how you would make that character come alive.

Your voice will come on its own. You might even think about writing an anonymous blog under a pen name, which might free you to experiment with different styles and topics that you might not be comfortable tackling under your real name. Who knows? Maybe your pen name might become popular.

To Anonymously Blog or Not: The Line Between Public and Private

This has nothing to do with the length of your post. It has to do with depth. How much information about yourself do you put out there for public consumption? Family? Pets? Your hometown? Spouse? Love life?

These are difficult questions, huh? I know you're thinking that you would not talk about your spouse on your blog or about the date you had last night. Yes, all bloggers think that, too, but as you become more comfortable blogging and as you build an audience for your words, it gets easier and easier to let personal details slip; details you might not otherwise want to share. Sometimes it just happens and sometimes that's okay. Other times, it can blow up in your face.

Although it is assumed that most people blog as themselves, and use their real names, some of the best and most famous blogs are written anonymously. Washingtonienne and Belle de Jour were both written by women who chronicled their sexual escapades online and became very famous for it. Washingtonienne was revealed to be an aide to a U.S. Senator, and Belle has recently revealed herself and is a highly respected researcher. Belle's anonymity didn't stop several books and a TV series based from being created based on her blog. Although names were never revealed by either blogger, the writing experiences were very much real. There was a blog penned by "Fake Steve Jobs," who wrote as if he were Steve Jobs, but in a mock parody of all that is Apple. It was witty, biting, and damn good stuff. People loved it and in the tech world, the discussions about who Fake Steve Jobs really was were almost as good as Fake Steve's writing.

It was an interesting day, almost anti-climatic when Fake Steve revealed himself to be Daniel Lyons of *Newsweek Magazine*. All the speculation was over—no more guessing who might be behind the satirical and funny posts. Sadly I was never considered to be one of the possible people behind the blog.

Washingtonienne and Belle de Jour might be two extreme examples, but they aren't alone. People pen blogs for many reasons (and books and articles) anonymously. Maybe they don't want their friends to know they write; maybe the topic clashes with their public persona. Maybe, like Fake Steve Jobs, they wanted to write some parody or satire that could only be done behind the safety of a pen name. Whatever the reason, nine times out of ten, it's a good one.

What can happen if you blog publicly or if you blog anonymously and you're outed? I've seen friends I've known for years fired from their jobs. There have been court battles where blog posts have been used as evidence against parents in custody fights. That doesn't even start to cover the standard libel suits that have been filed (and some have been successful).

CAUTION

Anonymous or not, you have to stand by and live with what you write. There are real consequences to telling tales out of school, speaking ill of someone, or any other unsavory thing. You can't hide behind "oh, it's just a blog" because a public blog on the public Internet is just like any other publication.

IDEA GALLERY

http://www.belledejour-uk.blogspot.com

BELLE DE JOUR

Belle was crass, frank, gritty, brazen—and real. The stories of Belle's life as a high-end London call girl fascinated people. Even if some might have been offended at her frank and open discussions of sex, sexuality, and the sex trade, you couldn't ignore her vulnerability or humanity. Her writing pulled people in because it was so real, not to mention the fact that it laid bare (couldn't resist the pun) the sex trade. She didn't name names, but the look into her life was—and still is—enthralling.

Her blog became a TV series and a series of books not because she wrote about sex, but because her writing gripped us. Her writing struck a chord with people. We all understood the need to love and be loved. We understood that sometimes you have to make hard, unpopular choices. Belle chose to become a call girl and she doesn't paint a rosy picture of it. She paints a *real* picture of it.

This isn't career day at school mind you; she doesn't advocate a life in the sex trade. Even if her topic isn't your cup of tea, you should read a few of her posts to see how she pulls you into a conversation and makes you feel like she is talking to you across a café table. I bet you'll go back to read more. All good writers, like Belle, leave you craving *more*.

Now, what about you? Are you going to write as you or under a pen name? Before you decide, you don't actually have to decide. I'll tell you right now that I have a couple anonymous blogs out there. I have anonymous blogs to explore different sides of my writing. Writing about different topics stretches my creativity. Stretching and pushing yourself is a critical aspect of being a writer.

When you're deciding whether or not to be anonymous, think about whether you would mind someone from your job, church, or local watering hole reading your posts and knowing that you wrote them. None of that should necessarily stop you from writing about what you want, but it just might stop you from writing about these things so openly. You might also not want the whole Internet to know exactly who you are, where you live, or the names of your family members. Although I do blog as myself, my children don't choose to (my daughter has a private blog), so they are only mentioned by initials and I don't post their pictures publicly. The same goes for other people in my life. They didn't ask to be drug into the wide-open land of the Internet, so I keep a lot private. I also make a lot public.

I've taken strong stands on mental illness, education, learning disabilities, my own health, and sometimes politics. I take those stands because sometimes it's the right thing to do; sometimes individuals need that chorus of voices calling for change. I feel I've been given a tremendous responsibility by having an audience. Even if it isn't a huge audience, I know it's a far-reaching one. So, I take a stand. Sometimes it isn't popular; sometimes I cringe

as I select "Publish," but I haven't had many posts that I regretted posting. If nothing else, anonymous or not, always write from your heart, be proud of what you write, and stand by your words.

> *If nothing else, anonymous or not, always write from your heart, be proud of what you write, and stand by your words.*

There are degrees of anonymity. You can blog as Jane Smith, but just not tell all about where you live, or blog as Bob the Delivery Guy and be a pen name. It's your choice. One of my friends is a "Daddy Blogger" and blogs under the name "Genuine." His family members are Mrs. Genuine, Genuine Girl, Genuine Boy 1, and so on. There is a layer between the world at large and his family. Is he anonymous? Nope. His name is Jim Turner. He and I were business partners in a company together. Oddly enough, he's far more famous as Genuine than as Jim (at conferences he writes "Genuine" below his real name). Go figure. Just mull that over for a minute, because now you're getting to the really fun stuff.

So the question is "Where does your public life end and private life start?" This isn't a question I can answer for you. Bloggers usually find out by crossing the line. In doing so, you'll learn from experience what topics you want to keep off limits.

Write Until You've Said Your Piece

One of the most common questions I'm asked is "How long should a blog post be?" I often give a rather impish answer of "as long as it takes for you to say what you have to say," but that is a cop-out answer. Generally a blog post is short, about 200 words or so. I think it became that way because geeks have notoriously short attention spans. That's not to say that people, including myself, don't write longer pieces. It's just in general, blog posts are short. The short-form post is something that seems to fit in well with today's fast-paced society; however, there is a *huge* drawback to it: People often just regurgitate the same ideas and links without adding anything to the conversation. Trying to squeeze some original analysis into 200 words isn't the easiest thing to do, but it is worth it when you really pull it off.

I've read great posts that are around 6–10 words long (a single sentence) as well as epics of thousands of words. One isn't better than the other. When you're writing a post, just write it out. Don't worry if it's too short or too long. Say what you want to say and when you're done, see what it looks like. You might want to split a longer post into a part 1 and part 2 (or 3, 4 …); series posts are *great* ways to keep readers coming back (don't forget the age-old cliffhanger!).

CAUTION

I do place one caveat on longer posts (500 words and greater): People find it hard to read a lot of text onscreen. If you have long paragraphs without breaks, readers might skim through the post. The solution to this is pretty easy: shorter paragraphs!

If You Post It, They Will Come: Posting Frequency Answered

How often should I post? This might be the number one question people ask about blogging, along with "How do I post links and images?" The honest answer is that it's up to you, but if you are trying to build traffic and a profile for a professional or business blog, you need to post *at least* three times a week, and not all in one day. Honestly, a post a day should be your goal if you want to build a readership and traffic. Yes, that might seem difficult at first and it does require a significant time commitment, but once you get going you might not be able to shut up.

If you feel like you have to post more than once a day, I suggest spreading the posts out over the day. You can do this two ways: One is to just hold off on posting, and the other is to use the post to the future feature available in most blog engines (see Figure 3.3). I recommend the latter, because it gets the post out of your system.

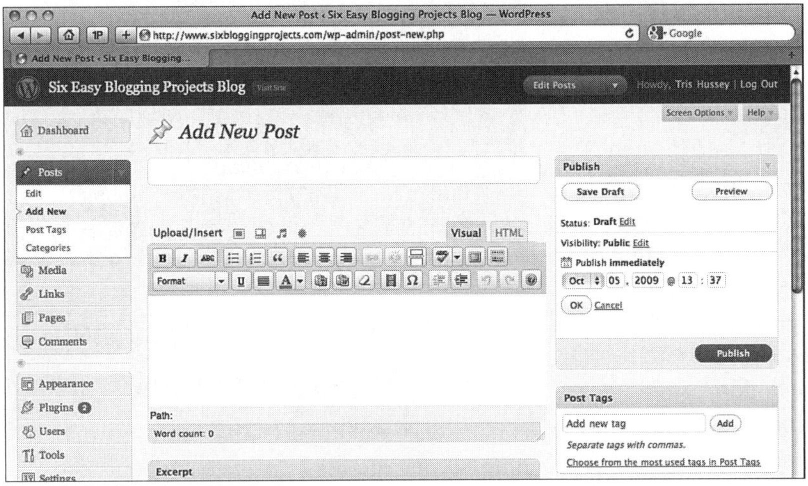

FIGURE 3.3
Part of the WordPress post editor showing the time-date adjustment panel.

In addition to gaining *readers* by posting every day, search engines index your blog more frequently, if you post frequently. Each post ties into the previous ones and strengthens the associate between your blog and the keywords you use. After a solid month of posting five times per week (or more), your ranking in the search engines will increase significantly.

Your First Post

So your first post. The "Hello world, here I am. Time to listen up" statement.

Uh huh.

Right.

Chances are your first post will suck. Oh yeah, it is pretty much guaranteed that you're going to look at it in month or so and die a little inside. You'll want to delete it. Expunge this dreck from the world.

Don't.

Your first post is something of a birthday state-ment. It's what you're going to look back on and smile after your blog has been around for a year or so. But, yeah, it will still suck and really that's okay. Just get the first post out there and out of the way. No, you don't have to write some great expressive post about what your blog is about; just a "Hi, yeah this is the first post, I'm going to talk about [insert topic], hope you enjoy it…" is great. Don't worry or stress about post number one.

This Is Practice

As you're writing, remember that these posts are practice. You might hesitate to post them. You might want to read and edit them over and over again. You might think that they aren't good enough. Well, they *are* good enough and you *should* post them. Sure, check for spelling and grammatical errors, but don't go and edit the post over and over. Don't try to work and rework your post for just the right turn of phrase. It isn't worth it. I've said it before and I'm going to repeat it again, ready? Listen. No, seriously, this is important.

Your first post will suck, and that's okay because all first posts suck.

I think my first post, which I wish I could share, but I lost it in a blog move, was something like this:

Here's a cool thing I found today. I think this collaboration tool is cool. [Link]

This is a riveting piece of writing, isn't it? This is a post full of passion and depth, inspiring you to think in a whole new way about collaboration tools. Yeah, not so much. This is why you just keep writing. It gets easier and eventually you find a voice to write in that expresses who you are. Experiment with short posts, long posts, lists, reviews, a brain dump of links, and so on.

Your first post will suck, and that's okay because all first posts suck.

At the beginning, writing and posting might seem like a struggle, especially if you're not used to writing on a regular basis. It *does* get easier—I promise. When I talk about sources of inspiration, you'll see that I don't just pull ideas out of thin air. Nor do I think my writing needs no improvement. I appreciate the feedback I get on my posts, and especially this book, because often a gentle critical look can help bring out the great writer that you are.

Before you get worried or excited about the content of your blog posts, always remember that blogging isn't rocket science. There aren't rules that you must follow to make a good blog post. When my friends and colleagues ask me "Is this an okay post?" I generally say that it's

fine. Sure I might help them fix a link or move a picture around, but generally that's it. Why? Because it's *their* story not mine. Yes, if it's a post trying to make a point, I'll read and offer suggestions for clarity, but that isn't often.

I hope that you are more inspired and think that I'm dead wrong about writing. Stop shaking your head because it's absolutely true. I want to get you *thinking* about *your* voice and story, and if you don't agree with me about my take on writing, that's great. It's your blog, not mine.

Writing Your First Post

Let's get into the nuts and bolts of posting. The following examples use WordPress' post editor, but many blog engines use the same components and icons in their editors so it shouldn't be too difficult to make the transition.

CAUTION

As much as it is the word processor of choice for most of us, regardless of platform, Microsoft Word *sucks* as the tool for you to write your posts. Why? Because when you copy and paste from Word into your post, Word brings along a ton of extra "stuff" in the formatting code that makes it not display properly when someone views it in your blog. Yes, you can avoid this problem with a couple extra steps, but frankly everyone forgets to take those steps, so just write in a simple text editor or a blog editor, which is even better.

The post/page editor in WordPress should look familiar to you if you've used a web-based email service like Hotmail, Yahoo Mail, or Gmail (see Figure 3.4). All of these online writing tools share similar icon sets and even sometimes background technology!

The post editor in WordPress, which is similar to other online writing tools.

The layout should be pretty easy to follow. The title goes in the skinny bar at the top, the post itself goes in the larger box below the formatting buttons, and the tags go to the right in their own box. Categories are also set on the right, chosen with check boxes (or created ad hoc by clicking the Add New Category link).

When you are ready to post, click the Publish button, and you are done! If you are worried about losing your work, or want to finish a post later, click the Save Draft button. The draft post shows up in the post list noted with "Draft" next to the title. WordPress has a handy autosave feature that stores a copy of the post as you write it. The default is to save every five minutes, so if you accidentally close your browser tab or window (that has happened to me more times than I like to remember), your browser crashes, or your whole computer crashes, WordPress will have a version (the last saved one) for you. I, however, don't trust autosave functions. I still proactively click Save Draft if I'm working in the browser, and you should too.

Let's pull this all together now. There is a button, located in the upper right corner of the WordPress dashboard, called New Post (refer to Figure 2.11). When you click this button, you get a blank post. If you fast forward in your mind, once you've written something to post, it will look something like Figure 3.5.

This post is ready to go. The title is there, the post is all there, and I have tags set (right side) and categories chosen (right side, below tags). I skipped putting an image into this post because for your first post, just write and get something out there. If you are confident enough to include an image, go for it. The only thing left to do is click the Publish button and make the post live on the Internet as shown in Figure 3.6.

THE MAGIC PASTE FROM WORD BUTTON

If you're like me, you have a love-hate relationship with Microsoft Word. Sure you *have* to use it (because everyone else does), but you don't have to *like it*. Earlier I mentioned how copying text from Word to your blog engine brings along extra stuff. This extra code changes the font of that post from all the other posts and the rest of the blog. The extra codes could even turn the whole layout of your blog into a jumbled mess. Don't do it.

But wait, "I like or even need to write in Word," you say. Whether it's a dictate from the boss or a personal preference, there are valid reasons to use Word, and it's because of them that the Paste from Word button was created (I call it magic).

Here's how you find it.

In WordPress, look in the post editor for an icon that looks like two lines of colored squares (it's the last button in the top row—or only row until you click it) and click it. You should see a button that looks like a clipboard with a very familiar "W" on it. That's it.

Select your post in Word and copy it to the clipboard (Edit menu, Copy or control-c). Next, click in the post area where you want the text to start (usually the top) and then click the Paste from Word button to paste your post into the window that pops up. Finally, click Insert. If the little window doesn't go away after you click Insert, click its close box in the upper right-hand corner.

If your text has underline, italics, or bold text, that formatting will be preserved in the post and put in as proper HTML code.

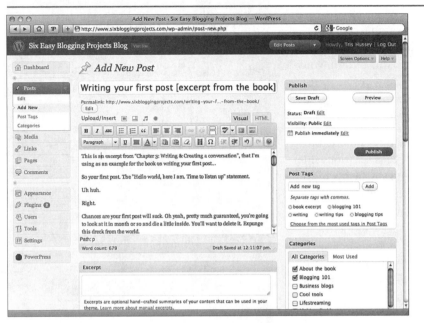

FIGURE 3.5

Post in WordPress' post editor ready to be published.

FIGURE 3.6

The post now published and live on the Internet.

If you look carefully at Figures 3.5 and 3.6, you'll notice that the body of the post in the editor looks like it's in Times New Roman font (it is actually). In the post, it's in a different font (Lucida Grand, for the fontahoics like me). This is all part of the magic of blog themes and style sheets. Often people tell me they want to change the font in the post editor, because they want it to look like that when it's published. Sure, you *can* do that, but you *shouldn't* do that because this is what your theme's style sheet does. If you don't like the font your theme uses, changing it isn't difficult, but that's a little advanced for right now.

That's it, really. Keep your first post simple, don't over think it, and just do it. It is as simple, and as hard, as that.

Drinking from the Information Fire Hose: Using the Internet to Power Your Posts

"But what should I write *about*?" I'm asked that over and over again, and sometimes when I suggest topics I even get "Oh, no one would want to read about *that*." No, you're right, I suggested it because I want to see you write really bad stuff (sarcasm).

In seriousness, getting that spark of inspiration is something that is hard to explain. The bolt from the blue *does* happen, just not often. I get most of my ideas from other people who intersect with me. Sometimes it's an electronic intersection; sometimes it's in real life (IRL). The key I've found is when you become inspired, don't

dismiss it. Run with it for a bit in your head, on paper, or electronically. Just see where it takes you.

Now, let's get to those intersection points.

Other Bloggers

I can't speak for everyone's friends, but I am lucky enough to be surrounded by some of the most brilliant, creative, and scary-smart people I've ever known. Looking at the things *they* create, share, and link to always gets something going in my head.

I talk more specifically about building your online community in Chapter 4, "Building Community," but within your community there are always people who send you interesting links and such directly. Many of them inspire you with a comment they leave on your blog. The real great stuff from you often comes from all the other "stuff" they do online. Bloggers call all that stuff, when it is all put together, a *lifestream*. I cover building a blog from *your* lifestream in Chapter 10, "Creating a Lifestreaming Blog." For now, just visualize a website where *everything* someone puts online can be read—pictures, shared playlists, shared links, posts, and updates from Twitter. Yes, that's *a lot* of information.

> **NEW TERM**
>
> The notion of a lifestream is a pretty new concept (late 2008 to be exact) that means pulling all the things you post online into one flow of information. For example, blog posts, pictures on Flickr, shared bookmarks, and favorite songs from music sharing sites are all shown together on one page.

Let's start small though. My two favorite ways to get inspiration from the community (and just small segments of larger lifestreams) are Twitter and Shared items from Google Reader.

Twitter is a *microblogging* service where people share "tweets" of 140 characters or fewer with people who follow them (like being friends on Facebook) and read the tweets of the people *they* follow. I follow and am followed by several thousand people right now.

NOTE

You can follow me, too, on Twitter. Go to www.twitter.com/trishussey to find my Twitter profile.

NEW TERM

Microblogging emerged in 2006 to describe services like Twitter where you post content that is very short in length (in Twitter's case, there can be no more that 140 characters).

I read the tweets from the people I follow in an application called TweetDeck (www.tweetdeck.com) that enables me to segment people into groups (like Friends, News, and Folks) so I can read more and not miss something that is important to me (see Figure 3.7).

FIGURE 3.7
Organizing tweets using TweetDeck.

So along with the wit and news my friends share, I also get updates from sources like CNN, CBC (Canadian Broadcasting Corporation), and a myriad of tech websites. Combined, this makes for a lot of potential inspiration, but it doesn't end there. Google Reader is the leading *RSS* reader and has a function where you can share articles you like as a public list. Like Twitter, people follow your shared items list and vice versa. The larger and more diverse the number of people you follow, the more varied kinds of articles you will see. Figure 3.8 gives you a look at a small portion of the shared items I've received in one day.

NEW TERM

RSS stands for "Really Simple Syndication" and is, simply, a series of technologies that produces a computer readable version of the posts on a blog that other computers can use to check for new posts. People use RSS readers to follow the sites they enjoy. The RSS reader checks the feed for the sites you've subscribed to and automatically downloads new posts for you. It's like getting an email from all your favorite websites whenever they publish something.

It doesn't matter what time of day or night, what the topic is, and so on, the community of people I follow and who follow me as well are a *constant* source of inspiration and support. So, if your community doesn't inspire you, come visit mine, we'd love to meet you.

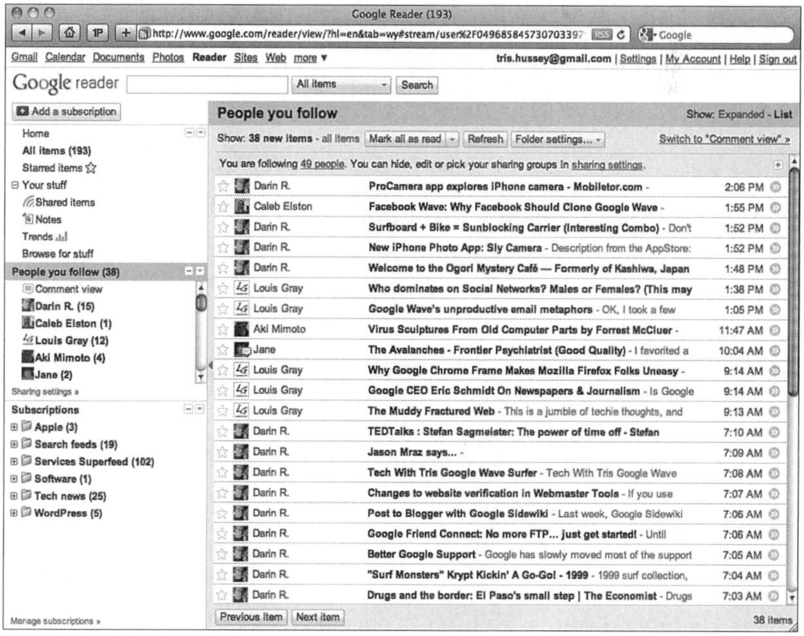

FIGURE 3.8

A look at my shared items in Google Reader for one day.

"Real" World

Contrary to popular belief, geeks do have lives and do venture outside. Fine, geeks often carry laptops, cameras, iPhones/Blackberries, but they're out in the "real" world. As you would expect, the real world can always provide something to write about. Going to a conference, a store, the local coffee place, and even walking down the street can provide you with much needed fodder. If you aren't inspired by real life, you need to get out more.

Geeks like to share what they know and have learned. To do this, they like to hang out together and generally geek out. In Vancouver, they have regular meetups for bloggers and people interested in PR and social media, and photowalks to just wander around and take pictures. There are even Tweetups, which are meetups organized through Twitter. Often, meetups are purely social, just time after work in a pub. But meetups, like Third Tuesday, bring in guest speakers to talk about blogging, social media, and society. These semi-structured social times are only *part* of the inspiration the real world brings.

The world around you is inspiring— remember to open your eyes.

How about a good or bad encounter with someone at a store? Did you get awesome, over-the-top service or something that makes you want to never go there again? How about just something you see on the street that strikes you funny. Take a picture of it with your cell phone if you can, and use that as the seed of a post.

The world around you is inspiring— remember to open your eyes.

Reader Comments

Chapter 4 goes more in depth with comments, but here is a short bit on how comments inspire me and my writing. As a reminder, part of blog posts and blogging is the capability of people to leave comments on the posts you've written. These comments can be everything from "That was awesome" to "You're completely wrong!" to "Yes, but have you thought about this angle..." and all of these can be sources of inspiration for your writing.

Sometimes there is nothing more inspiring than people reading your post and taking it in a whole new direction. It's very gratifying to me when someone reads what I wrote and then sees something else in the post that is *more* interesting than what I wrote. When that happens, and it will, build on it by writing a follow-up post. You might even think about asking the commenter to contribute to the post. This kind of writing symbiosis is one of the greatest parts of blogging. When your readers feel that they are also *contributors* to your blog, it only serves to strengthen your larger community. You also start to build a loyal following who will cheer you on when you get that book deal!

Great comments like that are amazing gifts. Don't waste them!

Writing with Search Engines in Mind

"Well, just look it up on Google..."

How many times have you heard or said that? If you're like the majority of North Americans, you've probably said it a lot. Looking up information through a search engine—Google being the reigning champion—has become standard practice. The take home of this idea is that if you want people to get to *your* site/blog/whatever, then you need to make sure that not only Google knows about you (that isn't very hard), but that you're *writing* so people will find your content when they are looking for your topic.

How do you get to this search engine nirvana? Believe it or not, just by starting off with a blogging engine, you're already ahead of the game. Search engines love blogs because they automatically link all of your site's content together. Even better, as you link to your own work, use categories, and tag your posts, you build connections that search engines can use to better understand and index your content. As great as blog engines are at the basics of SEO, there are some really easy things you can do to dial your SEO up to an 11. Now let's get you the rest of the way there with a few tips.

> **TIP**
>
> Did you know that Google does math? Oh yeah, and that's not all. The following are some of my favorites, which can be entered into Google's search field:
>
> Who is [put in a name]?
>
> What is 30c in f (converts from Celsius to Fahrenheit)
>
> What is $1 CAD in USD (converts from Canadian dollars to U.S. dollars)

For the moment you're going to take for granted that Google and the other search engines have found you. Yes, I know it doesn't happen overnight, but most blog engines automatically ping all the search engines when you post, so within a few weeks to a month you're being indexed.

> **TIP**
>
> If you've gone the DIY/self-hosted route for WordPress, then I recommend you install the plug-ins: Google Sitemap Generator and All In One SEO. These two plug-ins help all the tips I'm going to give you work even better. WordPress plug-ins can be found at www.wordpress.org/extend/plugins/.

One of the key parts to having people find your blog via search engines is understanding how people actually search for things: *keywords*.

> **NEW TERM**
>
> A keyword is the term used for the words people use to find something through a search engine.

Keywords

Put yourself into the shoes of someone searching for your topic. What words would you use to find a topic? What words in the title or the excerpt will get you to click that result? Don't just think, "Oh, of course someone will search for x." If you follow that track, very often you'll be wrong. It's okay. Initially, your gut will be wrong, but there are some tools for you to try out to check how often certain words are used.

These tools include:

▶ Google Adwords Keyword tool
   (https://adwords.google.com/select/
   KeywordToolExternal)

▶ WordTracker free keyword tool
   (http://freekeywords.wordtracker.com/)

For example, Figure 3.9 shows what Google's tool shows for the term "blog."

When you're writing posts, it's a good idea to learn what keywords people use to look for information on your topic. Because so many people use the word "blog" (and variants), using a term like weblog might not bring many people to my site. However, there are some ways to use the variety of terms people use to search for things to your advantage.

Once you have your keywords, run a few searches with them. What results do you get? What catches your eye? Follow the links to those sites and see how the content is written. I bet you'll notice how important terms are repeated often in the text, not in a strange way, just often. You should also notice how the authors use synonyms and variations of the keyword terms as well. This is because Google and the other search engines are putting more weight on the *content of the page* than they were in the past. It isn't a battle between who could write better code for pages; it's between who can *write better content for pages*.

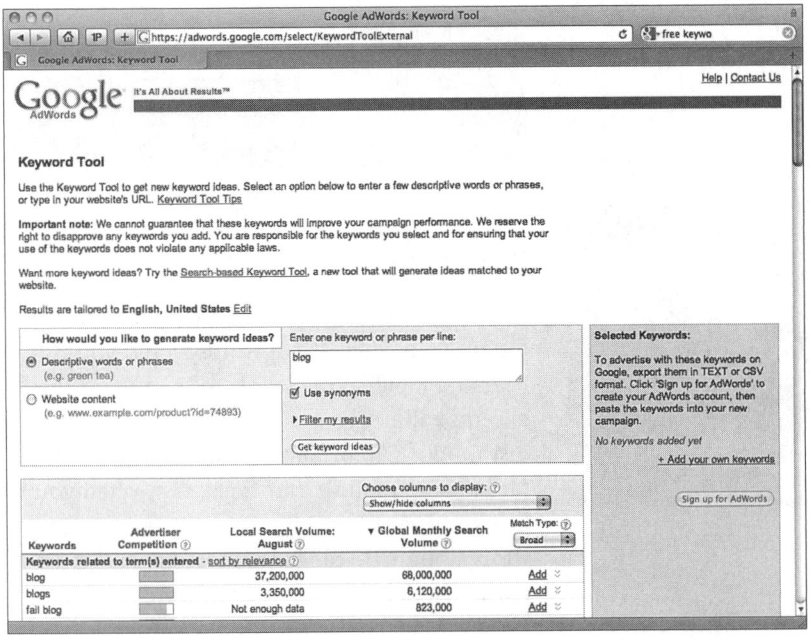

FIGURE 3.9

The Google Adwords Keyword tool to see how often people search for "blog" and similar terms.

Writing for Search Engines

Diversity is critical to your success with search engines. How many different ways do you know to express an idea? How many words do you know that mean pretty much the same thing? Can you distill an idea into a short sentence?

These are all key to writing for search engines.

> *It isn't a battle between who could write better code for pages; it's between who can write better content for pages.*

The operating principle is to write keyword rich. The title of any blog post you write should have the words that describe what the post is about. If your post is about investments and the stock market, then those words should be in the title. By the same token, the content of your post should include words like investing, stocks, securities, and so on. Write normally, but write *diversely*. Flex that vocabulary. Use different words and phrases in the post to explain the point. This makes your copy keyword rich. Your post will be indexed for the breadth of those keywords, which means that when people search for something like investing, your post is strongly associated with not only investing, but all the other shades of meaning. Search engines will take this to mean that your site might be more *relevant* to the searcher.

Google and other search engines strive to learn human language and shades of meaning. They try to tie words to ideas and concepts so the more words that you use to describe a concept, the better your post will be indexed.

Categories and Tags

Blog engines, like WordPress, use categories and tags to help you organize your posts into topic areas. Categories and tags are very similar, but easy to differentiate by just thinking about your kitchen's silverware drawer.

A category is like the silverware drawer itself; the drawer holds a lot of similar and related objects. In the drawer you have those metal objects you use to eat. If you were writing a post about those objects, you would put it in the category of "Silverware Drawer" but then tag the post with "utensil, fork, stainless steel, desert fork, and Oneida."

I'm betting that you have figured out the post is about stainless steel desert forks made by Oneida. The tags help readers and search engines connect all the dots together to put your post into *context* with other posts on your blog and blogs all over the Internet. You can see by extension if the tags for another post were "utensil, knife, stainless steel, steak, serrated, and Oneida" you'd know what that was about. If someone wanted to see all of the posts you wrote about your vast collection of Oneida silverware, clicking on the tag name in any of the posts with that tag brings up *all* the posts with that tag (knives, forks, and even spoons).

So, categories are big buckets for content. When you're thinking of good names for categories, think of the major concepts you'd use to look for your topic and what you're writing about. Categories might be the keywords that are *almost* too general, but still enough to get you in the right general direction. You don't want to have too many categories on your blog. My rule of thumb is around a maximum of 10.

Summary

This has been a very diverse chapter, hasn't it? A lot goes into writing good blog posts— finding sources of inspiration *and* remembering them for later, and then going through the process of just writing, getting that idea down. Posting is, really, just a small step, just one click. Then you need to think about how people will find you and your nascent blog.

It's not about learning tricks for search engines, but rather *habits*. Writing, creating categories, choosing tags, and even writing titles are all *proven* ways to help search engines find and index you properly.

The next chapter focuses on writing to encourage discussion and reaching out to other bloggers in your area of interest.

CHAPTER 4
Building Community

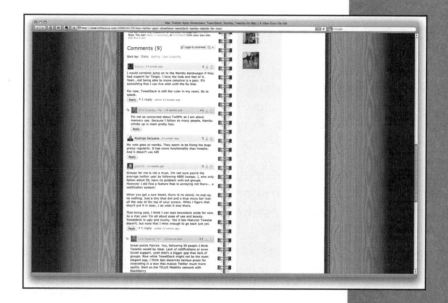

Even from the beginning, blogs weren't something that existed alone on the Net. They connected to each other. You found other bloggers like you found early websites back in the day: following links and trusting in a little bit of luck. Although finding great blogs isn't difficult now, getting your blog found is another matter. When there are only a half dozen people on the dance floor, it's pretty easy to find people. Add a few dozen more and you have a challenge on your hands. Blogs are no different.

It used to be there weren't many blogs on any given topic, so getting found was pretty easy. Today you can't be the proverbial wallflower; you have to get yourself to the dance floor and bust a move. The easiest way to get some attention for yourself is to get out there and look for people. Before you get into that part of the finding, let's handle the people who are going to start knocking on your door pretty much from day one—blog commenters.

Encouraging Comments and Discussion

Comments are what keep blogging going. The dialogue and feedback you get from readers not only helps you grow as a writer, but also ensures that you stay on track. Through comments you learn, interact, and gain inspiration. I've written entire follow-up posts based on a comment from a post. I've also received cease-and-desist letters because of comments (more on that later).

Part of getting comments is writing to encourage comments. First, make sure comments are enabled (that is, turned on) for all your posts. Nine times out of ten the default setting for blog engines is to have comments on, but sometimes they get turned off, so it's important to double check. Whether or not anyone can post a comment or whether there is some kind of moderation in place is up to you, and I'll get to that shortly.

With comments turned on, the next part is subtler: getting people to leave comments. There isn't a magic formula for you to get lots of comments. Sometimes I pull it off; sometimes I don't. In any case, the following are simple things you can do to help encourage comments:

▶ Leave examples out on purpose. People love to feel that they are contributing by adding to your post.

▶ Ask open-ended questions.

▶ Ask for comments directly.

▶ Take a contrary or controversial stance to the status quo. (Just make sure you believe in it. Few things in the blogging world are more annoying than a blogger whose only stance on anything is that he believes the exact opposite of what everyone else thinks.)

Even with these tips, including soliciting for comments, sometimes a great post just doesn't get any comments. This happens whether there's a lot of traffic through your blog or not, and it can happen to the very best of posts. Sometimes it's the posts that you don't expect to receive any comments that are the ones that get the most commentary. You just never know.

Once you do get comments, to keep the flow going you have to respond to the comments you receive. Be open and willing to be proved wrong or challenged and never lose your temper. Some commenters are just *trolls*. Don't take the bait.

NEW TERM

As discussed later in this chapter, a troll is Internet speak for someone who posts obnoxious or inflammatory comments with the express aim of stirring up trouble. The intent of a troll is not healthy dialog, but to provoke a hostile response.

Engaging in a healthy dialogue makes your blog a place where people will go for ideas and inspiration, which means that you will gain inspiration as well. Every blog, no matter what the topic, is made better with comments.

REASONS TO TURN COMMENTS OFF

Although the culture of the blogosphere is supposed to be one of openness and transparency, sometimes things can get a little *too* open. As a general rule, I keep comments turned *on* for all my posts and *off* for all my pages. Comments for posts are on because I want commentary on what I've written. I have them off on pages because that's information I've put up for reference and I don't want commentary or feedback.

There are good reasons to turn comments off on a post. If a post is controversial, often the comments can get out of hand quickly. Even if the comments are civil, just the shear number can become a management problem! So, closing off additional comments (and putting an update in the post) can be the only way to stem the tide. People also close off comments if comments in a previously written post turn nasty, which is a painful thing to see. This is often a last resort if moderation and deleting comments isn't working.

Finally, closing off posts on a topic that is sensitive or painful might be a choice you make for yourself. Although I've often received my best and most fulfilling comments on my most heart-wrenching posts, you just might not want that. It's up to you. It is your blog.

If you are a business blogger and afraid of having comments on your business blog, the *worst* thing you can do is close off all comments. This shows to other bloggers that you aren't really serious about having conversations; you just want to talk to people. Just keep the comments open and moderate all comments for a while until you are comfortable with the kinds of comments you get.

Yes, it might seem scary at first, but closing off all comments entirely can only backfire on you.

Yes, to an extent. If a blogger is exercising due care and not allowing clearly libelous comments through, the remainder should fall under the purview of free speech. However, this has not always stood up well in court. The safest thing to do for a questionable comment is to hold it in the moderation queue until you can talk about the comment with the commenter. Sometimes a person might be willing to edit the comment. Remember this is your blog, and you don't have to accept any comments that you feel cross the line.

Earlier I mentioned receiving a cease-and-desist letter because of comments on a post on one of my blogs. The post was about accusations of wrongdoing at an Internet-based charity. The accusations were pretty serious, including things like tax issues and how much people were paid to do things for the company. The comments started to raise some disturbing questions. The story didn't seem to be as cut and dry as I thought. (When is it ever, really?)

At one point, the comments started to become ad hominem attacks on the founder of the company and his personal integrity. I received a letter from his lawyer demanding that I take down the post and all comments. Lucky for me, I was working for a blog network and they stood behind their bloggers. In the end, we (within our company) agreed that there was some merit to saying that as a blogger if I allowed a potentially libelous comment to be published, I could be liable for that.

The compromise was easy, actually. I reviewed all the comments. Any comment that I thought was borderline, I sent to the management team to review. Together we made a decision on keeping or pulling it. In the end, I only had to remove one comment. Nothing ever went to court, and everything worked out in the end.

Commenting on Other Blogs

There is another way to help increase the comments on your blog: Comment on other people's blogs. Yes, it might seem odd, but this is the community aspect to blogging. You should be reading blogs on a regular basis (we'll get to RSS readers later). When you find a post you enjoy and feel you have something to add to the discussion ("great post" doesn't count, sorry), leave a comment.

The trick here is that there is a field in the comment form for the URL to your blog. See where I'm going here? Yes, leave a good comment, with your name linked to your blog, and you can bet that the author of the post is going to check out your blog. It's almost 100% guaranteed that you'll get a visit from the author, but only if it's a good comment.

To get good comments, you need to give good comments. It is simple as that. Conversations take two people, so start your conversations off on the right foot with good comments. As you get to know more people through your blog, make sure you support what they are doing with comments (and links) on their posts.

Remember, though, that just like real life, however, some people like to stir up trouble and leave comments that aren't only off topic, but malicious as well. These folks are your aforementioned trolls, and they don't just live under bridges anymore.

Spam, Trolls, and Vermin: The Comments You Don't Want

Although commenters can be a source of support, gratification, and inspiration, they can also be a royal pain in the, well you know. Often the problem isn't really a "person" but a computer sending out "comments" filled with links to the dreckiest dreck of the Internet. People run these charming little programs to leave thousands of spam comments on blogs. These comments are full of links to porn, online pharmacies, cheap car insurance, generally the same things you see in your email. There are also people who get a lot of enjoyment from making other people's lives miserable—these trolls are some of the worst vermin online. Like their fairytale counterparts, they don't like the light of day and can be managed. Both comment spam and more human vermin can be managed if you employ some pretty simple tricks and techniques.

Spam

Dealing with comment spam isn't as bad as it used to be. When comment and trackback/pingback spam first hit the blogosphere, it was just a trickle. It was nothing huge, nothing that you couldn't manage with a few minutes a day, and then the storm hit. When the first blog spam storm hit, bloggers were caught off guard. It was so big that many blogs and whole-hosted blog platforms ground to a halt. Yeah, imagine if a newspaper was flooded with so many letters to the editor that the printing presses overheated and shut down. That's pretty much what happened (see Figure 4.1). Bloggers were not amused.

> **NOTE**
>
> Why is it called spam? This term comes from the Monty Python skit and song "Spam, Spam, Spam." At the resturant where you can get anything you want, but with Spam and you couldn't order something without Spam. So email and blog comments that you didn't want or ask for became—wait for it—spam!

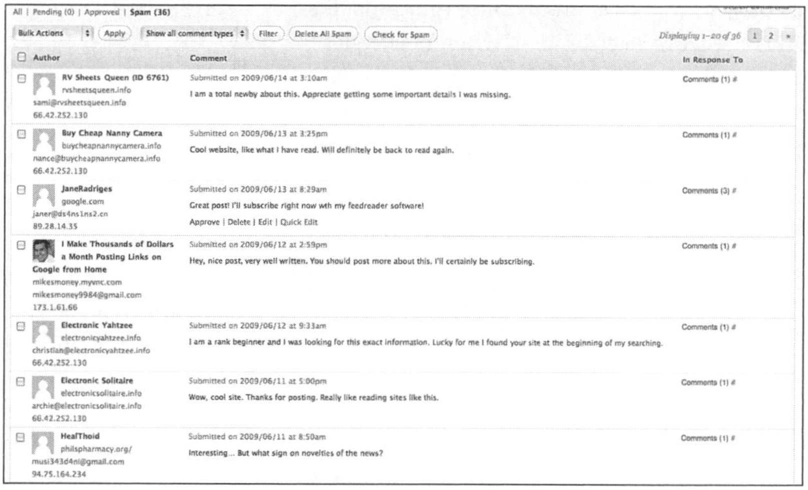

FIGURE 4.1

A selection of typical comment spam from my personal blog.

Being just as smart as the spammers, the blog community quickly figured out ways to combat them. Plug-ins were written, server rules were created, blacklists were made, and it was under control. Today, you don't have to "deal" with spam as much as be aware of it.

If you're using a hosted service like TypePad or WordPress.com, these services have anti-spam countermeasures already set up—it's in their best interest to. If you are self hosting, you'll need to install the anti-spam plug-ins yourself. With Movable Type and WordPress, you can use Akismet. For other blog platforms, there are anti-spam countermeasures available. Because comment spam can be a huge problem if it isn't managed, all major blogging platforms have ways to manage it.

Managing spam means that you have to look at the comments and pingbacks you get with a bit of a critical eye.

Managing spam means that you have to look at the comments and pingbacks you get with a bit of a critical eye. Legitimate ones stand out clearly, as well as spammy ones (plug-ins like Akismet learn over time, so when new styles come out you have to help by marking them spam). It's the subtle ones that you have to watch for. The following is how I separate the wheat from the chaff:

▶ Follow the link in the pingback. The spammy sites are obvious for their copious advertising and just posting excerpts from other blogs without original content.

▶ Sometimes comment spammers probe blogs with seemingly legitimate comments to get a comment approved. Generally once a commenter has been approved, he can comment without moderation after that. Look at the email address and site the commenter links to, which are often the giveaways to look for. If the email address looks a bit odd, you can probably bet it's a spammer testing the defenses.

▶ Don't worry if you accidentally mark a legitimate comment spam, because you can get a commenter or site off the black-list easily. As a community, bloggers would rather people be overcautious than overly kind.

Like email spam, comment spam thrives because there are people who let it get through. The spammers can make profits even if an infinitesimal fraction of blogs let spam through. So the fewer blogs that allow it through, the better off bloggers will be.

Trolls and Other Vermin

One of the facts of human nature is that no matter where or how people communicate or gather, there is always a jerk to be found. These are people who bait others into a fight or say something wholly inappropriate just to get attention or make people uncomfortable. You know who these people are in real life and if you see them at a party or meeting, you groan and try your best to avoid them. Sometimes they get the hint, sometimes they don't, and sometimes the bouncer tosses them out of the bar on their tush.

In the online world, the virtual equivalent is the troll. A troll is a person who just likes to stir things up and make trouble. They are often vulgar, insulting, and hateful.

Trolls are usually out for attention. Some people get their kicks being a jerk because the anonymity of the Internet makes it very easy to "be" someone else online. Although it's best to just ignore them, that's easy to say when someone isn't personally attacking you. Sometimes it is not enough to just ignore the troll; you might have to go beyond that. Blocking the person from commenting can be tricky because it is hard to isolate a single person on the Internet all of the time. What turns out to happen most often is to just keep deleting their comments. It might not be an automatic solution, but it is certainly a deterrent. The majority of the time, trolls are just a royal pain who will go away once they realize no one's taking their bait, but sometimes they cross the line, and when they do it often gets ugly.

Although you want to encourage conversation, you want to encourage thoughtful, witty conversations, not personal attacks, rants, or diatribes. (Okay, if you're the one ranting, that's different.) Having a comment policy is a first step, but better is just standing firm and standing your ground when someone crosses the line (or maybe strays a wee too close to the line). Remember, feed the conversation, but Do Not Feed The Trolls (DNFTT).

How does one feed the conversation? Ah, that is easier than you think.

IDEA GALLERY

http://headrush.typepad.com

KATHY SIERRA STORY

One the blogosphere's most (in)famous cases of trolls crossing the line surrounds blogger and technologist Kathy Sierra. Kathy was writing some amazing and influential blog posts and like anyone who starts getting attention, there is always a dark side to fame (I've had my share as well).

In March 2007, a line was crossed and the technology blogging community was aghast and horrified. Comments on Kathy's blog started to go from nasty and insensitive to threatening and downright scary. There were pictures of her posted next to a noose and worse. Personal information including her home address and Social Security number were posted online, in addition to (perceived) threats to her life. Kathy abruptly canceled all her speaking engagements, closed down her blog (although it still exists online), and withdrew completely from public life.

This incident highlighted not only the problem of trolls and other online vermin, but also the role of women in technology. In the end, the people who made the comments were called out and apologized. About a year later, Kathy returned to blogging and is stepping slowly back into public life.

This is an extreme example of the dark side of the Internet. 99.9% of comments on my blogs since 2004 have been positive and on point. A few of my friends have regular trolls, but often their comments are more laughable than anything serious. The point is to remember that it's your blog. Yes, there is an ethos of allowing all comments through if they aren't spam, but just as you have rules of conversation in your home, you have rules on your blog. If someone crosses the line, just delete, edit, or spam the comment.

Finding Other Blogs in Your Niche

One of the most fun and gratifying parts of being a part of the blogosphere and social media is connecting with people all over the world who share interests and passions. Whether it's technology, books, pens, cameras, or cooking, I have met some truly amazing (and inspiring) people through my various blogs. Many of these people are close friends, even if I only get to see them once a year at most. So, how did I find these people? The answer is only a click away.

Part of blogging is reading other blogs. If you're into fly tying or indie neo-classical music, you want to read what other people are doing and saying. So, do what everyone else does: Google it. Specifically, Google Blog Search it.

Google Blog Search is a subset of Google that focuses solely on returning results from blogs. So if you're interested in opera and do a search, it might look something like Figure 4.2.

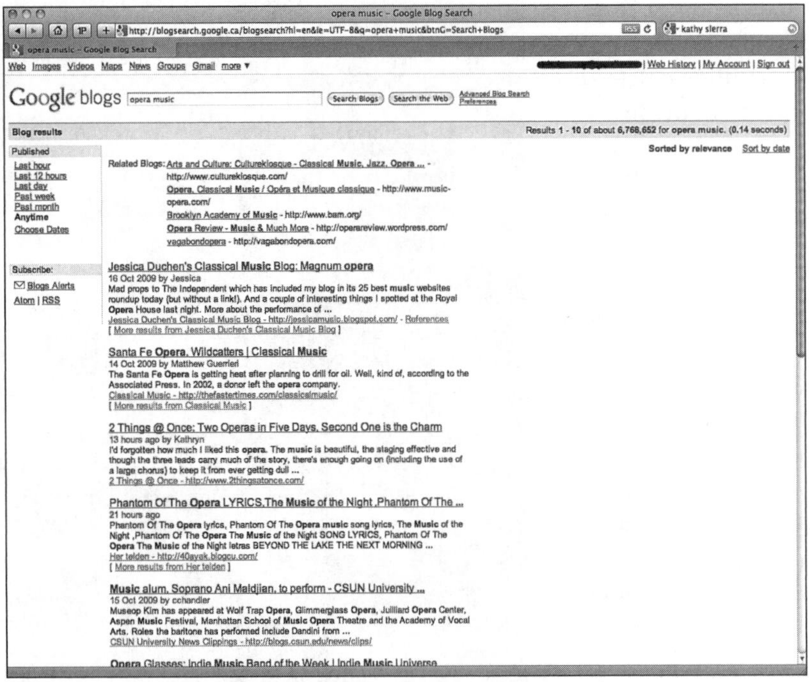

FIGURE 4.2

Searching for opera music on Google Blog Search.

Now, some of the entries might not all be from blogs, but a lot are. Follow the links. Read the posts. Because bloggers usually have links on their blogs to other blogs that offer similar content that they respect, follow their links to the other blogs. Now you've got the idea.

Using an RSS reader like Google Reader, FeedDemon, or NetNewsWire, you can subscribe to a virtually unlimited number of blogs and easily keep up with particular bloggers posts. If nothing else, bookmark them to come back to regularly read their new posts. I discuss more about RSS readers as part of your blogging toolkit in Chapter 3, "Writing and Creating a Conversation." To give you a taste of the range of blogs I follow, Figure 4.3 shows a screenshot from my RSS reader.

Read these posts, leave comments, write posts based on the ideas you get from them (giving credit and linking of course), and build a connection. Once you start finding blogs in your niche, you will find many, many others.

> **TIP**
>
> It's easy to find sites with RSS feeds. Just look in the address bar of your browser! If an RSS feed is included, you will see a special icon that looks like a dot with radio waves coming from it.

As Twitter and FriendFeed have begun to move into the mainstream, you can find new blogs just by connecting with people on social networks. When I start following and interacting with new people on Twitter, for example, I always check out their blog. Even if I might not think I'm interested in the topic they write about, reading their blogs gives me a new sense of who they are. Reading these blogs leads to other blogs because bloggers link to bloggers. I've lost hours just reading and clicking and clicking. I guess I can't say I "lost" the hours, because I generally leave enriched, better informed, and sometimes with nifty new techie toys to play with.

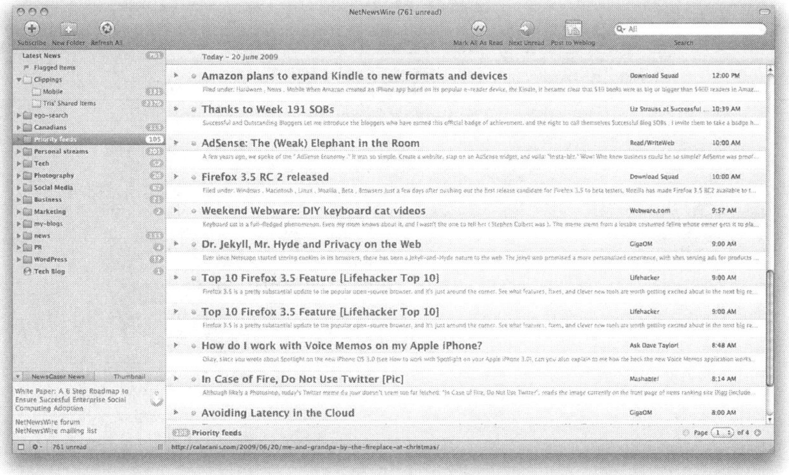

FIGURE 4.3

Just a few posts from the 700+ feeds I monitor on topics including technology, books, software, music, and beyond.

Linking to Other Blogs

It is essential to link to other blogs if you want to be successful and noticed. Linking to others shows appreciation to others, gives credit for the inspiration, and gives your readers more background or information on the topic.

Bloggers know when you link to their posts because they get a pingback on the post and most bloggers have searches send them results for links to them, mentions of their names, or mentions of their blogs (these are called "ego feeds").

Like getting a great comment, getting a link back is a great feeling. The more you link out, the more the search engines will love you. Search engines love sites that are content rich, updated frequently, and link to a lot of other relevant sites. When you link to someone, make the text of the link something descriptive like "as John said in his brilliant post…" instead of "click here." Beyond giving your readers some context for the link, you also give search

engines context for both your post and the other person's post. This amplifying effect helps both of you get better search engine rankings on a given topic.

Yes, there are times when you just want to write a long post to stand on its own. This is perfectly okay. I do this when I'm feeling a little more academic or verbose, but just make sure that you do link to other blogs in the majority of posts.

The easiest way to include other blogs in your posts is with the "Blog this…" *bookmarklet* that all blogging platforms have, and many editors as well. All of them work in the same, simple fashion. When you're on a page that you'd like to blog about, just click the bookmarklet on your bookmark bar, and a new post will be opened for you with a link to that original post (see Figure 4.4). If you select some text from the post, that becomes part of the post as well along with the link to the post. Nothing could be easier, and it's how I started blogging with Blogger back in the day and for the most part haven't changed that workflow substantially in five years.

FIGURE 4.4

Using WordPress' Press This bookmarklet to start a post on making a pizza oven.

NEW TERM

A bookmarlet is like a regular bookmark, but it contains a little Javascript script instead of a link to a website. This Javascript tells your browser to go to a certain site and perform some action. In the case of Posterous or WordPress, these bookmarlets help you quickly create new posts.

So remember, no blog is or should be an island. You need to link out, a lot. Remember to keep it relevant to the topic at hand or not only will your readers be confused, so will the search engines.

Connecting with Other Bloggers

As you might have gathered, commenting, linking, and reading other blogs are all the foundations to connecting with other bloggers. After a few comments on my blog, especially if they have been good comments, I'll often email the commenter, in addition to reading his or her blog, linking to it, and commenting. The blogosphere isn't really any different than the world as a whole. You start friendships one step at a time. Emails move into instant messages that, distance or timing permitting, move into meeting in person over a coffee. Because blogging is global in scale, there are a lot of people I consider friends who I've never met in person.

The blogosphere isn't really different than the world as a whole. You start friendships one step at a time. Emails move into instant messages that, distance or timing permitting, move into meeting in person over a coffee.

IS THE BLOGROLL DEAD?

When blogging was young, your "blogroll" was de rigueur for your sidebar. A blogroll was a list of links to your favorite blogs and bloggers you were friends with. Being included, or excluded, from a prominent blogger's blogroll was a big deal. But today with Facebook, FriendFeed, and Twitter on the scene, the blogroll is fading from importance. I will often not bother with a blogroll at all or only use it to link to other blogs or my own (or on a client's site, their other websites). Whether you bother with a blogroll or not is up to you, but you can just leave the drama in the past, thank you.

Regardless of the distance, the key is a global meeting of mind and common interests. This is what gives bloggers the strength in numbers. It's the friendships and professional rapport that builds up over time that gives bloggers the ability to call on friends and colleagues to repost, retweet, and otherwise get the word out on a particular issue or topic. Public relations crises aren't created by just one blogger; it's one blogger tapping into his or her network that can cause giant corporations to stand up and take notice.

When it comes down to it, a certain kind of person is attracted to this medium, and that person is inherently social. People like to chat, engage, and share. Yes, many people prefer to stay at home with the safety and distance the virtual world brings, but would enjoy social interaction and company.

So, no matter how you reach out and connect to other bloggers, do it. Send that email, follow them on Twitter, connect, and engage. There are a lot of amazing people out there.

Twitter, Microblogging, and Lifestreams

In case you hadn't noticed by now, the topics and sections of this book are more like a tapestry than a linear set of steps. Comments are for connecting with other bloggers, conversation, and inspiration. Linking isn't just to improve your SEO standings, but also to show appreciation and give your readers more depth and insight.

The phenomena of Twitter/microblogging and FriendFeed/lifestreaming are no different. Both of these new classes of tools/services serve to connect, inspire, converse, and promote. One trick ponies they are not. As you might also expect, their rise is intertwined with both each other and social media overall. Let's take a closer look at them both in terms of conversation and promotion.

Twitter can be very hard to explain. It started off as a service where you told your friends what you were up to answering the question: What are you doing? For the first six months of its life, Twitter was something only the geekiest of geeks paid much attention to. In March 2007, it exploded and hasn't stopped yet.

So, what good is it? Your messages can only be 140 characters long. The more people you follow, the harder it is to keep in touch with your friends.

You'd be surprised at how much you can say in 140 characters. In fact, it's a great exercise in brevity to distill a complex idea into a few words. As for the fire hose effect, well that is handled with good applications that help you manage your Twitter stream.

For the first six months of its life, Twitter was something only the geekiest of geeks paid much attention to. In March 2007, it exploded and hasn't stopped yet.

Fine, it isn't so bad, but still, why?

Because Twitter has become an online nexus of information and communication. Twitter is where people come together and not only update people on their thoughts, but share links, pass on headlines, and just chat. Twitter is one of those, you have to see it to get it, things and even then a lot of people don't like it or get it. That's okay. It is like trying to talk with a flock of hummingbirds on amphetamines (and you're one of the hummingbirds), but once you get the knack of it you might find that it is one of the best places for news and conversation.

> **NOTE**
>
> Twitter started as a side project for the folks at Odeo to break a creative slump and have a way to let each other know what they were up to. Today, Twitter is growing by leaps and bounds and even celebrities of all stripes use it. So, what are you doing?

Facebook and Social Networks

I'm going to tell you right now that I'm a certified Facebook curmudgeon. If I know you, I'll accept your friend request, but I don't necessarily participate in a lot of the reindeer games that go on there. Sure I'll respond to an event, but throw a sheep or sic a zombie on me and I'm just going to ignore that.

Regardless, Facebook and the myriad of personal and professional social networks are great places to connect with people and their blogs. The key way you're going to start the

GROUPING INFORMATION LETS YOU MANAGE IT

Without a doubt, Twitter can dump an unfathomable amount of information into your lap, but only if you let it. Even though I follow about 6,800 people on Twitter (some Twitter accounts are just news feeds from BBC and CNN), I can manage the flow of information *and* still keep up with my friends (which is what Twitter was originally designed to do). How? Simply by grouping people together, and having an application that lets me look at those groups easily.

TweetDeck is a free application (Mac, PC, and Linux) for Twitter that enables me to build groups of Twitter accounts that I follow and put those groups into separate columns. For example, I have a column just for news sources and a column just for tweets that mention me. I have columns for friends and one for colleagues. I also build columns for searches of interesting topics. These searches let me search through all the tweets posted on Twitter, not just from the people I follow.

TweetDeck is just one example of a Twitter tool with this sort of functionality. Web-based services Hootsuite (www.hootsuite.com) and Brizzly (www.brizzly.com) both have this capability as well as applications like Nambu (Mac only) and Mixero (Mac, PC, and Linux). I think looking at the deluge of content that Twitter can unleash makes it pretty obvious why bloggers need tools to group, filter, and search through Twitter.

Now if I could only do this for email.

connecting process is to make sure you have a link to your blog in your profile on these networks. If you have more than one blog (yes, sometimes that happens), add as many as you can or just pick a blog to be your hub online.

Facebook is the hot thing right now, but other social networking sites like LinkedIn and MySpace are still going strong. All social networks do one thing well: They connect people. Part of this connecting is giving people a little about yourself to not only learn more about you, but also match you with similar affinity groups. For example, if a social network asks in your profile what you do for a living (say writer) and a hobby or two (reading and cooking), then it will be easier for other writers to find you. Likewise if you can add geographic info, you might be able to find other bloggers near you. In Vancouver, there are several social media-blogging groups like the Vancouver Bloggers Meetup, Third Tuesday, WordPress Meetup, and Drupal users groups.

I found all of these through one social network or another. Maybe I saw a mention of it on Twitter or was invited through Facebook or read about it on a blog. Regardless of source, these groups are a lot of fun and a great way to meet like-minded people in real life.

Just remember that it isn't the site or program or whatever that makes a social network; it's the people in it. Facebook might implode on itself (I can only hope so), but the desire to connect with each other will remain as strong as ever and people will find (and build) a site or service to do just that. Count on it.

Summary

This chapter discussed the ways you can expand your readership and build a community around your blog. Whether it's leaving comments, linking, social networks, or meeting people in real life, the central premise is that what people are doing is social. Humans are social animals. We like to gather together. People like to find other people interested in the same things, whether specifically (the left-handed fly tiers club) or generally (Vancouver bloggers meetup), through that meeting and connecting, experiences, writing, and blogs become richer and more fulfilling to everyone.

It's about community, and community is one factor that can separate a blog from the crowd. Whether it's comments on your blog or other's, these are the first steps to building a community. Once you start writing your blog, look for other blogs in your niche. Use these blogs as both inspiration, part of your community, and connections to other social networks. Make sure you leverage the networks you're already a part of, like Twitter and Facebook, to promote your blog and also connect to your community of readers in another place.

Like any society, the Internet and Blogosphere has a darker side as well. Like your email, there is spam to handle, which is easy to manage, but also people who like to just cause trouble. These trolls are best left ignored and comments either deleted or just left to sit. If a troll crosses the line, then you might need to take additional steps, but that is a rare occurrence.

Building a community around your blog is just like building a community of friends; it takes time, but is a very rewarding experience.

CHAPTER 5

Creating a Personal Blog

It seems a little redundant to talk about creating a personal blog, because in the beginning all blogs were personal. To have a business blog was anathema to bloggers. Making a blog that is all about "you" is what's at the heart of personal blogging. You is in quotes because, as you've learned, who "you" are online really depends on how much or how little you want to reveal. Because this is a personal blog, it's intended to reflect your beliefs, hobbies, family, essentially who you are.

I think many people dismiss personal blogs as less serious than "professional" or "business" blogs, but I think it's just the opposite. Personal blogs are very serious, even if the subject matter isn't. What's more important than who you are? Because the origins of blogging center on the personal blog, it's important not to just dismiss them out of hand.

I first started blogging to learn about it for professional reasons and to be an outlet for things I wasn't doing at work. It was the epitome of the personal blog. Of course in my case, my blog was mostly about collaboration tools, software, and other geek esoterica. Still it was personal and, because I expressed myself well and made some local connections, my humble blog became a springboard to my present career. That said, there is a strange hybrid here that is worth noting, the personal-business blog. My blog falls under that category because it is my personal blog, but it serves to drive and support my professional career and business life. If you want into this category, I suggest you read both this chapter and the next one on business blogs. Take what you learn in both chapters and run with those ideas.

This chapter takes what you've learned in the previous four chapters and builds on it so you can go from a general blog to something that's more your style. Roll up your sleeves here and get to work.

What to Put in a Personal Blog

Because this is a personal blog, what kind of content you post is up to you. So you might have posts, videos, podcasts, pictures, or whatever suits you at the moment—whatever tells your story. This is fantastic really because it gives you a nice depth and breadth into the range of things you can have on a blog. This range of ideas is perfect for when you get hired for your first professional blogging gig or your boss asks you to write, set up, or own the company's blog.

NOTE

If you are like most technology folks, you might also have a professional or business blog at work where you can't talk about everything freely, so having a personal blog frees you to do that. I do this myself because there are things that I want to write about that just aren't appropriate for my work blog (even if my personal blog is admittedly somewhat of a business blog, too).

If you intend to run both personal and professional blogs it won't take long to realize it's a bit of a high wire act. I was fortunate in this regard because my bosses accept that I have both kinds of blogs and, because I keep those lines very clear, they don't censor me at work or at home. Okay, sometimes I slip a bit from one side to another and so will you, but we are all human after all.

What do you put on a personal blog? Well, the sky's the limit really. Throughout this chapter I'll cover the different ways you can fill your personal blog with content. Let's start with the simplest; the basic blog post.

Writing

Chapter 3, "Writing and Creating a Conversation," discusses writing in a general way, but in a personal blog, giving readers a look into your life is what brings people back to read more posts. Some of my favorite blogs have been ones where the posts were about the lighter side of family life or a person's struggle with cancer or a recovery from an accident. A very popular blog told the stories of a paramedic in London, UK. He related what life was like for him when saving lives, witnessing tragedy, and even the drudgery of his job. This was a great read.

What pulled it all together was the writing style or voice. Personal blogs are more informal. This isn't where you'd expect a long treatise on the meaning of life; it's where you might find the funniest street signs you see on your way to work. How about the guy you buy your paper from? There can be great stories there.

TIP

It's hard to just sit down and pound stories out on command, so if you're trying to capture these kinds of stories try to jot them down as they happen.

Don't worry that your writing isn't "good enough," because it is good enough; just write your stories. No matter what your stories are, write them with passion and realism, and people will enjoy them.

IDEA GALLERY

A FEW OF MY FAVORITE PERSONAL BLOGS

There are a ton of personal blogs out there that I like and respect, but the following are a few of my favorites:

- ▶ Joey deVilla "The Adventures of Accordion Guy in the 21st Century"— www.joeydevilla.com
- ▶ Marshall Kirkpatrick—marshallk.com
- ▶ Matt Mullenweg (creator of WordPress)— ma.tt
- ▶ Derek Miller—www.penmachine.com
- ▶ Erin Koteki Vest "Queen of Spain"— queenofspainblog.com

Spend some time reviewing these blogs, because they might give you some ideas for what to do with your own blog.

Topics

One of the unfortunate examples of blogger stereotypes is the infamous "cat blogging," which refers to personal blogs that are just writing about and having lots of pictures of an owner's cat (or dog). Okay, it's true. Cat owners often do mention them from time to time, some people far too often.

You can gather a lot, though, from the way people write about their cats. They love their cats and want to share their cats' lives with the world. The topic is close to them and, most of all, personal. It's something with which other obsessive pet owners can identify. This is the key for your blog. You're not writing for the people who have no interest in your passion, but rather those who share it. It doesn't matter if the topic is cats, crocheting, or reflecting on the nature of humanity; topics for your personal blog are entirely of your own choosing.

With that said, let's take a look at some popular categories of personal blogs.

TIP

Ideas for topics and posts come at the strangest times and places. Keep a small notebook and pen handy to jot them down! You could even email them to yourself, and that's really geeky.

Hobbies

We all have hobbies, even geeks like me. Often it's a hobby that you're really passionate about (such as woodworking, stamp collecting, fishing, wines, cooking, trains, and photography) that are often some of the best and most rewarding topics for personal blogs.

Write your blog like you'd talk about it to another enthusiast. Share tips, tricks, pictures of your latest creation, and in-jokes that only a true aficionado would get.

On my personal blog (which does get professional often), I have talked about my passions for cooking and photography. I've shared recipe creations and photography tips/finds. The comments I get on those posts are something that I truly look forward to. How often do you get to "geek out" on your hobby?

Write your blog like you'd talk about it to another enthusiast. Share tips, tricks, pictures of your latest creation, and in-jokes that only a true aficionado would get.

I know that often the other people in our lives get a wee tired of hearing about how you just found a great way to store all your grades of sandpaper so you could both find them and keep them sorted by grade or the awesome new pattern for knitted laptop covers you found. An audience of like-minded enthusiasts never gets tired of it. Whether it's just one facet of your personal blog or the primary focus, talk about your hobbies. Make this your little corner of the world where you can wax poetic on good-fitting lens caps and not feel like it's strange at all. (It isn't strange, by the way. I hate poorly fitting lens caps!)

Life

Yes, "Life" is a broad category, I know, but life is like that, isn't it? Whether you talk about love found or love lost, your partner, or your kids, sharing the stories of your life is something that can be very therapeutic. Savoring the victories and sharing the defeats is something everyone can relate to and enjoy reading. Not in a shallow schadenfreude kind of way, mind you, but rather in that more positive and constructive way all individuals like to share their lives.

In my personal blog, for example, you can find entries about dealing with divorce and loss, mourning and marking the anniversary of my father's passing, and marking the rite of passage of my first "heart scare." These are the real, gritty parts of life, which are the things that connect humans and people. Don't shy away from them; embrace them.

Yes, there is a limit to what you should share. As I'll delve into later in this chapter, there are some things that you might not feel comfortable sharing or that you feel comfortable sharing but the other people in your life don't. Respect that line and try to stay on the "good" side of it. Yes, you will slip now and then, but if your heart is in the right place it might escape unscathed.

One note that I reiterate later as well is that once you publish something online, it's there forever. Delete isn't really delete because the content might be cached and stored all over the Internet. As my friend and journalist for the Vancouver Sun Gillian Shaw says, "Don't put something online that you don't want to see printed on the front page of the paper."

> **TIP**
>
> Think about using an offline blog editor to enable you to blog offline and work on drafts more easily. Blog editors are like conventional word processors, but for blogs. My favorites are Windows Live Writer (Windows), Scribefire (Firefox extension), Ecto (Mac), and Blogo (Mac).

Just "Stuff"

Of course there is a lot of space between life and hobbies, so I've called that space stuff. No, it's not the most eloquent descriptor, but it works. This category includes movies, music, books, and day-to-day issues that are just general chit-chat. For like-minded people, it's always good to read about what someone thinks about a movie or book. Where else can you post those silly pictures you find online or those bad jokes that proliferate on the Internet like rabbits?

Privacy

When you choose to blog, you are choosing to live a portion of your life in the public eye. Sure, most of the things you write are innocuous, but sometimes they aren't. Again, that's fine because you're choosing to reveal those things about yourself. What about the other people in your life? Yes, there's the rub. Although deciding your own level of privacy online, and that "line" will float and change over time, is relatively easy, you have to also consider other people as well and how they might or might not be included in your writing.

> *"Don't put something online that you don't want to see printed on the front page of the paper." – Gillian Shaw, Vancouver Sun*

Relationships

Because this is a personal blog, delving into the world of relationships seems like a natural topic area. Many of the women I know write about their (mis)adventures in dating, being married, or being a parent. Interestingly, not as many write about the same things, with the exception of parenting. In any case, my friends who write about their relationships do so either with the full knowledge of their partners or write so their partners (usually dates) remain anonymous.

For married couples who both blog, there is an even more interesting dynamic there, but again there are agreed-upon rules. Don't be surprised that the first question you're asked when you announce, "Honey, I'm starting a blog!" is "What are you going to write about?" which isn't really about your topic per se as much it is asking, "Are you going to be blogging about me/us/the kids?" This is the moment to have the ground rules established.

When you write about your partner, show him or her the post before you post it. If your partner wants something gone, make it gone.

Even if you're going to be blogging about your pets, model trains, or knitting patterns, because blogs become a personal outlet the other people in your life creep into your writing. Figure out early on how comfortable your partner is with being included in your writing. When you write about your partner, show him or her the post before you post it. If your partner wants something gone, make it gone. Even if you're just referring to his or her

as "my dear hubs" or "my darling wife" or "the love of my life," give your snookie-poo a chance to say no. Yes, as time goes on, the rules and lines might change. This is a natural evolution, so there's no need to push it at the beginning. Respect the boundaries that have been established and if, later on, you want to push him or her, ask first.

Children

Where kids are concerned, it's a horse of a different color. The world today is not like the world I grew up in as a kid—not at all. My personal line is that pictures of my children online are private to friends and family only. I don't use their full names and make a point of avoiding discussion that makes them personally identifiable online. Other friends of mine have pictures of their children online and use their names. The line you draw is up to you and your partner. Where children are concerned, you're not just talking about personal privacy but their personal safety. When your children are old enough, they can participate to a degree in the discussion. My daughter has veto rights on pictures that I put up even for friends and family to see. In the end, you are going to have to make your own decision. Honestly, don't take it lightly.

Comments

Chapter 4, "Building Community," explores more about comments in detail, mostly in terms of how they relate to building a community. For a personal blog, commentary is just continuing the discussion or the story. As discussed in Chapter 4, although individuals might leave comments that are inappropriate or abusive the best way to engage them is to not engage them at all. Sadly, these sorts of comments are one of the dark sides of the Internet. I've known bloggers who have had serious run-ins with people who crossed the line, but these have been the glaring exceptions and not the rule. I have found comfort, solace, support, congratulations, and good laughs from the comments left on my blogs over the years. Rarely have I ever had a comment that strayed into the realm of troll and when they did, the comments were so asinine that I let them stand as a testament to their own stupidity.

Although I started this section with the caveat of the bad things that commenters can bring, let me close with the good. I have found that when I have written deeply personal posts, ones that talk about life struggles or successes, the comments have always been the best parts of the posts. They have not only shown me the depth and warmth of the human sprit, but also that as a writer that I moved people. When the story I tell elicits the emotions in my readers that I felt while writing it, then "I done good." People relate to, and comment on, things like struggles with grief and loss but also successes. I've written about missing my father, but also how he is still my greatest inspiration (this book is dedicated to him). When I've written about topics that everyone can relate to, I get the best and most heart-warming comments. Enjoy your comments. They might very well be the best part of the blog.

SHOULD KIDS HAVE THEIR OWN BLOG?

This is a great question both for parents who blog and for those who don't. Pretty soon, your kids might ask about having their own blogs. Before you say, "No," there are safe and secure ways for your kids to blog. My favorite, and easiest, is to set up a private blog on WordPress.com. Not only can you shield a WP.com blog from search engines, you can set it so it is only visible to approved members. To everyone else, it just isn't there. My daughter has had a blog like this for years. It's nice and safe and secure. When your kids are old enough you can talk about making the blog public, but in the meantime, think of how much the grandparents, aunts, and uncles would like to read updates online? Yeah, it's pretty cool.

It's important if your child is active online, and especially if they blog in semi-public, that you set some ground rules about how they conduct themselves online, such as the following:

- ▶ Emailing people you, as a parent, don't know
- ▶ IMing people you don't know
- ▶ Giving out personal information like real name, hometown, address, or phone number
- ▶ Meeting people you meet online in the real world
- ▶ Using webcams and voice chat

One thing that will probably grate on your kids is having the computer in a public part of the house and not their rooms. Yes, there will come a time when they are old enough for the computer to be in their rooms, but early on (elementary age, especially) kids' computer use should be supervised. In the age of inexpensive laptops and netbooks, this is going to get harder and harder to enforce, but it's important to make sure your child is safe online.

Multimedia

In 2009, The World Wide Web turned 20 years old and the Internet itself turned 40. From the beginning of the Web and the first web sites, it was more than just text, images, and sounds that played a huge role in bringing it to life. These days, seeing a webpage barren of pictures seems like an error, and often it is. Although you might not think your personal blog will contain "multimedia," you'd be wrong. Pictures, videos, music, and podcasts are all forms of multimedia that are getting richer and richer by the day—you're likely to find a use for at least some of them on your blog.

This section explores using pictures, video, and audio (podcasts) in your personal blog. Let's take it from the hobbyist perspective and focus on simple tools and techniques. If your hobby is photography (like me), video, or audio, clearly you might take things up a notch or three. You might also read Chapters 7, "Creating a Podcast Blog," 8, "Video Blogging," and 9, "Creating a Portfolio Blog." These chapters offer a far more detailed look into each of these areas. Now, because a picture is worth a thousand words, and I'm a lazy typist, let's start with pictures.

Pictures

Putting pictures, whether yours or ones you like by others, on your blog is one of the easiest ways to punch up your blog and add some color and spice. The technical "how" you do it varies from blog platform to blog platform, but keep in mind the general points in this section when adding pictures to your blog. Before discussing how you get a picture in your post, let's talk about copyright.

Make Sure You Have the Right to Post It

I know this seems like a really strange thing to say, but one of the biggest problems online is people posting and republishing images without the permission of the artist or even giving artists attribution for the work. Clearly this doesn't apply to photos you've taken or other works you create yourself, but it starts to apply to pictures other people take and other art online. Often the easiest way to find out whether you can use the image is to just look at the information around it. For example, I put this as part of the description of pictures I post online: ©Tris Hussey, 2009.

When you see "Non-commercial use permitted with attribution," it means that if you aren't a company who makes money through your website, you are free to re-post/use my picture as long as you give me credit. If you're a company, you're not allowed to just use the image without my permission. Sometimes that permission comes with a price tag; sometimes not. Often I love to see my works used on my friends' websites. If someone really likes a picture I took of him or her, well I can't think of a higher compliment than for him or her to want to use it to represent himself or herself online. To do this, my friends ask me before posting the picture, and you should do the same for other artists.

Always remember that just because it's posted online doesn't mean that you have the right to use the work of art. It doesn't really matter even if your intentions are good (for example, promoting the artist), because in most cases it's illegal. So, look at the picture and determine what the "rights" are. See whether you can just use it free and clear (public domain) or have limited rights (non-commercial use only) or all rights reserved (hands off, buddy). If you're not sure, you need to ask.

Posting and Sharing Pictures Online

Putting your pictures into your blog posts is really only half the battle. Due to the advent of the digital camera, the number of pictures people can take and save has become tremendous. Because the pictures are already digital, moving them from your computer to blog is a pretty straightforward process. What if you want to have whole albums online, or even just a whole bunch of pictures? The answer is right there on your computer.

First, start with iPhoto (Mac), Windows Live Photo Gallery (Windows), or Picasa (Mac and Windows), which are all great solutions for managing your pictures on your machine. iPhoto is pictured in Figure 5.1.

Once you start organizing your pictures on your computer, you can then start posting them online as well. There are lots of photo-sharing services out there ranging from Picasa and Flickr to SmugMug and SnapFish. Each of them offer its own additional services, but in the end its core service is uploading your pictures to the Internet and sharing them. Most services enable you to mark the pictures public or private, title them, and share them with family and friends through email. Some additional services include grouping pictures into sets, tagging, editing, and requesting physical prints (and other items) of the pictures. When you view a photo-sharing site, look at what you get free versus what you have to pay for. Look at how long the company has been around and how many users it has. For example, Picasa is owned by Google and Flickr by Yahoo!. Both of these Internet giants aren't going anywhere anytime soon and have tens

FIGURE 5.1

A look at iPhoto and my collection of pictures.

TO RESIZE IMAGES OR NOT

Today's images from most digital cameras are very large files sizes, like 5+ megabytes, and dimensions of over 4000 × 2000 *pixels*. Many blog engines, like WordPress, automatically create smaller versions for you, but the original is still stored on the server taking up space in your account, and the server has to work pretty hard to resize those images. For my blog posts, I always resize images when I export them from iPhoto or other photo-management tools. I reserve my full-sized, high-resolution images for Flickr.com, which is designed to host and manage high-resolution pictures.

Photo management tools like iPhoto and Picasa have an option to resize the picture when you export a copy to your hard disk. For a standard picture that you'd like to have people be able to click and see a larger version, having the longest edge scaled to 800 pixels is fine. If you are going to just put the image into a post, resize images to about 500 pixels max.

This is an example of what this export process looks like in Picasa.

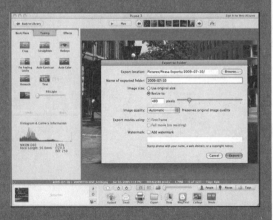

of thousands of users each. In my opinion, either of them is a safe bet. Personally, I use Flickr and have tens of thousands of pictures stored there.

TIP

There are a lot of popular online photo-sharing sites: Flickr (my preferred), Picasa, SnapFish, and SmugMug (more for pros).

Having your pictures online at one of these services does two things for you. The first is obvious, you can point readers easily to your set of pictures about your new project. The second is actually much cooler. You can often post pictures to your blog right from the online photo service. Flickr does a good job of this enabling you to post all pictures as you upload them, or ad hoc as you need them. You can also get easy to copy-and-paste code for a given picture that you can use in a blog post (I usually do the latter).

As a personal blogger, this saves you time in uploading *and* server space because Flickr or Picasa are storing the actual file not your server or host (this is very important for WordPress.com users). How do you get a picture into a post? That's what I'm going to show you next!

Getting a Picture into Your Post

The good part is how to get those stupid pictures into your post. Assume for this example that your picture is on your local drive. You've exported it from iPhoto or Live Photo Gallery (optional) and you've already resized it to fit your blog (optional). From there, use the following steps.

NEW TERM

A pixel is a unit of measurement used to measure the size and resolution of images. For example, your monitor might be set to a resolution of 1024 × 768, which means 1024 pixels wide by 768 pixels high. A 3.1-megapixel camera captures images at 2048 × 1536 (2048 × 1536 = 3,145,728 pixels or 3.1 megapixels).

toolbar and looks like a white square with a black square inside it.

1. Click the Insert image button in your post editor. This takes many forms but generally looks like a picture or a circle, triangle, and square. If you're not sure what the button looks like, try to pass your mouse point over each icon in the toolbar and see what comes up for a tool tip. In WordPress, the button is located above the formatting

2. Find the image on your hard drive (see Figure 5.2). You should already know where the picture is, but if you're unsure, start your search in the My Pictures (PC) or Pictures (Mac) folders.

3. Upload it. This should be an obvious button in the window. Once you find it, click it.

4. Tweak how it will show up. This is where wrapping text around the image or having it stand alone comes in. What you're looking for are buttons or radio buttons that say things like align left, align right, or no alignment. Align left puts the text on the right, and align right places text on the left (see Figure 5.3).

FIGURE 5.2

Choosing a picture from your hard drive to upload to WordPress.

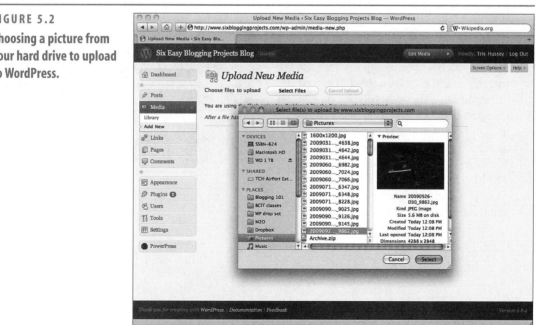

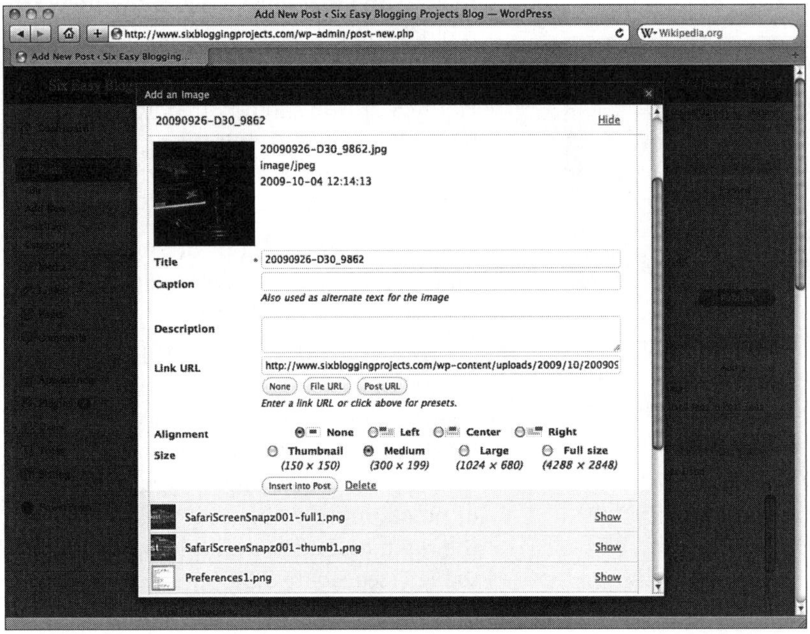

FIGURE 5.3
Adjusting images setting in WordPress.

If you are seeing the changes live as you make the tweaks, you might think, "Yuck! All the text is smooshed up against the image!" Yes, it is, so you need to give it a little padding. There should be boxes to set margins or padding parameters for the image. Enter a number in pixels to serve as a buffer between the text and image. You can play with the amount of space you like, but personally I like 5 pixels. After you insert the picture, the result should look something like Figure 5.4.

NOTE

When you upload an image, WordPress 2.7 automatically does all the resizing for you. It creates a thumbnail, small, medium, and large versions of your image so it is less of an issue than it was previously, although I still resize images myself. It's just a good habit to be in!

FIGURE 5.4
Image in place in a draft post.

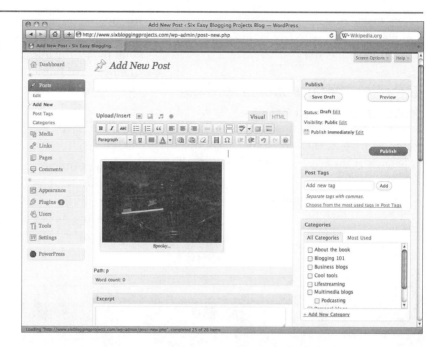

That's pretty much it. It's not exactly rocket science, is it? People often feel that placing images in a post is difficult, but like most things, once you get the hang of it, it really isn't. If you'd like to make it harder on yourself, be my guest (maybe try doing it blindfolded), but I don't think you really need to do that.

Podcasting

Podcasting is like video blogging, except it's audio only. Podcasting was initially more popular than video blogging. The files are much smaller and generally easier to deal with. Like video blogging, podcasting for the personal blogger is something that you should keep pretty simple. If you use a laptop as your primary computer, you are likely to find a

microphone is built-in. If you're using a desktop machine or a laptop without a microphone, then just go out and buy a basic headset with microphone. I've used headsets for podcasting and video conferencing that cost about $20 and were perfectly adequate to the task of recording a podcast for a personal blog. You don't have to break the bank getting a super-duper headset. If you catch the podcasting bug after doing a few episodes, then read Chapter 7. For now, though, you are going to keep this simple and low to no cost.

There are two ways to record your podcast. The first is to use a recording program like GarageBand for the Mac or Audacity (Windows/Mac/Linux, free) to record directly to your hard drive. The second way is a little more interesting because it combines high tech and low tech into a cool solution: using the phone to call into a service to record your episode. Let's start with recording the podcast on your machine first.

Recording Podcasts on Your Machine

Recording and editing podcasts is a simple process. First, open the application that will record your voice, then edit it to remove the little gaps at the beginning and end. I usually add in some intro music with a nice fade in and out. Sometimes I'll add background music to the entire show, but that's trickier because you have to find music that can still be heard, but not overwhelm your voice. Often I've found great tracks for background music, but couldn't get the music low enough (and still be intelligible as music) or vocals high enough to be able to hear either one well. The only way to know is to try and experiment. Now, let's get into recording and editing in a little more depth.

Although GarageBand (for the Mac) contains a lot of powerful tools (see Figure 5.5), it sometimes seems like overkill for a simple recording. For new and novice users, I suggest starting with Audacity.

FIGURE 5.5

Apple's GarageBand for recording podcasts.

Audacity is an open-source software project to create a great, basic (actually it has grown to be more than basic) sound and recording editor that is available to everyone (see Figure 5.6). You can download the latest version from audacity.sourceforce.net.

Recording with Audacity

After you download, install, and launch Audacity, you might think that you're in for a really complicated application. The good thing is that you're not—not at all. Audacity automatically finds and chooses the microphone (called input devices) you have set as a default. I've learned, through trial, error, and swearing, that if you want to connect a new device to use as a microphone, you need to quit Audacity and relaunch it in order for Audacity to "see" the new device.

To start recording, just click the familiar red circle on the toolbar. Audacity automatically creates a new audio track with the default settings (which are fine, by the way) and begins to record. I find it's always best to click record, wait a few seconds, and then start talking. Even though you're saving to your hard drive and not tape, it does take just a moment for things to get up to speed. Just delete the extra dead air at the beginning of the recording when you're done (the same with the extra stuff at the end).

Once you're done recording, save the file. Saving as an Audacity file and not as an MP3 is a good idea at this point. You'll want to do more edits on it before you export it as an MP3. Editing in Audacity is simple. To remove a section (for example, the beginning dead air

FIGURE 5.6
Audacity with one vocal track recorded as an example.

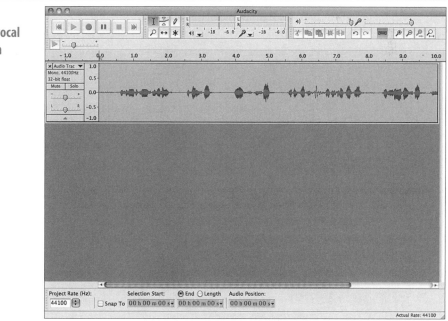

before you started talking), just select the area of the recording you want to remove and click the Delete key. Stop and listen to the recording to make sure you got it right. If not, click Control-z or Command-z to undo the deletion and try again.

Audacity has a large number of powerful audio tools for adding additional tracks, adding fades, cleaning up noise in the record-ing, and a lot of things that would even impress a professional audio engineer. For an in depth look at Audacity, read the tutorials on the Audacity website.

When you have finished recording, it's time to export it. When you downloaded Audacity, you might have noticed the note to download the LAME encoder for MP3s. Again, this is a free download, but for licensing reasons Audacity can't include it with the download, so you

have to do it on your own. Both the Audacity website and site where you download the LAME encoder have all the information you need to get it installed (it takes just a couple minutes and is essentially just downloading a file and saving it to a folder).

CAUTION

You can't export to an MP3 until you download and save the LAME encoder to your computer.

To export to MP3, go to the File menu in Audacity and choose Export. In the first screen, add the ID3 tags to your file (see Figure 5.7). ID3 tags are what iTunes and other MP3 players use to recognize the artist, song, album, track, genre, and year. In the following figure, I have the basics filled in for this export. For Album, use the name of your show and Track the episode.

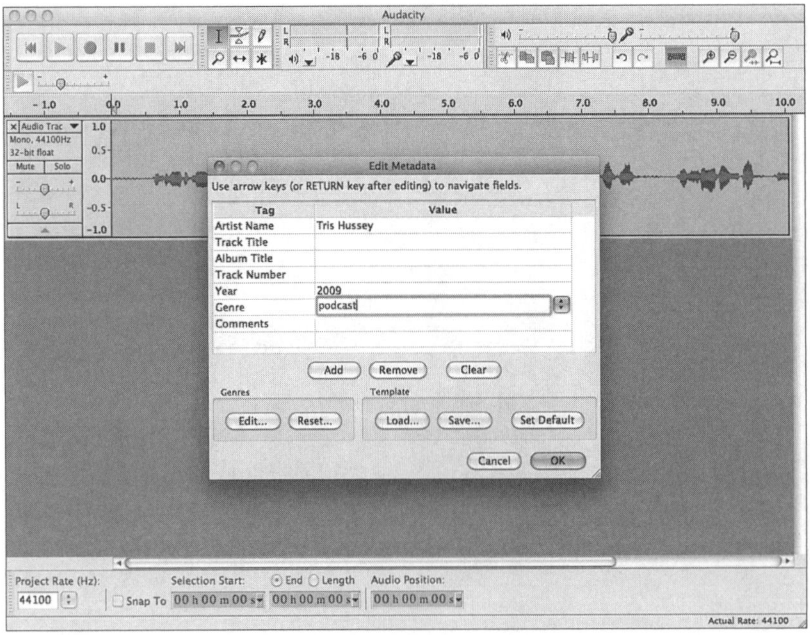

FIGURE 5.7

Step one of exporting to MP3 from Audacity: Setting the ID3 tags.

After you click next, you come to the familiar save window. I chose MP3 from the list and then clicked Options to bring up the MP3 Export Setup window (see Figure 5.8). For now, just leave the options as they are.

> **TIP**
>
> **ID3 tags are an internationally agreed-upon format for including artist information into an audio file. There is a newer version called ID4 with more options, but for most people ID3 is fine.**

Posting Your Recording

Once you've recorded and exported your podcast, you just need a place for it to live. Although there used to be free services like YouTube for hosting podcasts, most are gone now. Now people host their podcasts on their own servers (DIY) or put them on video-blogging services. Once you get going, if you want to pay for a place to host your podcast, libsyn (Liberate Syndication at libsyn.com) is one of the last remaining (and reliable) podcasting hosts.

So, as a personal blogger, if you're using WordPress.com, you can't upload your audio (or video files for that matter) to your blog without buying the space upgrade. This, I think, is very sad. There are several free video hosts that allow you to upload a short (10 minutes or less) podcast, but all the free podcasting hosts have fallen by the way side. While podcasting is still popular and there are more and more podcasts available, people have had to get pretty creative to host their podcasts.

FIGURE 5.8

Final step of exporting to MP3 from Audacity: Saving the file.

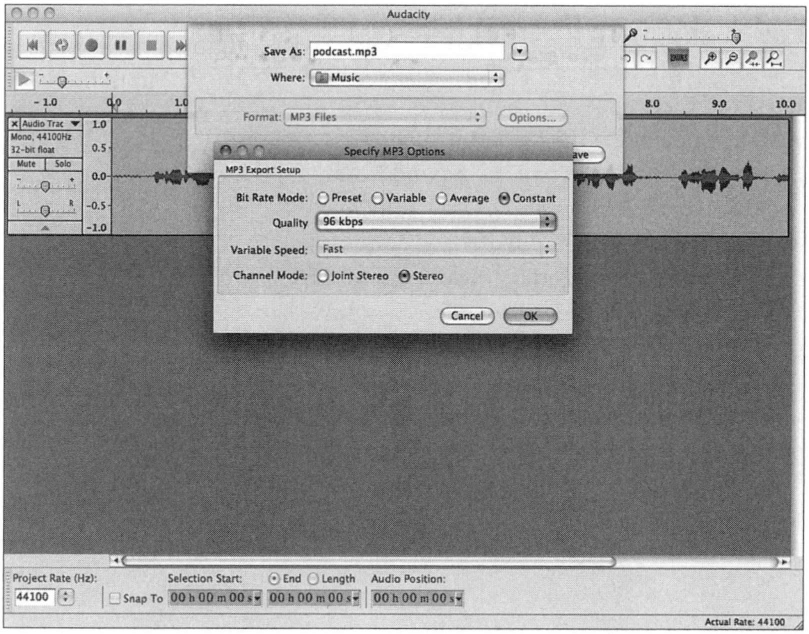

For a podcasting plug-in, go with PowerPress from Blubrry.com. It's simple, easy to configure, and best of all actively developed and improved.

If, however, you've already gone for the DIY install route, you just need to fire up the FTP client and upload the file! If you're using WordPress, I recommend uploading your files to /wp-content/uploads. You can organize the files more there if you want, but that is a good start. For a podcasting plug-in, go with PowerPress from Blubrry.com. It's simple, easy to configure, and best of all actively developed and improved. PowerPress includes a nice, basic player that you don't have to configure to make work.

Now, there is an alternative to all this self-recording stuff, and it's as close as your phone. Welcome to Internet radio.

Podcasting with Internet Radio

Even though recording a podcast yourself isn't too hard, there are some technical bits to deal with (hosting being the biggest issue now). Enter telephone-based podcasting and Internet radio. There are two main services, TalkShoe (talkshoe.com) and BlogTalkRadio (blogtalkradio.com), and both work essentially the same way. You sign up for a free account (BlogTalkRadio has paid plans, but free is just fine) and you're given a phone number that you call into to record your show. You schedule your show and when the time comes, you call in and … well that's it. The rest is taken care of for you.

The episode is recorded and converted to an MP3 for you (that process usually takes about 20 minutes after the show is over). During the call, you can have guests call in and live chat as well. I've done several of these, and frankly they are a great solution.

I've used BlogTalkRadio for a regular show and for one-off interviews. There is a caveat here though, because if you use the phone, you are calling long distance. I know a lot of people have unlimited long-distance calling, but both these services are also based in the U.S. so international podcasters need to plan for that potential charge. Another service, TalkShoe, has a way around this by using the Internet as a gateway for your call (see Figure 5.9). You download a small program and it lets you talk over the Internet, just like voice chat in IM programs like MSN and Yahoo!. BlogTalkRadio has something like this as well, but it's only for call-in guests, not hosts (TalkShoe's application is for both).

Both services also suggest trying the Voice over IP (VoIP) program Skype, where you can buy credits to call landline numbers. In practice, however, Skype calls aren't always the best quality and when you download or play back the recording you notice a real difference.

Despite all these caveats, try both of these options for your podcast. Both are easy and free. Both offer lots of great features like guest callers, chat, and even automatic submission to iTunes. If you ever wanted to host your own radio show, this is your chance.

FIGURE 5.9

TalkShoe homepage: one of two good Internet radio services for hosting podcasts.

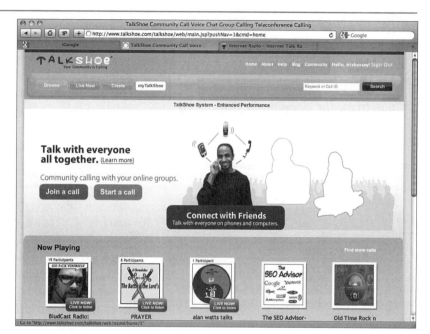

Video

Oddly enough, it seems that video blogging has leapt ahead of podcasting (audio only) as the most media popular after pictures. I say this not because people aren't making podcasts anymore or that video blogging is really easier than podcasting, but because a huge range of services and devices have cropped up in just the past couple years than have brought video itself to the fore.

At the first Northern Voice conference held in Downtown Vancouver in February 2005, there was an amazing session on creating podcasts. The room was packed. People were dying to know how to do it, and how to do it right, but video blogging? Bloggers all agreed that it was a fringe pursuit. The files were (and still are) huge, and the complexities of lighting, sound, compression, and gear were just too much for all but the hard-core techies in the audience, and let's face it, many people have faces made for radio.

Sites like YouTube and Seesmic enable you to record straight from your webcam to the Internet. There are even plug-ins for WordPress that enable you to record video posts straight to your blog.

Flash forward to 2009 and virtually every laptop and netbook comes with a built-in webcam. Sites like YouTube and Seesmic enable you to record straight from your webcam to the Internet. There are even plug-ins for WordPress that enable you to record video posts straight to your blog. With the popularity of LonelyGirl15 (or "Bree" real-life actress Jessica Rose) and Amanda Congdon's Rocketboom, people realized that it didn't take much technical savvy to make entertaining video blog posts, and so it began. There are two paths that most video bloggers take: One is the record, edit, and post model; the other is to just record and post it. When I do video blog posts, I'm mostly in the just post it group. I might pass the clip through a little compression program to resize the video and clean up the sound, but that's about it. Other folks, including people I work with, record parts, edit, mix with voiceovers, b-roll, and even add music.

For a personal blog, I'm going to put you in the just post it realm to start off. If you start to really enjoy videoblogging, then you just need to come back and read Chapter 8. First, let's talk about what sort of camera you might use for recording.

Webcam

Hands down the easiest way to start videoblogging is using a webcam. Any new laptop or netbook you buy now is likely to have one built in, and for desktop computers an adequate webcam can be had for less than $100. (Such webcams can also be used with a laptop should yours not have one built in.)

When you're using a webcam, you're going to be tethered to your machine to do your broadcasts. That means whatever lurks behind your computer desk is also going to be onscreen. Because you're going to be "stuck" in front of your computer, you're also going to be limited in terms of how dynamic you can be. There's no jumping up and arm-waving over some delicious rant because all the viewers will see is your belly button.

Live streaming is a whole different animal. This is just like live TV, so there are no second takes. It's all out there.

Using a webcam you can record to a file saved on your computer that you may or may not edit later before posting online, record "live" to the Web and when you select stop it is finished and posted for you, or you can stream live to the Web like a TV show with no delay (however, often saving these broadcasts for later is problematic).

Saving to your hard drive lets you record segments even when you're offline ("Look at me in this tent, I think there are people coming to get me…"), but it takes up hard drive space that you will have to deal with later. Recording up to YouTube (for example) is great, but doing several "takes" is more of a pain. On the plus side there isn't a large video file that you have to store and upload later. Live streaming is a whole different animal. This is just like live TV, so there are no second takes. It's all out there. Livestreaming is great for lectures or events, and if you have enough of a following, interviews, but often there is a hassle getting and keeping an archived version. So, recording with a webcam is easy and gives you some flexibility, but you're still tied to your computer to record and post online.

Camcorder

Hand-held camcorders have shrunk both in size and price while increasing the quality of the videos recorded. A small video camera that fits in your pocket can be capable of recording in HD and recording hours of video. As for cost, the small camcorders intended to produce web-ready video are less than $200.

The main benefit of a hand-held camcorder is that you can take it virtually anywhere to record. The downside is that you have to transfer the video from the device to your computer and then to the Internet.

With a camcorder you are in the record copy, edit if desired, upload model. Yes, with some cameras you can connect them as webcams for livestreaming, but this isn't always easy to set up.

At this point you might be wondering which I use—both. Sometimes it's just easier to do a quick missive while I'm sitting at the computer and when I do, I often post right to YouTube or

the like. When I'm out and about, I use a small camcorder. I try to avoid doing much editing only because the more barriers I put in front of me between recording, the less likely that I'll get the video up.

Halfway between a full-on camcorder and a webcam are little point-and-shoot video cameras like the Flip cam. These easy video cameras are essentially one-button devices. Besides the on/off button, there is a record button. Press to record; press again to stop. The focus is automatic and the microphone is built in. This new class of video cameras is pretty much idiot proof and have been selling like hotcakes. Often you might have a little zoom and basic settings for the recording, but it's minimal and easy. The best part of these devices is that they usually also have the USB connector on the device, and the videos are encoded for easy, fast transfer to your computer or directly online.

Editing basics

If you want to edit videos before you post them, you need some kind of editing software. For a personal blog, I think less is more. Keep it simple. Whether you use the free Windows Live Movie Maker (Windows) or iMovie (Mac), editing videos is as simple as drag and drop (see Figure 5.10).

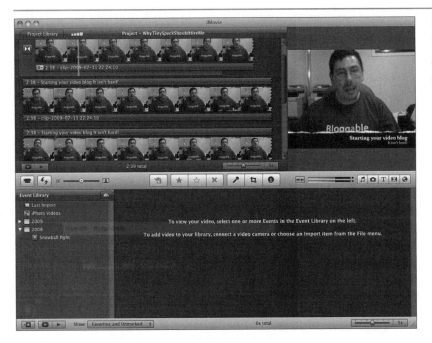

FIGURE 5.10
Editing a movie using Apple's built-in iMovie application.

Loading your movie onto your computer is a, thankfully, easy process now. First, launch iMovie or Windows Live Movie Maker, and then plug your camera into your computer. The program will either see that a movie camera is connected and start the import process for you or enable you to just import manually (the import functions are almost always under the File menu). How each program works is better left to the tutorial sections, but the following are the edits I usually make.

- ▶ Trim out the beginning and ending parts, which are the sections where you haven't started and the end where you are done, but clicking to stop recording.

- ▶ If you're feeling fancy, drop in an introductory title.

- ▶ Sometimes you'll want to cut out a part in the middle of the movie. That's fine, just put a transition between the cuts. Maybe a fade in and fade out will make it seem more natural.

- ▶ Movie Maker and iMovie have built-in tools to normalize the audio (speech) track to make it sound better. This helps your video sound better.

- ▶ Drop in some background music. Make sure you lower the volume on that audio track so you can hear the dialogue.

Once you've made your edits and previewed the movie, it's time for the moment of truth: exporting!

Unless you're using one of the point-and-shoot video cameras, the videos you get from other sources might need a little resizing/compression to make them suitable for online use. Yes, if you upload to YouTube and the like, they handle some of this, but remember you have to upload the video to YouTube. If the video is a large file size, it might take a while to post and process.

When exporting from iMovie to post online, I generally choose 480 × 272, which covers smart phones through computers. I have also been known to go a little higher and use 640 × 360 or 640 × 480 (depending on the aspect ratio of the clip). Whether to go big or small depends on the original quality of the video and what I'm going to use it for. Again, compressing personal blogs to 640 × 480 (which is still pretty large) or 480 × 272 and uploading will be just fine.

Right now the movie formats of choice are .m4v, .mpeg4, and .avi. If you're on a Mac, go with .m4v. Windows users should consider .avi. If you're not sure, use a simple export or export wizard to generate the export file. Once you're ready, export the file and get a snack. This will take a while.

Posting Online

So you have this great video of your cat chasing your dog around the yard (cliché, I know), and you want to post it online. What do you do? There are several ways to go and places to go. The 300-pound gorilla in the online video world is, of course, YouTube, but YouTube isn't alone. There is Flickr video, Vimeo, Blip.tv, and Viddler. At the highest level, all of the services are essentially the same. They let you upload videos, the video is re-encoded to stream/play over the Web, and codes are generated to enable you to link to or embed the video elsewhere. The Devil is in the details, however, when you look at these sites.

BASIC MULTIMEDIA STUDIO TOOLKIT

Video bloggers need a few basic tools in their toolkit. These tools often include:

- ▶ **Point-and-shoot digital camera**
- ▶ **Webcam**
- ▶ **Computer headset with microphone**
- ▶ **Audacity (sound editing) or GarageBand (Macs only)**
- ▶ **MovieMaker (PC) or iMovie (Mac) for video editing**

How big a file can you upload, what file types are supported, can you pay to get more/better bandwidth or faster processing times? So, when it comes right down to it, YouTube is your best choice. Even for a personal blog, YouTube gives you the largest potential reach and audience. Not to mention, it is free and they have made embedding videos in posts pretty painless.

Video embedding is what you do to put your video into a post. Here is the top-line process: Look for the embed or link code on the video page, copy it, and paste it into your post through your video embedding button. Let's go through it step by step:

1. Go to your video's page on YouTube and look for the URL field in the gray box located on the right next to the video (see

Figure 5.11). Click in the field and copy the link (Control-c or Command-c) to the clipboard.

2. Start a new post and click in the post where you'd like to put the video. It's a good idea to have a blank line above and below just in case you want more text around the video.

3. In WordPress click the Embed button (looks like a strip of film), click in the File/URL box, paste the URL of the video (Control-v or Command-v), and then select the tab key. The video appears in the box (see Figure 5.12). Click Insert.

4. The video looks like a big yellow box in your post. Click the Preview button to see what it will look like on your blog (see Figure 5.13).

FIGURE 5.11
Video on YouTube to put into a post. Look for URL box on the right side.

FIGURE 5.12
Inserting a YouTube
video into a post, video
insert window.

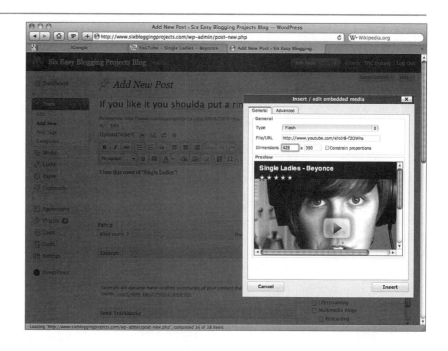

FIGURE 5.13
YouTube video in a post
and working.

That's it. Really. I know lots of steps for basically copying and pasting a link. Regardless I know lots of people who like to post short videos, just to mix things up a tad. Why not, it's pretty easy. So fire up that web cam and start recording. Movie Maker and iMovie have all the tools you need to get started.

Hosting Your Personal Blog

Chapter 2, "Installing and Setting Up Your First Blog," explored the different wasy to host a blog. Looking back at how I managed my blogs over the years, I don't think I would do too much differently. I started on Blogger, and then bought a domain and used that with my Blogger blog until I moved to Blogware and later to WordPress. Each step along the way, my blog grew as my blogging career grew. For most people I suggest starting off with a WordPress.com blog. Get used to blogging and see whether you enjoy it. Dip your toes into the blogosphere a little at a time. If you think you'd like to be more serious about blogging, then buy a domain name for yourself and pay for the domain mapping extra on WordPress.com.

If you grow beyond WordPress.com, then shop around for a good webhost and move your blog there. Moving a blog and domain is beyond the scope of this book, but trust me, it isn't hard. With each step along the path, you and your blog are growing with each other.

If you want to jump right in with both feet, or have a strong geek network to help you get set up, then by all means buy a domain straight away and sign up for a hosting plan. I caution you that you are putting money on the line for this. A good web host is about $10–12 a

month, plus your $10 a year for a domain. No, not a lot of money, but if you find yourself not blogging much after a month or two, you're paying for a blog to just sit there. However, if you start with WordPress.com, which is free, if you don't blog for awhile, you haven't spent any money to keep that blog there.

This is just something to think about.

There you have it. Everything you need to start a personal blog. Ready? Set? Blog!

Summary

Your personal blog is your own soapbox on the Internet, and building it is a rewarding experience. After deciding what you want to write about, even if it's just your day-to-day life and experiences, figure out whether you'd like to use a hosted blog service like WordPress.com or do it all yourself. Once you have your blog set up, pick a theme that pleases you and get going!

Don't forget about your own levels of personal privacy and the privacy of those around you. It's a good idea to know how much you want to share online and where you're going to draw the line.

Once you get going you might like to start adding video and start podcasting. Remember it's fun and easy and you might have everything you need to get going already! Most of all, have fun. Never lose sight of the fact that this is your space online and you are doing this to share your passions with the world, whatever they might be. That's how almost all bloggers started: They just wanted to tell their story.

CHAPTER 6

Creating a Business Blog

As described in Chapter 3, "Writing and Creating a Conversation," in the beginning all blogs were personal. Anything else just wasn't "blogging." In January 2005, all that changed in a short few days. January 24-25, 2005 was the first Blog Business Summit. It was a watershed moment when people started talking about not only the business of blogging (like being a professional blogger, which I was already at the time) but businesses using blogs to reach, connect, and communicate with their customers.

At the time, business blogging was something completely new and not terribly welcome in the blogosphere, but times have changed and businesses that don't have blogs and RSS feeds are getting left behind. That said, not every business needs or should even have a blog. Part of the key ethos of blogging is openness, transparency, and honesty. If your corporate culture cringes at an employee writing, "Yeah, we blew it on that one, but here's how we're going to fix it…" just stop here. If you're getting the dictum from on high that "We shall have a blog, and it shall be good. It shall be the best thing we've ever done," proceed with caution; the winds of corporate change can be fickle.

If you're getting the dictum from on high that "We shall have a blog, and it shall be good. It shall be the best thing we've ever done," proceed with caution; the winds of corporate change can be fickle.

Every company I've worked for since mid-2004 has had a blog, and I've generally been their primary blogger. Of course I've been either working for a tech, blogging, or media company, all of which need a blog to maintain competitive advantage in crowded markets. For you, dear reader, this begs the question, "Should my business even have a blog?"

I'm going to say, yes, even with the previous caveats. Remember, a blog is about writing. It's about expressing your passion for something. If you're really and truly passionate about what you do, you are probably your company's best cheerleader. Tell the world how proud you are. Tell the world when the CEO has been invited to speak somewhere. Just tell the world your thoughts on an industry topic, just to show the world how on the ball you are. Passion! Use your passion to make people take notice and think, "Wow, they've got it going on over there at John's Joinery Junction."

You might be worried that no one wants to know about your business and that you won't generate any traffic. Uh huh. You've got customers, right? Well, they probably want to know about your business. If you're an accountant, you can write about "The top 10 things you can do to make your accountant's life easier." Imagine how much easier your life would be if all your clients did that?

Are you a lawyer? Write about the "Things to consider when writing a will" or "Are online will kits legal in my state?" Are you getting the idea?

Although not every business can blog or is ready to blog, almost all businesses have a story to tell and something to say. You might be amazed with the results.

Content

A business blog is a somewhat different animal than the personal blog discussed in the preceding chapter. You have a business reputation to uphold and there is certainly some professional decorum to maintain. So "Pinup Fridays" probably isn't a good topic for you. Before you get too far into the "thou shalls and thou shall nots…," let's talk about writing.

Writing

Regardless of how good or bad a writer you *think* you are, chances are if you're thinking about writing a business blog, you're probably not a slouch in the writing department. Being a fairly decent writer is a core competency of everyone in business. With a personal blog, lapses in spelling, grammar, and structure can be overlooked, but on a business blog it reflects poorly on your business. You don't want a perspective client saying to themselves, "Jeez, they couldn't even spell check their posts. How will they handle my business?"

If you've had a personal blog for a while, it's time to step it up a notch. Time to break out Strunk and White's *Elements of Style* (required reading when I was in graduate school) and bone up on those rules of "affect" and "effect" and "further" and "farther."

> *You don't want a perspective client saying to themselves, "Jeez, they couldn't even spell check their posts. How will they handle my business?"*

This doesn't mean that you can't write with energy and passion; it just means that you

CAN A FICTIONAL ENTITY BLOG?

This was a huge question in the early days of blogging. Blogging stalwarts felt that only "real" people should be blogging, especially for a company. There were a couple notable character blogs that were pretty controversial at the time: the Denali Flavors Moose blog and T. Alexander from the Gourmet Station blog.

For a number of months this was an all-consuming tempest in a teacup, with all sorts of name-calling and unpleasantness, however when it all blew over… Sure, characters can blog. It became clear that whether it was fan fiction or a company mascot assuming the role of "spokesperson," it wasn't who the "author" was pro-ported to be, but rather what and how things were said.

Businesses find it helpful to have one "person" be the voice for the entire company, but have several folks write behind the scenes because there aren't enough people in the company to dedicate one person to blog. The hardest part of having multiple authors blogging is keeping the voice of the writing consistent. One easy fix is to divide the tasks up. Maybe only one person writes longer, more intricate posts, but others do things like a weekly post of interesting links, while still someone else does a photo of the week. Mix up the type of posts and the people writing them and you'll have a dynamic blog with a lot less effort!

need to write with energy, passion, and correct spelling. Everyone has a story to tell, you just have to find the right voice to tell it. Finding that voice is that much harder when you have the constraint of having to be more formal than a personal blog, but constraints can lead to more creativity. It's going to take time and practice, but you'll get it. Your writing voice will come out and be heard, and when it does, it's an amazing feeling. So let's start breaking down the components of your writing.

Tone and Style

The tone and style of a business blog is always a tough thing to establish. I've been lucky because I've always blogged, even on my business blogs, with a similar tone and style as my personal blogs, but that's because I came in with a tone and style that people wanted. If you're starting out fresh, the best thing to do is pass the post around. This doesn't mean blogging by committee (a sure, slow, and painful death for any blog); it means sitting down with a few people, and probably the boss, and saying, "Okay, here are a few posts that I'd like to put up on the blog over the next week. Do these sound right to people?" Take their feedback seriously. You might be too informal in your posts, and you need to tone it down a little. Maybe the boss really likes your less formal posts but wants to keep them for an online "casual Friday" approach.

The businesses I've worked for have typically been young start–up companies with young people running them. Our posts could be too informal sometimes. This is when having older advisors can help you (and give you a smack upside the head, if needed). I can't give you a perfect rule for tone and style, but I can say that if you wouldn't say it out loud to the boss, then don't post it on the blog. Beyond that, you just have to go by what your gut tells you. Your gut is usually right.

Topics

The range of topics you can cover in a business blog are surprisingly broad. Yes, I have seen some posts on business blogs that make me wonder "What were they thinking?" Very often those posts magically disappear (funny that). By and large, however, writing for a business blog is very much like being at a business networking event.

When you meet someone for the first time, you introduce yourself and what you do. You might get into what your business does and what your industry is all about, but it's going to be pretty superficial stuff for sure. If the person is interested in your particular business or industry, he or she might ask you a particular question, which being the polite person that you are, you will answer as best you can. If later in the evening you run into people who are also in your line of business, you might talk shop a little. What are the latest trends in your industry and what does everyone think about them?

Guess what? You have at least four solid posts right there. The following are some of my favorite business blog post topics:

▶ Description of your industry or niche

▶ Industry trends and your thoughts about them

▶ Answers to common questions about your business

▶ Current news (think informal press release with a link to the formal press release at the end)

▶ Community, charity, and volunteer work (see Figure 6.1)

▶ News from conferences

You get the idea here. Very often the stuff that you might otherwise brush off as boring are things people, potential customers in particular, find interesting.

FIGURE 6.1

Molson Coors Canada in the Community from its blog, which shows how large corporations give back to the community.

The Virtual Newsroom

One of the greatest changes that blogging and social media has wrought has been its effect on how news is gathered, reported, and disseminated. Today not only journalists, but also bloggers are looking for information on your company online. It is expected that at the very least you have your press releases on a section of your site (and a blog is a great place for them).

There is a lot of hype right now about the "social media press release" and how it is somehow different. My feeling is that you build your press materials (including photos, bios, and additional material) into a section of your blog. This does several things for you right off the bat. First, it makes the material much easier to update than traditional websites. Next, search engines find and index content much more easily (more on that later in the chapter). Finally, blogs are inherently social media enabled. With simple plug-ins, like "Share this" (available for most blogging engines), readers can share your content via email, Facebook, Twitter, and many other social networks.

I am often frustrated at how little information businesses post about themselves, *on their own websites*! If you want bloggers and mainstream media journalists (who often blog on their media outlets' website) to write and comment about you, help them by providing the information. If you don't provide the information, bloggers will try to find it elsewhere, and it might not be accurate or up to date.

The virtiual newsroom is a *great* way to leverage your blog and social media and can become a repository for all types of media on your company. I highly recommend that you at least give this a try.

Privacy

While personal bloggers think about privacy in terms of themselves, their family and friends, and so on, for a business blog you have to add a layer of complexity. You want to be open and transparent (key rules for blogging), but at the same time not give away trade secrets. It can be a fine line between sharing information that helps sell your company and disclosing information that could put you at a competitive disadvantage to other companies that offer similar services.

Like a personal blog, other people in the company might not want to be included in the blog by name or at all, and you need to respect their privacy. If you are posting pictures from a company picnic or the like, make sure people are okay with that going up before you post it online.

No, you can't control what people do on their personal blogs per se, but it could be considered a fireable offense if an employee divulges sensitive information to the public.

It's hard to say if privacy is more or less of an issue on a business blog versus a personal one. On one hand you *should* know better than to blab about company plans and strategies, but on the other hand there might be other people *within* your company who might not see things the same way and just do it on their own blogs. In a business blog, even if you have only one *official* blogger, you might have far more *unofficial* ones blogging on their own. If their own lines of personal privacy don't match yours, it can lead to trouble. An important thing to do in these cases is for you or your manager to make it clear in your company's blogging policy what is expected of employees who blog, whether it's for the company or for their own personal blog. No, you can't control what people do on their personal blogs *per se*, but it could be considered a fireable offense if an employee divulges sensitive information to the public. If you are clear from the beginning, then you significantly reduce that risk. As the unofficial blogging policy at Microsoft says, "Don't be stupid."

Comments

Chapter 4, "Building Community," explored comments, mostly in terms of how they relate to building a community around your blog. On a personal blog, commentary is just continuing the discussion or the story. For a business blog, the people in the community are your customers and colleagues. Many business bloggers have found their greatest product champions through their blogs. If someone cares enough about your company or product to leave you a comment, then *listen* to it! Even if it's something that you don't want to hear, like a product didn't meet expectations, listen and read. If you want to do what you do better, can you think of a better way to learn how than by getting comments straight from your customers? Feedback from someone who says, "I think your toasters are great, but the adjustment knob seems to go from untoasted to charcoal too easily. Can you put in finer gradations?" is gold! The person said that the toasters are great but... well now you know an area to work on!

Encourage comments on your business blog by keeping comments open on posts, even if they have to be moderated (which is fair), and respond to all the comments on your posts within 24 hours (at most). Moderation can be a very important part of a business blog's comment system because you don't want inappropriate comments on your blog, ever. It doesn't matter if those comments reflect badly on the company or just one person. There are two simple and easy solutions to this issue: a comment policy and comment moderation. By default, most blog engines have comment moderation turned on and the typical setting is that after one or two approved comments, that person's comments are posted without moderation. For a business blog, you might not want to take that risk, so keeping moderation on for everyone, all the time, is a sensible way to handle it. That said, you should make sure that in the comment form, you state that all comments are moderated and provide a link to your comment policy.

It's not unusual for commenters to complain that negative comments about a company aren't posted on a business blog. Well, duh! Sometimes fair, respectful criticism is a really good thing that you should allow. It shows that you, as a business, are open to change and criticism. However, comments filled with venom, obscenities, and *ad hominem* attacks aren't welcome on any blog, much less a business one. If there are valid points intermixed with the vitriol, you might consider asking the commenter to resubmit the comment (giving guidelines for language, and so on). If the commenter declines, then the original comment can be deleted without worry of offending someone.

A comment policy simply is writing out the level of decorum you expect on the blog.

AN EXAMPLE BUSINESS BLOG COMMENT POLICY

Discussion Guidelines for Molson Blog Readers

Molson Blog aims to brew honest, friendly and courteous conversation. Please be respectful and civil to bloggers and others members of the community, even if you disagree with them.

Do not post anything that could offend another member of the community. Anything containing profanity, sexually graphic, or offensive language, and so on, will be deleted. We do not allow harassing, threatening, racist, abusive, hateful, violent, or obscene language or behavior. Molson will decide (in its sole discretion) what is inappropriate for this blog. If you have complaints or questions regarding any of the content posted on this blog, please contact us.

Also note that:

1. Participation in, suggesting, or encouraging any illegal activity is cause for immediate deletion, and may be reported to the appropriate authorities.

2. Any articles, news reports, or other copyrighted material included in the posts must be with the permission of the relevant copyright owners.

3. Do not flood or spam, post chain letters, pyramid schemes, junk mail, or URLs for outside sites that violate any of these guidelines.

4. No commercial solicitation or advertising will be allowed.

continues

Continuing with the business networking function metaphor, there are rules that are followed in such a setting, such as topics that are allowed and not allowed, and what language is acceptable and what is over the line. Just make it clear that people leaving comments are doing so at your party in your living room and certain things will not be tolerated.

Blogging Policies

One of the hottest topics discussed at early business blogging conferences was company blogging policies. In larger companies like Sun Microsystems, Microsoft, and Boeing, employees were often writing personal/business blogs at work with the support and backing of their employer. Support didn't mean that the employees had carte blanche to do anything they pleased; it meant that employees wouldn't be fired out of hand for blogging and often the company provided the technical resources to have a blog. In general companies that originally started openly supporting their employees blogging were the ones that realized that the horse was already out of the barn and trying to stifle conversation would be worse than just trying to monitor it.

Sun Microsystems has one of the best corporate blog policies going. It was a detailed document that covered the gamut of topics and scenarios that could arise for a blogger, everything from your picture you used on your site to how to criticize Sun products. Microsoft didn't have an official policy per se, but had a mantra, "Don't be stupid," that covered the bases pretty well. Another piece of advice is if you don't feel comfortable with your boss/VP/manager reading that post, it's probably a good idea not to post it.

NOTE

Sun Microsystems led the business blogging/employee blogging charge for many years. Their blogging and comment policies are still referred to as best practices.

You can also implement an official or unofficial review and approval system where one person reads and approves posts before they go live. This can be frustrating for both the writer and the person approving the post. If time is of the essence, then waiting for an approval is maddening. Likewise, if you're busy and you get three or four posts to review and the authors are clamoring to get the posts up right now, that might cause your blood pressure to go up a few points.

A mid-way point is just asking people to read the post before you post it, but if they are busy you might be told to post it and maybe edit later. That kind of arrangement develops over time as people trust what you're posting is okay and not going to get the company in trouble. At my company, bloggers read over each others' posts before they go live to check for typos, clarity, and formatting. I usually harp on adding tags and selecting the right categories for the posts, but that's my role in the company (as the primary blogger).

Like comment policies, the best blogging policies are the simplest ones. The more you try to define, outline, delimit, or constrain the *more* questions you're going to have to deal with in the long run. Simple is good. Simple works. Simple is, well, simple. Sun Microsystems' blogging policy is a great example of a great blogging policy. It is clear, detailed (but not overwhelmingly so), not written in legalese,

Molson blog is about Molson's products and the community of Molson's customers. Please keep all comments related to the subject matter of the post as off-topic or spam entries will be immediately deleted. If you have a question or concern not relating to the topic of the post that you need to communicate to Molson, please contact 1-800-MOLSON1 to be directed to the best person to answer your question/comment.

We ask for your email address when you post a comment. Your email will never be published, but will be used to verify your comment and possibly to contact you in relation to your comment. We will not use it for any other purposes without your permission.

—From the Molson Coors Canada Blog

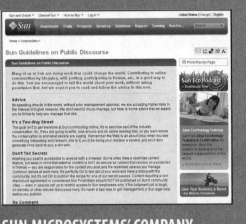

SUN MICROSYSTEMS' COMPANY BLOGGING POLICIES

Sun Microsystems led the way with corporate blogging policies for many years, and today I think it is still one of the best out there. It covers many common scenarios and questions, but without burying you in legalese. This blogging policy is available for not only Sun employees to read, but everyone else as well. The policy puts a clear stake in the ground on how it expects their bloggers to behave.

It's far too long to post in its entirety here, but here are a couple of relevant sections:

Be Interesting, but Be Honest

Writing is hard work. There's no point doing it if people don't read it. Fortunately, if you're writing about a product that a lot of people are using, or are waiting for, and you know what you're talking about, you're probably going to be interesting. And because of the magic of linking and the Web, if you're interesting, you're going to be popular, at least among the people who understand your specialty. Another way to be interesting is to expose your personality; almost all of the successful online voices write about themselves, about families or movies or books or games; or they post pictures. People like to know what kind of a person is writing what they're reading. Once again, balance is called for; a community site is a public place and you should avoid embarrassing the company and community members. One of Sun's core values is integrity, so review and follow Sun's Standards of Business Conduct in your online community contributions.

and current. Sun's blogging policy might seem a little intense, but remember this a company built on geeks. Geeks like detail and know how to handle lots of different scenarios.

Multimedia

When I say, "business blog," you might not automatically think "multimedia rich," but that's selling the potential of these blogs short. There are hundreds of easy ways to pull in pictures, audio, and video that not only liven up your posts, but also help make your point. I'm going to look at multimedia from the standpoint of busy business people whose job isn't to shoot video, take pictures, or record podcasts all day. I take a simple, pragmatic approach (in case you hadn't figured it out) to multimedia so don't worry about me telling you to turn an office into a recording studio. Adding pictures to illustrate a point or show off a product is obvious, but what about video and podcasts? As you get more and more into blogging, you might feel the desire to record a podcast or video interview. Just roll with it; audio and video are easy to record and post online. Be creative and note what other business blogs in your niche are doing. Imitation is the sincerest form of flattery! Learn from others and you might find yourself doing amazing things on your blog you might not have considered before.

Pictures

Business blogs are not usually associated with having lots of pictures in the posts, but remember, sometimes a picture tells... You get the idea. The most important things to remember when posting a picture online are

> ▶ Do you have the rights/permission to post it and if you do, have you attributed the photo to the artist correctly?

> ▶ How big is the file you are uploading? Remember to check the height and width and the number of KB the picture takes up.

> ▶ Did you insert the picture into the post correctly so it looks good?

Make Sure You Have the Right to Post It

As a business, you are under the section of "commercial use" under copyright law. For example, nearly all my pictures posted on Flickr are marked as non-commercial use only, a topic covered extensively in Chapter 5, "Creating a Personal Blog." Essentially that means to you as a business blogger: Hands off, unless you ask and receive permission first.

ABOUT CREATIVE COMMONS

The Creative Commons system is a universal, iconographic depiction of what the usage license is for a particular work. CC uses symbols to represent things like commercial use permitted or not, attribution required or not, and derivative works permitted or not and on what conditions. For example, my Creative Commons license for my photos looks like this:

Attribution-Noncommercial-No Derivative Works 2.0 Generic

You are free:

to Share — to copy, distribute and transmit the work

Under the following conditions:

Attribution — You must attribute the work in the manner specified by the author or licensor (but not in any way that suggests that they endorse you or your use of the work).

Noncommercial — You may not use this work for commercial purposes.

No Derivative Works — You may not alter, transform, or build upon this work.

With the understanding that:

Waiver — Any of the above conditions can be waived if you get permission from the copyright holder.

Other Rights — In no way are any of the following rights affected by the license:

- Your fair dealing or fair use rights;
- The author's moral rights;
- Rights other persons may have either in the work itself or in how the work is used, such as publicity or privacy rights.

Notice — For any reuse or distribution, you must make clear to others the licence terms of this work.

It means Attribution-Noncommercial-No Derivative Works. In English this means that you may use my works as long as you give me credit and it is for non-commercial use only. You may not take my work and use it as a part of another work.

Some people in the intellectual property field feel that CC isn't worth the paper it's printed on and there are too many loop holes to make it effective. I think it's better than nothing and it makes a clear statement about my intentions.

In the end, as a business blogger, if the work says "non-commercial" it's off limits unless you ask the artist. If you want to use such work for your commercial blog, you are likely to have to pay for a license to use the work.

Posting and Sharing Pictures Online

Depending on your business, you might like to upload pictures to one of the Internet photo-sharing sites like Flickr, SmugMug, Picasa, or SnapFish. The benefit of using a service is that you are, essentially, backing up your pictures to an offsite server and it makes posting your pictures online a bit easier. Photo-sharing sites give you easy-to-code html codes for embedding individual pictures into posts or your blog. For example, if you were just at a tradeshow and wanted to show off your booth, having the pictures on Flickr is a great way to share them. If you create software, having your screenshots and other visual materials not only makes it easier for you to use the pictures, but Flickr becomes another touch point for search engines to index your content.

Other than that, however, for most businesses, having photos on a photo-sharing site is a nice to have feature, but not a need to have. There are, of course, exceptions. If your business is involved in the arts, or is involved in tourism or can otherwise benefit from heavy use of photos, having an account with a capable photo-sharing site can be helpful. As previously mentioned, many of the software companies I know and work with host their screenshots on Flickr. Photo-sharing sites are for more than vacation and baby photos; these are great places to archive images and gain additional search engine traction.

If you'd like to learn more about photo-sharing sites, Chapter 8 "Video Blogging," has more in-depth information on these services. I recommend Flickr as a photo-sharing site for businesses and personal users. Creating a Flickr account is as simple as creating a Yahoo! account (Vancouver-born Flickr is owned by Yahoo!, Inc.). After creating your Flickr account, I strongly recommend upgrading to a Flickr Pro account for about $25 per year. You receive unlimited uploads per month as well as unlimited sets of photos. The cost is a real bargain and unlocks the power of Flickr for you.

Some businesses might also want to have a Flickr *group* to which the public can contribute. A good example of this is the group I set up for the Vancouver International Airport Authority (YVR) to let plane spotters and other aviation enthusiasts contribute their own pictures (see Figure 6.2). Initially the group was closed and invite only, but as YVR became more comfortable with the group, and *crowdsourcing* in general, the restrictions were opened up.

NEW TERM

Crowdsourcing is tapping into the Internet at large for feedback, content, or help. Crowdsourcing helped YVR find new and diverse images for the airport terminal by just searching and asking the photographer's permission. The additional cost was limited because many people were flattered to have their pictures displayed at Canada's second largest airport!

FIGURE 6.2

The YVR Connections Flickr group showing just some of the user submitted pictures (including my own).

Inserting Images into Your Posts

One of the best things about using blog engines is that they are so utilitarian. The process for putting an image into a business blog post is the same as a personal blog. Refer to Chapter 5, "Creating a Personal Blog," when you're ready to put an image in your post.

Logos and Corporate Images for the Media

As a blogger, when reviewing a company's product, I often need pictures of that product to use in my posts. I *could* try to find them elsewhere online, but wouldn't it be better if they provided images for me? The same goes for your company logo, pictures of your executive team, and anything else a blogger or reporter might need to do a story on you. You might not want to put the giant print-ready images on your site, but you can put web-scaled versions (images about 600 pixels wide are perfect) and

contact information for higher resolution images, if needed.

Don't dismiss this out of hand, even if you are a small business. What if the local paper wants to do an article on you and they need a picture? Wouldn't you rather they have a really good picture that you *like* than something they find online or send the photography intern to shoot? That's what I thought. Make this a part of your digital newsroom that I talked about earlier in this chapter, and you are well on your way to using a blog for serious business.

Podcasting

We've all had those moments when we're writing an email and just reach the point where we stop and think, "This would be easier if I called…" That's just one of the aspects of podcasting—saying more than you could easily write out. How about a short interview with people at your company? I use podcasts in my business life to educate and teach people about WordPress. I record a few short WordPress tips and post them. When people are searching for WordPress information, find it, and listen to it, they might learn something and think "I think this guy might be able to help me."

Certainly, not everyone is comfortable recording his or her voice, but if you have aspects of your business where your employees or customers *could* benefit from an audio tutorial or news break (think of people listening to their iPods on the way to work), you might give it a shot.

It is sometimes difficult to think of good topics for a podcast, so I like to build off a larger topic. I've done shows on several aspects of social media and a series of one-minute podcasts on WordPress. Very short podcasts can make the entire job of podcasting easier, because it's easier to focus on a single episode if you have a bigger picture in mind.

Let's get into recording that first podcast by starting off with the software aspect of it.

TIP

When you are recording any kind of audio, always do a mic check. Make sure your mic is working and the recording sounds good.

Getting a mic that works well for you is pretty easy, but getting *software* that you like is another matter. In Chapter 5, I focused mainly on using the free, open source application Audacity for recording. After you learn an application like Audacity, other applications, like GarageBand (which has very good tutorials

by the way), aren't very difficult to pick up. Like with photos in your posts, I'm going to shift your attention to Chapter 5 for the basics of recording podcasts and also telephone-based Internet radio. The mechanics are all the same, so here I'm going to focus on two more business-related ideas: Internet radio shows to build business and hosting considerations.

TIP

Applications like Audacity and GarageBand work off of "tracks." You have, for example, a vocal track and a music track. Video editors also work in the same way, so you'll find trying video a lot easier if you've practiced with audio first.

Internet Radio to Build Your Business

You've heard your share of "industry experts" on the radio, TV, and so on, right? Now is your chance to *be one*. Using services like TalkShoe or BlogTalkRadio, you can have your own call in show online, whenever you want. Like all Internet services, both services only take a couple minutes to set up. Both have free plans (TalkShoe only has free plans) so there is no harm in trying both of them out to see which you like better. Chapter 5 discussed how these services work in general, but let's see how they work for a business blog. In fact, I'll tell you how *I* used them in *my* business blogging.

I had a weekly show on BlogTalkRadio for almost a year. My business partner Jim Turner (Genuine Dad) talked about the latest news in social media and had a number of high-profile people as guests. We used the show as an industry round table. The purpose of the show wasn't for direct selling or pitches; it was to expand our profile and reach. It worked. The show ended up serving two purposes: Clients listened to it during the pitch phase, and a service we offered to clients. Jim and I helped clients set up their own shows and even be guests on the shows, so we could help them get their feet under themselves.

Jim and I barely scratched the surface with using Internet radio for business. We could have sold advertising spots on air and we could have done special "training" episodes to sell, but we didn't. Don't get me wrong—that's fine; we were making the choice to do it how we were doing it. Lots of other businesses are going the extra mile in their shows and being far more commercial, and I think that's great.

TIP

If you're wearing a headset-based mic, the mic should be about the width of two fingers away from your mouth. This reduces "popping" and gives you better sound quality.

Having a show where you get to be the host, have guests call in, and have live text chat is a potential gold mine for advertisers and potential business leads for you. You might be thinking about now that no one would be interested in your show. I think you're wrong. Do you have industry trade shows? Association meetings on a regular basis? When you sit and talk shop with people, don't you wish you could capture all that great discussion for later?

Now imagine firing up the speakerphone, calling in, and having a live show from the convention floor? How about an interview with someone well known in your industry? With a podcast you can do that no problem, and then edit the show later. With something like BlogTalkRadio or TalkShoe, you can do it right then and there. Live radio at its best.

I encourage you to at least try a couple of shows. If you have cheap or unlimited long-distance calling, I don't think you have anything to lose. You might, in fact, get bitten by the radio bug like I did.

Hosting Considerations

Once you have an MP3 file of your podcast, you need to upload it somewhere. Unlike video, the number of services that are dedicated to podcasting has declined rapidly over the past three years. Right now only PodBean, Libsyn, and Blubrry remain as hosts in the podcasting world. Unlike most online video hosts, podcasting hosts generally charge for storing your files on their servers. For my own podcasting, I upload my file to my own server space and use a WordPress plug-in called Powerpress (from Blubrry.com) to insert a player into the post. As a business blogger, you should own your own domain to start with and use either a service like WordPress.com (with premium features), pay for a service like Libsyn, or host your blog yourself (I think the last option is best).

Video hosts, as I'll get to in a moment, are very generous with free space. I think it's because people tend to watch videos right there (and, therefore, see more ads) while podcasts are things you listen to often while doing other things. I think this is unfortunate and limits how many people can publish podcasts.

The final step for podcasting is submitting to iTunes. (See Chapter 7, "Creating a Podcast Blog," for more information.) Without going into a lot of detail, it's a two-part process. The first part is setting up the information about the feed (which is easily done regardless of using TalkShoe, BlogTalkRadio, or Powerpress on your own) then using a form on Apple's website to let them know to index the feed for inclusion.

Video

Business and online video aren't two things that many people put together. However, more and more businesses are using simple, easy videos as ways to showcase who they are and what they do. With today's low-cost video cameras (the Pure Digital Flip is the best example), it is very easy to shoot a video you can be proud to post online. I recommend that businesses put some time and effort into a video that they are going to post online. A little work in iMovie or Windows Movie Maker goes a long way to separate your video from the waterskiing squirrels. Both programs are very easy to use, as I talked about at a high level in Chapter 5 and will in much more detail in Chapter 8. Like Audacity or GarageBand, iMovie and Movie Maker work off the idea of "tracks" that come together to make a final movie.

Show People How It's Done with a Screencast

One great application of video on a business blog is the use of *screencasts* of your product or service in the form of how-to videos. Say you have an online order form and are getting a lot of questions about how to use it; you could record a little video with a voice-over explaining the form and demonstrating how to fill it out properly. An example I often see, and refer to often myself, is when you have a piece of software that you'd like to explain. Nothing explains how to use a piece of software like watching and listening to someone use it.

If your business does anything related to computers (online order forms, software, websites, and so on), a screencast can reduce the number of questions you have to field *tremendously*. Screencasts even work fantastically for employee training or just explaining the steps to do something on the computer. I think once you start using screencasts for your blog, you'll find yourself using them for more and more things.

> **NEW TERM**
>
> A screencast is a video recording of a computer screen. It's great for all sorts of applications, whether it's showing off an application demo or explaining how to use a program or website.

One of the best screencasting applications I know (and use) is called Jing (www.jingproject.com) from Techsmith (the makers of Camtasia and Snaggit). Jing is a free screencasting and screenshot program for both PCs and Macs. Jing is dead simple to use and makes recording a screencast easy. There aren't a lot of bells and whistles to it, but as a starting point, you can't beat it. If you find that you need more than what Jing has to offer, its big brother Camtasia is available for both Macs and PCs and is a very powerful and easy screencasting tool (see Figure 6.3).

FIGURE 6.3
Camtasia for Mac in action as I record taking a screenshot to email to a friend.

If screencasting just takes a computer, what about a *real* video? What does it take to shoot great-looking video without breaking the bank?

Hardware

The webcam built into your laptop is great for video chatting or even as part of the picture-in-picture of a larger screencast, but for a stand alone video, it just won't cut it. The quality you can get out of a webcam just isn't good enough for videos that you want to represent your business.

Small HD video cameras have come down in price significantly in the last year, and I expect the prices to drop even more in the future. If you are interested in starting to shoot good video, you should at least start there. Once you have the camera, think about how you're going to shoot the video. If you've watched home movies at all, you know that they have

a lot of extra movement just from the person not being able to hold the camera perfectly still. Even the professional camera people I know have trouble shooting steady video with hand-held cameras—there just isn't a lot of weight to help keep them still. The solution is putting the camera on a table, or better, a tripod. Small tabletop tripods are also not expensive and are a great help at not only getting a nice steady shot, but also lining up the shot in the first place.

> **TIP**
>
> Need a tripod in a pinch? Look for a lamp with a screw-on shade. It just so happens that the size of threads that are standard on all still and video cameras is the same size as lampshades. Take off the shade, screw on the camera, and shoot away. Turn the light off first to avoid glare.

After you get the shot set up, check the lighting. Overhead fluorescent lights make almost everyone look like the undead. Having just a couple basic lamps with regular lightbulbs (or better daylight bulbs) will make sure you look good on video. Try to arrange the lights above the person being videoed so there aren't hard shadows across her face. It might take a couple minutes to get the lights right, but it pays off in having people look "normal." And don't think you have to break the bank with lights. Regular home lighting is great; just making sure it's nice, even, and without hard shadows is the essential part.

Of course, the more you spend on cameras, the better your videos will look. Before you start spending a lot of money on equipment, borrow or rent equipment first. For an occasional project, asking your friend with a better than average camcorder might be just the thing you need to make that awesome video.

The final bit of hardware that makes a huge difference is switching from a built-in camera microphone to an external one. You'll have to move beyond the entry-level video camera for this and decent mics aren't cheap (but you don't have to break the bank to get good quality either), but the results are *immediately* noticeable. There is less background noise, voices sound more natural, and the sound level remains constant.

Of course all of these hardware choices are things you should build on over time. Jumping into expensive video gear can be daunting if you're shooting just a couple videos, so start simple, start small, and work up from there.

Editing Beyond the Basics

Chapter 5 explored the basics of editing video, and Chapter 8 gets into even more detail, but for this level of video there is a nice spot in between. One thing that really makes a business blog video stand out is using titles in the video. Even just a simple intro and outro title set with a transition into the actual video makes a huge difference. Speaking of transitions—keep them simple. Just a nice fade in/fade out is perfect. I know that iMovie and Movie Maker have all the awesome effects you can drag and drop into your project, but trust me, skip them, especially when you're just starting out. I know we'd all like to be George Lucas or Ken Burns, but we're not and trying to rarely comes off looking professional.

The last bit of editing magic you can do is work with the audio levels and noise. Even basic movie editors have some simple tools for "normalizing" (evening out the louder and quieter parts of the audio track) and even noise removal. Depending on your camera's mic, how far away the person was from you, and the amount of noise in the background, you will have greater and lesser degrees of success. However at least *trying* to clean up the audio is a simple step that almost always helps to some degree.

Posting Online

So you have this great video of your CEO being interviewed by the local paper, and you want to post it online. What do you do? Although there are many alternatives to YouTube (Viddler, Blip.tv, and Flickr), some of which have "professional" or "premium" plans that offer more options and sometimes the ability to upload larger videos, YouTube is a huge destination for people searching for video. You might think that using YouTube isn't "professional" enough, but you'd be wrong. Because you can now customize your YouTube profile and channel your page to your liking, your space on YouTube can look great and reflect well on you as a business. Like photo-sharing sites, putting your videos on YouTube gives your company another SEO boost. Your company name, link to your website and blog, plus all the other data you include with the videos can only *help* you be indexed by search engines and found by potential customers.

Since the birth of the iPhone, more and more sites are trying to make their videos and sites compatible with iPhones and other mobile devices. As I'm writing this, the race is ongoing with YouTube and a few others making the main sites iPhone friendly, but few have made the videos embedded on other sites iPhone compatible. My bet is that YouTube, because it is part of Google, will likely be the first to offer the best range of mobile-compatible video options, which is another reason to post your videos to YouTube. You are future-proofing your space there when the mobile revolution finally takes off.

Because everyone wants to post videos into his or her blogs, at least at one time or another, blog engines have all made inserting a video into a post as simple as copying the URL of the video from your browser's address bar and pasting it into a simple tool in the post editor.

The WordPress Insert Video window shown in Figure 6.4 looks like a strip of film.

FIGURE 6.4
Inserting a YouTube video into a WordPress post.

Start with your post, click in your post where you'd like the video inserted, and then click the Insert Video button. After pasting the video URL, hit the Tab key, then click Insert. That's it!

That's a wrap on the video section for this chapter. Although I don't think business blogs will be posting (many) videos of waterskiing squirrels or cats chasing dogs (a Friday funny isn't a bad idea though), there are many ways you as a business blogger can use video in new and creative ways. Experiment a little and check out what other people are doing. I'm sure you'll see something that you'd like to try on your own blog!

Building and Hosting Your Business Blog

Chapter 2, "Installing and Setting Up Your First Blog," discussed where to host your blog and a little about choosing a host as well. In Chapter 5, I recommended starting out with WordPress.com because it's free and easy, but for business bloggers I recommend stepping things up a notch or two.

Choosing to use WordPress.com is still a great option, especially if you don't want to have to bother with web hosts and servers, but you should at the very least purchase a domain name and sign up for the premium domain mapping option. This gives you a blog that has the address of www.yourgreatbusinessblog.com but still has the comfort of knowing that you have all of WordPress.com and Automattic's support staff behind you. If you want to podcast, purchase the extra space option as well. Now, if you start to do the math, you might find that it is better to pay about $10–15/month for a web host of your own.

> **TIP**
>
> Remember that WordPress.*com* is the hosted service. WordPress.org is where you download WordPress to install yourself on your own web host.

You still need to purchase a domain name (you were going to do that regardless, right?), but with a web host secured you can easily host your own podcast files. Additionally, on WordPress.com, you are limited in the number of available themes and you can't install additional plug-ins. You have neither of these restrictions when you have your own web host.

Although I know a number of business bloggers that use WordPress.com, personally I think it is well worth the investment to have your own web host. If you already have a website, you might just be able to add a blog onto it for no additional cost per month. You just need to install WordPress yourself (or find someone to help you with it) to have your blog up and running in short order.

Choosing a Template for Your Business Blog

A business blog has to look professional, so choosing the right template is critical. There are thousands of free themes and templates available for WordPress, Movable Type, and Drupal blogs. There are also hundreds of premium themes you can purchase. With either option, look at free themes first. You want to find something that complements your company's image and doesn't look like everyone else's blog. Starting with free options gives you a fantastic range of options that you can quickly review and try out. This way, if you later opt to pay for a custom theme, you have a much better idea of what you like and don't like.

Theme developers are becoming more and more sophisticated in how their themes are built and what additional features they offer. Some themes now have built-in SEO tools, media galleries, and choices of layouts. It is well worth your time looking at the range of blogs out there and what themes they are using (look at the bottom blog's page for a link to the theme developer's site). I think you'll be very surprised to see how many "regular websites" are actually built on top of WordPress and Movable Type.

Stats

I discussed blog stats in Chapter 2, and here I have only to add that your boss will want to know what's going on pretty often. Google Analytics has an easy way to keep your boss informed of all the latest info on the blog. Look for the email button located above a report (I usually choose the main dashboard report) and click it. There you can choose to send out a one-off email or schedule reports to be emailed out periodically (see Figure 6.5).

FREE VERSUS PREMIUM THEMES

In your search for themes, it's not going to take long before you come across links, banners, and ads for premium themes in which you might wonder if paying money for a theme is worth it. Personally, I use both free and premium themes in my work. Often, premium themes are better designed, better supported, and better coded then their free brethren. However, free themes are, well, free and you can't beat that price. My advice is for your first blog, stick to free when you're starting out. See how you like "this blogging thing" and take it from there. I suggest giving premium themes a serious look, though, after a short while. The professional and polished look of the premium themes is well worth the price. Of the current crop of theme designers, I really like the themes from Studiopress.com and DIYThemes.com (I have developer licenses for both that give me access to all their themes). The developers and designers of both sets of themes are great. Using themes from either designer saves me hours of development time on a project. As a business blogger, you get the benefit of a professionally designed, technically sophisticated, and supported (you can ask questions if something doesn't look or work correctly) theme.

Look at free themes, and then look at premium themes to see whether they both match your budget and the look and feel you want for your blog.

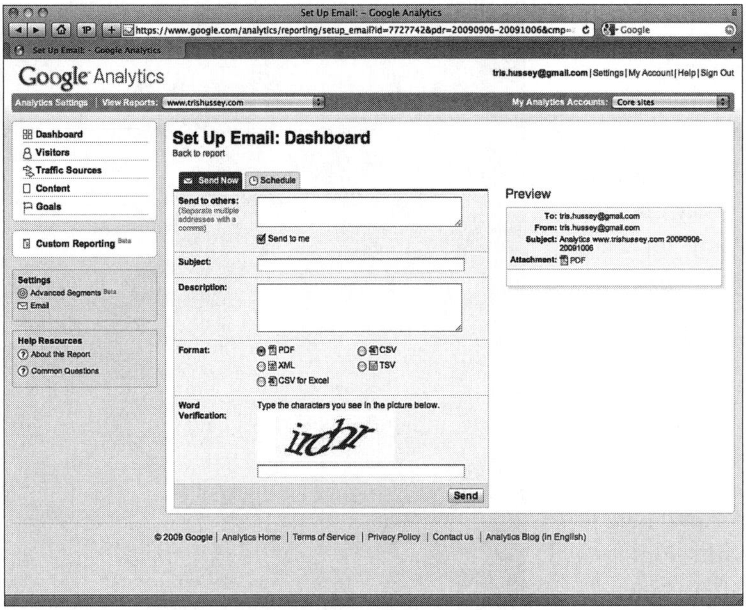

FIGURE 6.5

The scheduled report page at Google Analytics—a great way to keep people informed of how the blog is doing.

Business bloggers should also leverage the power of Google Blog search to see who is linking to you and talking about your posts. It's a very simple search to do and you can add that search to your RSS reader and check it frequently. In Figure 6.6, you can see I entered "link:trishussey.com" into Google Blog Search (blogsearch.google.com) and it returned a list of all the posts that linked to my personal blog.

Think about your blog stats in a larger fashion. Getting tied up in specific numbers will, I promise, drive you crazy. Look at the trends. Are visits and page views increasing or decreasing? Are there certain days that have more traffic than others? Are certain search terms being used to find your blog that you find surprising (on my personal blog "yam fries recipe" is often number one, and I only posted about that once!)?

These are the stats and metrics that will really matter in the longer term. I promise—worry about writing great content and engaging with your readers, and the rest will work itself out.

FIGURE 6.6

Google Blog search looking for links to my personal blog.

Summary

Although a personal blog is all about you, a business blog is all about your business. Choosing to start a business blog is opening a conversation with your customers, colleagues, and the world. This might seem like a scary thing at first, but the rewards can be tremendous. Having a direct line out to the world to talk about your successes, new products, and even let people see the human side of your business is advertising that money just can't buy.

Because you already know what you're going to talk about, the next step is just setting up the blog. I recommend the business always buy a domain name. Even if you use a hosted service like WordPress.com, ensure that your blog is using your domain name. I also recommend running your business blog on a regular web hosting account so you have complete flexibility and control over the look and feel of your blog and you have the freedom to expand into podcasting or video blogging without very many barriers in front of you.

Don't forget to consider implementing a blogging and comments policy for your company (if one doesn't exist already). Because this is the public face of your company online, you need to make sure you put your best foot forward.

Regardless of all these considerations, this is still your place to show off your business and show the world what you know and think about your field in general. Just get out there and say your piece, show your passion for what you do, and share with the world.

CHAPTER 7

Creating a Podcast Blog

This is a different sort of chapter because it isn't as much about blogging as one aspect of blogging: podcasting. Podcasting is essentially an audio blog post saved as an MP3 file. Think of it as a downloadable radio show if you like, but in reality, podcasts are blog posts (and often "group" blog posts). Although recording and posting a podcast to send out to the world might seem both daunting and overly technical, neither is true. I've found podcasting to be one of the most fun and easy parts of blogging and social media. Because a podcast, generally, lives as a part of a larger blog, you will need all the info discussed in the first four chapters to get going. Skimming Chapters 5-6 isn't a bad idea either. Don't worry—I'll still cover the basics here, but the majority of this chapter is going to be more about audio than text.

Content

If you haven't figured it out by now, the primary content of a podcast blog is the podcast. The sky is the limit when it comes to podcasts. I think podcasts are more flexible than writing content because you can have music, interviews, sound effects, as well as your narrative. So unlike *writing* a blog, you're going to be *speaking* a blog. I would, however, encourage you to write posts as well as your audio work. I like to provide some show notes and links to the things I'm talking about in the podcast, which not only gives your reader some context, but the search engines something to index.

I first started podcasting in 2005 with my "Walkabout Podcast." The idea was that I would take a walk (usually to town when I lived on Salt Spring Island, BC) while recording my thoughts on a small MP3 player-digital recorder. It was *very* rough stuff. There was a lot of background noise (cars, gravel crunching under my feet, and so on), and I often would convert the files to MP3s and upload them without post-processing or editing. Very often this is a recipe for a disastrous listening experience, but people loved them. The amateur, off-the-cuff feel became my shtick and I've kept it ever since.

The question for you is "What do you have to say?" You can do a solo recording, or team up with some friends. You can talk politics, tech, or sports—music or no music. You can even decide if you want to host your own show live on the Internet.

Today I have much better equipment, like a professional microphone, and I do add music, but I avoid doing a lot of other editing. My topics have generally been focused on social media, blogging, and technology area. Because I generally would record what was on my mind, my topics became quite varied. I even did a podcast of a (poor) imitation of Yoda (which strangely enough became very popular) talking about business blogging.

The question for you is "What do you have to say?" You can do a solo recording, or team up with some friends. You can talk politics, tech, or sports—music or no music. You can even decide if you want to host your own show live on the Internet. Like writing, podcasting is open to what you want to give it.

> **NOTE**
>
> The term podcast is often attributed to Dannie Gregoire when it started to enter tech "audioblogging" parlance in September 2004.

Recording Your Podcast

In many ways, recording your podcast can be even *easier* than picking a topic to podcast about! If you have a relatively new laptop, it probably has an adequate microphone built in, and that can be your first start. If you'd like something easier, there are several free services where you can call a phone number and your podcast will be recorded and turned into an MP3 file for you.

Unlike traditional blogging, the end result of your podcast has a lot to do with the quality of the equipment on which it is recorded. Don't get worried about needing professional audio gear and instead think about your basic nightly news show on TV. Think of the difference between all the ways correspondents call in their stories. The differences among studio to studio communications, regular phone, cell phone, and satellite are all pretty evident. So, a podcast recorded with your laptop's built-in microphone wouldn't sound as good as one recorded with an external headset, but it will sound *much* better than something recorded over the phone. So while writing is writing and there is no difference in the quality of your posts whether you write them in Word or a text editor or online, podcasts are input dependent. The great thing, however, is that recording an awesome sounding podcast isn't an expensive undertaking.

On that note, quiet in the studio. Recording your podcast, take one…

Tools

Recording a podcast is one of the simplest and easiest things you can do online. I already mentioned that if you have a laptop, you are already halfway there because chances are that your laptop has a microphone built in. No, it might not be the best mic in the world, but it's a start. If you don't have a laptop or your laptop doesn't have a mic built in, you can buy a basic computer headset and microphone at your local computer store. Don't feel like you need a very expensive one to start out with. First off, you're just starting out and second when you publish the podcast you're going to compress and down-sample it, which generally eliminates a lot of the benefits of a more expensive mic.

Yes, if you invest in higher-end, professional gear, you will notice the difference, but let's start out simple. Look for a nice headset with stereo headphones. I like having a mute switch on my mic, but that isn't a deal breaker for most people. (I do a lot of audio conferencing so I like to be able to mute the conversation.) Most good mics are going to be on a stick (or boom) coming from the headphones. You should be able to adjust the mic up and down at least. If you can adjust it closer or farther away from your mouth, that's even better.

WHAT MAKES A GOOD MICROPHONE?

If you're looking in the aisle with all the headsets and microphones at your local computer store, you're going to ask yourself "Okay, seriously, is $40 for a USB headset worth it?" Yes, it is. In fact, having gone through lots of headsets over the years, there is one thing that I learned: Cheap is still just cheap.

For headsets and microphones, there are two places where cheap lets you down: the connectors and the microphone. The cheaper the headset, the flimsier the connectors. Because the wires are thinner, the connection to the plug and wire isn't as good. At first this won't be a problem, but after a couple months it will be. It won't take long for those wires to start to weaken. I've had my worst problems right at the plug and at the microphone-headset junction (where it moves a lot). Once you start hearing audio clip in and out or the microphone levels wander up and down, you should start looking for a replacement headset.

The next big jump in quality was going to a USB headset. Not only could I hear better, but my recordings were clearer, and when I was using Internet voice chat, people noticed *immediately*.

What makes a headset good is how well the connectors are constructed and how well the headphone-microphone junction is built. I've found the headphone part to come along for the ride if the rest of the headset is good.

If you are really going to set up and get a professional USB mic, shop around. Go to a music store and see what they offer, and read online reviews. I have a strong suspicion that you're going to find microphones made by Blue Microphones to come up in your search. The Blue SnowBall is nothing short of *amazing*. It isn't cheap, but it's a mic to look at if you get serious about podcasting.

TIP

Why a headset? A headset does two things: One, it keeps unwanted sounds from your computer getting into your recording (the beeps and such) and, two, it also makes it easier to hear how the recording will sound. Even if I don't record with headphones (I mute the speakers when I do that), I do use them when I edit.

You will see two kinds of connections: analog (plug-in jacks) and USB. I used to be a proponent of audio jacks, but now that computers and audio cards are so much faster, I prefer USB. Another reason to opt for a USB-based microphone is that not all laptop or desktop machines have both a headset and microphone jack and for those that do, they're not always close to each other. Conversely, you're all but guaranteed to find a USB port on any computer. Buying a USB headset lets you go to pretty much any computer and start recording. As far as sound quality goes, I can't hear a difference and my professional-grade microphone that I use is also USB, so going with a USB headset is going to be just fine.

Now that you have the hardware set, you need software to do the recording. If you are lucky enough to have a Mac that came with iLife, then GarageBand is the obvious choice for you. On Windows (or Mac if you don't have GarageBand), the choice is Audacity (see Figure 7.1).

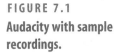

FIGURE 7.1
Audacity with sample recordings.

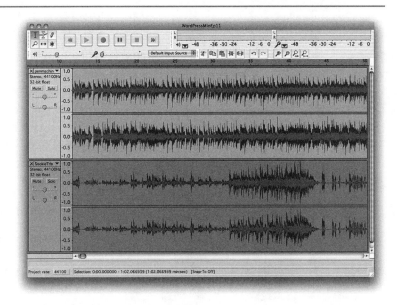

Yes, the Sound Recorder application comes with Windows, but it's ill-equipped for the job. Even Microsoft's own support site says that Sound Recorder is not for podcasting and to use Audacity instead. Before you panic about spending more money, Audacity is a free, open-source application for recording and mixing audio tracks. You can download it from audacity.sourceforge.net along with extra plug-ins and tutorials. To export your masterwork as an MP3 file, you need to download the *LAME* encoder for MP3s. It is also free, and the Audacity website gives you step-by-step directions to assist with the download. Hardware, check. Software, check. Topic, check. So, next must be recording.

NEW TERM

LAME stands for, wait for it, "LAME Ain't an MP3 Encoder" because originally the open-source project wasn't actually an encoder to make MP3s. Now it is, but it is still called LAME. It is the free library that lets you turn a sound file into an MP3.

Your First Recording

I've put recording before talking about building your blog because it's a good idea to have a couple episodes of your show "in the can" (complete) before you launch your site to the world. Giving yourself the target to have three episodes done before launch also gives you plenty of impetus to get things done quickly. If you already have a blog with plenty of written content and you want to add podcasts to the

TRIS' TIPS FOR A GOOD RECORDING

There is no magic to good recordings. Getting a good podcast recorded takes practice. Just do it over and over until you are comfortable when you click record. If you are more comfortable with it, use a script and talking point for your recording. If you're working with a friend or two, make sure everyone knows the plan *and* what hand signals to use for non-verbal communication.

I often do a quick run-through, and even record it, to warm up my voice (this isn't nonsense— you need to warm up your voice a bit). I don't do vocal exercises, but the run-through gives my vocal cords time to wake up and be ready for work.

▶ Relax.

▶ Take a sip of water (or something) before you start.

▶ Don't try to have a "radio voice"; just speak naturally.

▶ Slow down. You're probably speaking too quickly even though you don't realize it.

▶ Choose a quiet location.

▶ Turn off your cell phone ringer, computer speakers, and so on.

▶ Relax (I know I said this already, but this is important).

mix, feel free to post your podcast as soon as you feel your recording is ready to post.

When I started podcasting, the hardest part was starting the show. The "well, what do I say" feeling hit me and I would be stuck. Once I got the first few words out of my mouth, I was fine and by the end I had to remember to shut up and stop recording. Sometimes the best openings are the simple ones. Something like "Hi, this is Tris. Welcome to This Week in Social Media. [pause for 2–3 seconds] This week we're talking all about Facebook…"

It's a very basic and simple opening that tells listeners exactly what they need to know. The pause after the introduction gives you a nice, clean break to insert theme music. When the music fades out, you get the second half of the introduction. Unlike live radio, you don't have to hit start and stop to bring music into the recording, rather you can splice a music track in after you're finished recording. Sure, you could play and record the music all at once, but that is more difficult than you might think. If you're doing a show with a guest or more than one person, make sure they know how you do the intro so they don't inadvertently interrupt it or remain quiet when it comes time for them to say something.

When I started podcasting the hardest part was starting the show. The "well, what do I say" feeling hit me and I would be stuck. Once I got the first few words out of my mouth, I was fine and by the end I had to remember to shut up and stop recording.

When preparing for a podcast, there's also the question of whether to go in with some kind of prepared script or just winging it. Although I don't usually work off a script or show notes, I don't recommend the "flying by the seat of your pants" route. Reading from a script is sure to make you sound robotic and unnatural, but working without any notes at all makes it difficult to stay on topic and avoid rambling. If you do ramble a bit at first, don't worry. It takes practice.

One good trick worth trying is to rehearse what you're going to talk about in your head, so it's not like you're doing it cold. I can tell you that the fact that I usually don't work from notes has driven several co-hosts nuts, but it still works for me.

> **TIP**
>
> If you use show notes, print them in a large font, like 18 point or greater, so you can read and skim them quickly.

Next you need to think about length. The question of how long your show should be is a tough one. Right now, I'm doing a 5–10 minute show and a one minute show. I've also done a one-hour live show streamed over the Internet (complete with call-in guests and listener comments), and there are plenty of successful podcasts out there that run even longer. Consider the following questions on show length:

> ▸ How long do you need to say what you want to say?
>
> ▸ How long do you think people will be willing to listen?

▸ Where do you expect your audience to be listening to your show?

▸ What format(s) will you use to distribute your show?

If you're doing something like an online class, you might be able to have a longer show (especially if people are paying for it), but an hour-long podcast might not work for the commuter listening to you on the bus. I'm leaning towards shorter podcasts now because it seems that all media are getting shorter. Yes, I could be accused of pandering to shorter attention spans, but I'm one of those people with shorter attention spans. I often haven't listened to podcasts because they were too long. I like to multitask and I can't multitask to a podcast (because I need to pay attention to them).

> **TIP**
>
> Asking your audience or trying different show lengths and gauging the traffic patterns might be the best ways to decide on a show length. Then again, if you have the desire to record a two-hour podcast, more power to you; just don't expect a lot of people to listen in regularly.

Laying Down the Main Track

Regardless of whether you're using Audacity or GarageBand, the process of recording is essentially the same. You open a new project/episode file, create a base vocal track, and record. In GarageBand when you create a new podcast episode, you get default male and female tracks, a music/jingle track, and a track for images (podcasts can have an image associated with them for branding). Audacity is a blank canvas, but when you click the record button, a default track is created that becomes the base for the project (see Figure 7.2).

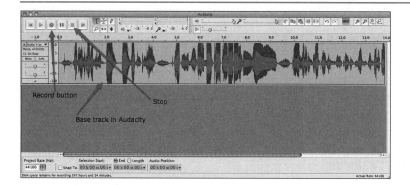

FIGURE 7.2
Audacity with a main track, and record and stop buttons highlighted.

If you're wondering about recording or mic technique, I'm not going to go into a lot of detail. Mic technique is something that you will master over time, and it takes a certain amount of practice. Although every mic is a little different, especially built-in mics, the general rules of thumb are the same: Speak clearly, speak normally, and be about 4—6 inches from the mic.

No matter how many podcasts I've recorded, I always do a mic check. In fact, no matter how many times I record voice-overs in the studio, I do a mic and level check first. I've done whole interviews not realizing that the mic was turned off or the battery was dead and have been pretty mortified and angry when I figured it out. So word to the wise...do a mic check. Mic and level checks are easy. I get my mic set up, plugged in, and positioned, then hit record. An easy standard to adopt is to say, "Mic check, mic check, one two," and then stop and play back what you recorded. Sometimes the mic is "too hot" (loud) or soft, and in those cases you need to adjust the recording levels or your positioning relative to the mic.

NOTE

Ever wonder why people do mic checks saying, "check one two"? It's simple. Like "the quick brown fox jumps over the lazy dog" uses all the letters of the (English) alphabet, "check one two" covers a good part of the range of normal speaking frequencies. And now you know.

Ready to record? Okay, take a sip of water, swallow, take a breath, hit record, and pause for about two seconds. Even though you're not using tape, it still takes the computer a second or two to record the audio, so if you don't wait you might get an intro that starts off a little clipped. If the opening gap is too long, you can always trim the excess when you're done.

When you're recording, make sure all other programs that make noise are closed, your cell phone is off, and that you won't be interrupted. Background noise happens, but the more you can eliminate it, the better the podcast will sound. You don't need a professional sound booth, just a quiet room. Personally I find it strange to record in a sound booth; it's too quiet in there (the strange sound and quiet hurts my ears). Just to be sure, often

I mute my speakers so if I missed an app that beeps, it won't interfere. Just remember to *unmute* the speakers before playback; it's rather hard to hear what you've recorded when the speakers are turned off.

> *Just remember to **unmute** the speakers before playback; it's rather hard to hear what you've recorded when the speakers are turned off.*

As you record your podcast, be ready to flub. We all do, even professional voice-over people flub up (and it's always funny) and have to start over. When I started out and shied away from editing, I just kept going. Now, I might stop and start over or just pause and keep going. Sometimes you can edit out the flub "in post"; it just depends on how you flub. The first few times you record, you'll probably need some time to warm up before you can relax. I generally do a first take that I discard, and then record a second (or third or fourth) for real. In the first take, I often haven't quite got my point condensed or solidified in my mind. Because I fly without a net, sometimes I need a little practice first.

> **TIP**
>
> In studio, I just keep recording when someone flubs; it's easier than getting things going again. If you're going to keep recording, when you flub pause for a few seconds, and then restate what you flubbed. When you edit the recording, you'll have a nice, clean place to cut and seamlessly edit the flub out.

Editing Basics

Once you have your show recorded, you might want to do a little editing. This is where GarageBand and Audacity come in—they let you take the vocal track you just laid down, mix it with some music, normalize the volume, and otherwise make it sound really cool.

There are several basic edits that you should do. First, trim off the extra dead air at the beginning and the end. It's easy to identify because the track line goes flat in places where no sound is recorded. I find that trimming a bit at a time and listening is the safest way to go. You still want a bit of silence at the beginning of the recording before you start talking. Try it both ways and you'll see that it just sounds better to have a bit of a pause there.

If you made mistakes and want to edit those out, go ahead. As for pauses that just came naturally, leave those in. Listen to the way DJs and other people do voice-over narratives, and you'll notice that they let the natural pauses give their words more strength and drama than if they just had several minutes of talking. Not to mention that it would sound very strange to have someone talk without pause for five minutes, or even one for that matter. It goes without saying to save often and play back your edits to see whether they sound right. Once you have the vocal track done, let's add some music.

> **TIP**
>
> Good editing takes time. The trick is to listen, rewind, listen, edit, listen, and save—often. Then save even more.

Mixing in Music

Both GarageBand and Audacity are multi-track editing programs, which means to add music to the podcast, you just create another track alongside your recorded audio track and put the music there. The mechanics of how to do this are simple; you either import the song into a new track or create the track and then import it.

That said, once you dump some music into a new track, you're not nearly finished. If you play the podcast like it is right now, chances are it will be hard to hear your recording over the music or vice-versa. Not to mention if you wanted an intro track to fit into a pause like "Welcome to the knitting podcast. I'm your host Darning Needle. [pause] Today we're talking about angora…," it might not fit exactly right. This is the fun part of editing podcasts, getting the music in the right place, fading in and out, and in the right places. It's fun because when you get it just right, it sounds awesome.

In most editing programs, you can cut and splice the music into sections, move it to differ-ent parts of the time line, and adjust the volume of just a section of the audio track. GarageBand makes this process a little easier by using automatic "ducking" of the Jingle or Music track. Ducking is just keeping the volume of the music lower than the other tracks above it (in this case, your voice track). Although ducking helps with making sure that you can hear your words over the music, it isn't 100% perfect. My process is to place the audio track in and listen to the ducked version without adjustments. Then, still listening to the playback, I turn down the track volume of the music to a point where I can hear the music, but still hear my voice clearly. There is a subtle point where you can hear and make out the music and still hear your voice. If you set the music too low, people will strain to listen to the music, which will be distracting to them.

Fades

Deciding how and when to fade music in or out during your podcast depends a lot on the nature of your particular podcast. For example, if I start the voice and music tracks at the same point I adjust the volume so that when I stop talking for the pause after the intro, the music is louder (see Figure 7.3). Often I have picked music of a certain length for just the part after "Welcome to Social Media this week…" and before the main content of the show. I fade in the music at the end of the intro and fade out as I begin to start the show. If this doesn't entirely make sense to you, don't worry, listen to radio, and you'll hear exactly what I'm talking about.

Ducking, fade ins, and fade outs are nice touches that are easy to include but also give your podcast a nice polished sound. At the end of the podcast I might fade in some outro music, but just let it run for a bit then fade it out.

FIGURE 7.3
Audio fade in and out in GarageBand '09.

Where do you get awesome music for your podcast? If you answered, "my CD/MP3 collection," *Bzzzttt!* Wrong answer—thanks for playing. You can't just use any old music in your podcast; you need the *rights and license* to use it as well. What kind of music is that? Podsafe music.

Podsafe Music

Just because you can find a song online, doesn't mean you should or have the rights to use it in your podcast. Music, like pictures, are copyrighted. Artistic works are protected by copyright laws. Although you might scoff at this, that's pretty hypocritical because you, by creating a podcast (or a written work), are also a copyright-protected artist. Yes, a little different now, isn't it?

Music is a very interesting, not to mention touchy, subject online. People love music and love to share the music they love with others. This isn't necessarily bad; it's just how it's all done that gets sticky. In the case of podcasts, the issue is payment to the artists for the exhibition of their works. When a radio station plays a song, a royalty is paid to both the performing artist and the composer(s). Radio stations keep detailed logs of what songs are played and how many times. These numbers are then reported back to the recording companies, along with the royalties due to the artists. So when you use your favorite song in your podcast, you are technically broadcasting that song and, therefore, should pay royalties.

When podcasting first started, this became a huge issue. If you use an excerpt of a song for a review, is it covered under fair use? If you do a parody, is it fair use? Can you play a song, giving credit to the artist, and be okay if you were actually promoting the artist? All these questions were debated and hashed out in the early days of podcasting and there turned out to be a great solution: "podsafe" music.

WHAT DOES "FAIR USE" MEAN?

Fair use is, essentially, an exception made in copyright law to allow people to use portions of a copyrighted work for the purpose of review, criticism, parody, and other artistic or journalistic reasons. Fair use was first brought into Common Law in 1740 as part of "fair abridgement" from a 1709 British law. Fair use wasn't officially on the books as part of copyright law in the U.S. until 1976.

There are lots of misconceptions about fair use. Wikipedia has a thorough discussion (meaning get a cup of coffee to read) of fair use— http://en.wikipedia.org/wiki/Fair_use—that is worth a read.

One of the key parts of fair use is that it is a legal *defense* not *a right*. You don't have the *right* to infringe (use without authorization) on copyrighted works, but if you're sued then you can call upon fair use as your defense. It is the *defendant's* burden to prove fair use; the assumption is that there has been a violation of copyright.

Where does this leave you? After all, it's perfectly acceptable for a book reviewer to quote passages of a book in his or her review. Would it then be acceptable to play a portion of a song for a review? What if you really wanted to play a *whole* song as part of a review of a larger *album*?

These are important questions that are still being worked out for the online world. I will say that part of proving copyright infringement is both how much of the material was copied *and* the intent. So, perhaps playing one song to talk about the whole album might be okay (especially if you wax poetic about the album exhorting people to buy it from iTunes).

I don't know all the answers, and the jury is still out (pun intended) on this issue. My advice is to be cautious.

Podsafe music is music that is released online for use in podcasts. The creators of the works are not relinquishing their ownership or copyright, but giving you the right or license to be able to use the work, under certain conditions. Generally the conditions were that your podcast was noncommercial and that you gave credit back to the artist (usually a link back to the artist's site). It was a simple and effective way to handle the problem. In fact, many popular musicians released some of their works under Creative Commons podsafe licenses to get additional play and attention.

NOTE

In November, 2004, *Wired Magazine*, together with Creative Commons, released a CD of 16 tracks that were shared by artists to sample and use for podcasts. The tracks are still available for download—http://creativecommons.org/wired/ (I used a few of the tracks in my own podcasts). This was a great step for both podcasters and artists. This was also during the height of Napster/music downloading fracas, so having artists release their music like this was very well received (by geeks as least).

Finding podsafe music is as easy as doing a Google search for podsafe music. Of course to save you a step, visit my friend Derek Miller's website penmachine.com and check out his podsafe music. I'm rather fond of it, especially because he wrote one especially for me (Mighty Mullane). You can use commercial music in your podcast, if you ask permission and are granted a license. I did this for my early podcasting efforts. I really wanted to use the beginning of one of my favorite songs ("Basement Apartment" by Sarah Harmer) as my intro music, so I asked her label and received permission. It was that simple. As daunting as it might seem to ask for permission from some big record label, you never know until you ask.

Exporting to MP3

Regardless of the tool you use to edit your podcast, it isn't ready for distribution until you export it as an MP3 file. Audacity, GarageBand, and other audio-editing tools save your work in their own file format so you can edit them, add tracks, and generally tweak your recording. Also, until your recording is exported, it is *uncompressed*. The audio is just as you recorded it, but that file would be useless if you tried to share it with people online. When you export your podcast as an MP3, you are combining the tracks together *and* compressing the file to make it smaller. You're probably very familiar with MP3s already; a lot of the music you already listen to is saved in this format. The trick with MP3s is finding the right amount of compression for the audio track.

SUZANNE VEGA "MOTHER OF THE MP3"

When Karlheinz Bradenburg was working on the new MP3 codec to compress music, he needed a song to test the compression against to ensure he wasn't losing audio quality. According to Internet lore, he was walking down the hall and heard someone playing "Tom's Diner" by Suzanne Vega. He felt that the complexities of that song (a cappella singing and harmonics) would be the perfect test for his new file format. And thus, Suzanne Vega became the unofficial Mother of the MP3.

The MP3 codec is a "lossy" compression scheme, meaning data are removed from the file to make it smaller, but done in such a way that you won't notice a loss of quality—to a certain point. Any audiophile will tell you that any time you compress something, there is a loss of fidelity. The trick is to get the right balance between not enough compression (large file sizes) and too much (small file size, but sounds terrible). For podcasts that are mostly spoken word, I suggest 64 kbps (kilobits per second) stereo (which also happens to be GarageBand's settings for "Good" quality). If you have more music in your podcast, try exporting at 96 or 128 kbps, but before you upload listen to all three files. You might not be able to tell the difference between 96 and 128 (much less 192 kbps), and if you can't discern a difference then go with the smaller file size. Smaller file sizes not only take up less space on the server, but also take less time to download (therefore people don't have to wait as long before they start hearing the podcast).

In case you're wondering, the uncompressed songs on an audio CD are 1411.2 kbps. This is why when you copy songs to your computer from a CD or download them, they are compressed to 128, 192, or even 320 kbps (for very high quality) because the uncompressed files are huge. A CD only holds 700 MB of data with maybe 13 songs on a disc. If the songs weren't compressed when you copied them over, you'd fill up your hard drive pretty fast! Both GarageBand and Audacity have presets for exporting the audio you've created into MP3s, so don't worry about remembering specific kbps settings (I certainly don't).

There's one last thing before you post your masterwork—setting the ID3 tags.

ID3 Tags: Like Dog Tags, but for Music

When you buy a song online or copy it to your hard drive, your computer "knows" a lot about the song already, like artist, album, composer, genre, year, and so on? This data is stored with the MP3 file as additional information collectively called the ID3 tag. The ID3 tag gives software, and therefore listeners, that additional information about what they are listening to, like who the heck the person is or what the silly song is. When you export files with Audacity, as shown in Figure 7.4, you're presented with a dialogue box to fill in this information (some might be prefilled for you). GarageBand doesn't do this as well (shame on Apple), but you can use ID3 tag editors to tweak any MP3s you created in GarageBand.

FIGURE 7.4
Audacity ID3 tag dialog box.

For the sake of ease and clarity, don't worry about ID3v1 and instead select v2. For the genre, I pick spoken word or other, unless podcast is offered. If I edit the ID3 tags later and can change the genre to podcast, I do. In most cases, however, it doesn't make much difference for podcasts if the genre is specifically on the money. It's important to provide your name, the podcast title, and year as bare minimums because these are used by podcast servers and software to give the listener information about what they are listening to (see Figure 7.5).

FIGURE 7.5

Editing ID3 tags.

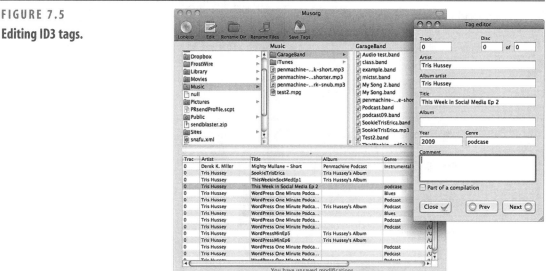

Internet Radio Renaissance

Sometimes I wish podcasting had become as popular as video is now, but maybe the era of the Internet radio just might come back into style. You never know. Speaking of Internet radio, what if you'd like to do a live radio show online? You can and all you need is a phone. As strange and ironic as it might seem, Internet-based radio had a renaissance using just the plain old telephone system (POTS).

Services like BlogTalkRadio (www.blogtalkradio.com) and TalkShoe (www.talkshoe.com) developed technologies to let people call a phone number from pretty much any phone and have it streamed live to the Internet. Not only that, you could have guests, co-hosts, music, and even an archived version as an MP3 to download. I had a show on BlogTalkRadio for a while and absolutely loved doing a live show (see Figure 7.6). Sure, my co-host and I had some bad shows, but we also had some awesome ones too.

FIGURE 7.6

BlogTalkRadio.com.

For both of these technologies, the key is the boring, old, low-tech phone system because it's everywhere. If you don't have access to a landline then you surely have a cell phone. The ubiquity of the phone and phone system makes it a great system to build on for putting together a radio show. Both services enable hosts and guests to call into the show via a phone number, and listeners can follow along online. Past shows are archived and can be sent to iTunes as podcasts.

There are some downsides to doing shows like this. The biggest is audio quality. The difference between one phone and another can be huge, resulting in one caller sounding great and others sounding like they are talking from inside a tin can. If you live outside the U.S. or don't have unlimited long distance, then you also have to pay for long-distance charges. For this reason alone, I haven't been doing as many BlogTalkRadio shows lately.

Both BlogTalkRadio and TalkShoe are working on using the Internet to run the entire system—BlogTalkRadio callers can use a click to talk system, but not the host. At the time of this writing, though, neither have made tremendous progress. Despite these limitations, both services are tremendously cool and powerful. With a free account, you can be your own radio show host. Now, come on, how cool is that? I've used BlogTalkRadio to record interviews with people, and then downloaded the MP3 to edit and post on its own. This, believe me, is a lot easier than trying to sync up recordings from different sources.

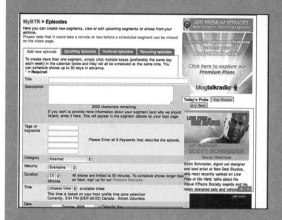

SETTING UP A PROFILE ON BLOGTALKRADIO AND SCHEDULING YOUR FIRST SHOW

Your profile on BlogTalkRadio is your gateway to listeners. The more you describe your show, the better. Take a quick look at the shows in Figure 7.6, and I'm sure there are a couple you might be interested in checking out. Do you have a good picture for your profile—it might take a few minutes to show up—and be descriptive. Visit blogtalkradio.com and see which shows catch your eye. Check out the profiles and get ideas of how to entice listeners.

Of course to have listeners, you have to have a show, so let's schedule one now. The page shown here is straightforward. Again, part of the trick to getting listeners to your show is telling people what the show is about. Saying "We're just going to talk about stuff" will work for a celebrity but not regular people like us.

What are you going to talk about? What's the issue at hand? Is there come controversy that you are going to address?

Think about real-life radio shows you like. What keeps you interested in the show? Often it's the interaction between the hosts that makes (or breaks) a show. Talking about how you and the host(s) will tackle an issue is a great addition to the profile and show description.

Oh, and have fun. This is also about having fun doing it.

For a personal blog, as discussed in Chapter 5, "Creating a Personal Blog," BlogTalkRadio and TalkShoe are great ways to easily record and host a podcast. For a serious podcaster, these services are best if you are just starting to get into doing a show or you want to be able to easily have guests on your show. Keep in mind that the audio quality is based on the phones and phone connection.

There are other ways to do group interviews, but these require a certain amount of tech savvy among *all* the participants to get a good recording in the end. There is no doubt that both BlogTalkRadio and TalkShoe are worth a look if you are interested in doing live shows with chat and guest callers, but if you want great sound and production value, you might think about doing it all yourself.

Hosting and Promoting Your Podcast

After you have your podcast recorded, it needs a place to live (hosting) and people need to be able to find out about it (promotion). Like setting up your blog itself, you can host your podcast yourself or use a hosted service. Unlike blogging or even videos, podcasting lacks free hosting options (there is one at the time of writing). Unless you are completely averse to doing it yourself, you are going to wind up paying for podcast hosting (which is the same cost as doing it yourself without the benefits of controlling all aspects of your online world).

Where and How to Host Your Podcast Blog

The key issue for all podcasters is storage space and bandwidth. Unlike a "regular blog" or a website, if your focus is on podcasting, you are going to be creating files that are much larger than everyone else. A five-minute podcast can easily be a couple of megabytes, even with compression applied. If planning for an episode a week, you have a few hundred megabytes of files to manage. Not only that, *every time* someone listens to your podcast, it uses up your allotted bandwidth. If you are allotted 30 gigabytes of bandwidth a month (that's my allotment) and have a 10 megabyte/episode podcast, you've used up 10 MB of your total allotment each time someone listens to it.

One listen isn't a lot, but multiply that by 100, and then by the number of posts you have, plus the bandwidth for the rest of the site. Yes, it can add up and quickly. Several friends I know had their websites shut down for periods of time because they used up all their allotted bandwidth before the end of the month (it happened to me once myself). This was a double-edged sword kind of event for them. First it meant that someone very popular had linked to them (therefore they had some high-profile attention and they had "made it"), but at the same time this popularity came at the price of being knocked offline.

Right now, only PodBean (podbean.com), Libsyn (libsyn.com), and Blubrry (blubrry.com) remain as hosts in the podcasting world, and PodBean is the only free one (compared to at least six for video). These services give you storage space and either generous or unlimited amounts of bandwidth for your podcast. Embed a player, like you might for YouTube, into your posts for each podcast. For my own podcasting, I upload my file to my own server space and use a WordPress plug-in to insert a player into the post. I suggest that you follow the same path. If you're going to be serious about podcasting (more than an episode or three), get server space and set up hosting. The cost you will pay for hosting is essentially the same as paying for hosting at a podcasting host service, without the benefit of being able to host and control your own site(s). Follow the self-hosted/DIY route discussed in Chapter 2, "Installing and Setting Up Your Blog." For more insight into tuning a blog, refer to Chapters 5 and 6 for tips on SEO, plug-ins, and other blog settings. Once you get your blog set up, there are a few tweaks needed to get it ready for iTunes.

Posts with Your Podcast

When you create a podcast episode, it needs to live within a blog post. This lets iTunes know it's there, and it gives content and context for your readers. Because your podcast lives both within iTunes and your larger blog, you can increase its chances of being found by search engines and visitors. Make sure that when you write the post, it isn't just a link to the podcast file, but rather has a little bit about the episode. Not only does describing your episode give your readers-listeners something to latch onto, it also gives the search engines something to index. Figure 7.7 shows an example from my friend Shane's Closing Bigger podcast.

FIGURE 7.7

Example post from Shane Gibson's ClosingBigger.net podcast (one of my favs, btw).

How do you get your podcast into your post and how do you get that awesome player? It is all part of using the right WordPress plug-ins. With either PodPress or PowerPress, adding a podcast episode is, frankly, just a few clicks away. Both plug-ins just need the URL of the episode that you've uploaded to your host and then you're off to the races. The easiest way to get this URL is to use the media uploader built into WordPress (see Figure 7.8).

FIGURE 7.8
Copying the URL of an uploaded media file.

Next, paste the URL into the space provided, write your post, and publish. The player, download links, even informing iTunes is all done for you. Snazzy, eh?

For WordPress.com users, if you paid for extra storage, the process for adding a podcast is nearly like regular WordPress, but even easier

(but less flexible). For other blog engines, especially self-hosted ones, the process is essentially the same as self-hosted WordPress. TypePad has simple podcasting, but they also suggest in their help documents that if you're worried about bandwidth charges, you might consider hosts like Libsyn.

Submitting Your Podcast to iTunes

Just like in the online music world, iTunes is the 300-pound gorilla for podcasting. This wasn't always so, however. Initially, iTunes didn't support podcasts, so the community relied on other software (podcatchers) and directories to promote their podcasts. At podcasting's peak, I remember at least a half dozen major podcast indices and directories. You had to submit your podcast to each one separately to have it listed. Then came iTunes tuning into podcasting.

When iTunes started to support podcasts, the best thing to do was to submit it to iTunes. Because iTunes has such *huge* reach, that and basic promotion of your site/blog, is all most folks need to do to get an audience for their podcasts. Before long most of the directories folded because listing with iTunes covered a lot of bases and if traffic is the basis for your business model, as traffic tanked, so did your business.

The process for submitting a podcast to iTunes is simple. Make sure iTunes is downloaded and installed on your computer. Launch iTunes and click iTunes Store. Click the Podcasts link located on the left side of the store window, and you should see something like Figure 7.9.

FIGURE 7.9
iTunes store podcast
section with Submit a
Podcast highlighted
(within iTunes).

Click on the Submit a Podcast button and you should see a screen like Figure 7.10. Insert your URL and include the "http" portion. It should look something like http://www. sixbloggingprojects.com/feed/, which is the standard format for WordPress-based blogs. For other blogs, go to your blog and copy the RSS feed URL by right-clicking the link and copying the link. Paste this into the submission box.

The next screen gives you the option to set the topics areas, but you'll get an error if you haven't created at least one episode (two or three is better).

That's all you need to get the process started. Note the word "started" here; this is because someone from Apple reviews each submission to iTunes to determine whether it is worthy of inclusion. Yes, most podcasts are accepted, and

FIGURE 7.10
Submit a podcast to the
iTunes directory screen
(within iTunes).

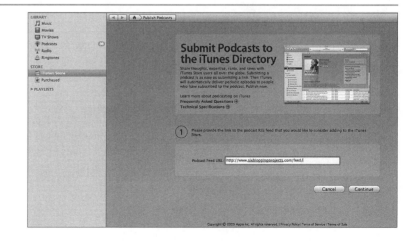

the process generally takes only a week or two, but you can see that Apple can (and does) decide what is allowed on iTunes. So some topics might be considered off limits, and because of this iTunes will never be the be all and end all of podcast listings.

Once you receive approval for your podcast, you can add categories and keywords. Apple, unfortunately, doesn't give you a lot of options for primary and secondary categories. I, personally, set the genres and such within my WordPress plug-in, because I have much more control and ability to define keywords better. The Blubrry's PowerPress plug-in example shown in Figure 7.11 shows you how detailed you can be when adding keywords and other data to your iTunes listing.

You can update or augment your iTunes keywords from the link Apple sent you. Making your updates through the plug-in is faster, easier, and takes effect as soon as you publish your next episode.

Like most things related to the technology of blogging, once you have the initial setup done, it runs itself. I don't worry about my iTunes feed or RSS feed or if my shows will keep playing. I know that if I set it up right, it should just keep working.

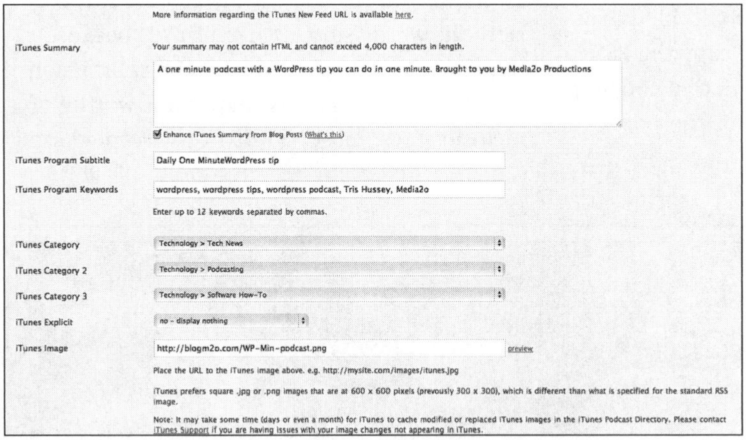

FIGURE 7.11
Additional iTunes settings through advanced options in the PowerPress plug-in.

Summary

Podcasting, short of writing and photography, is my favorite part of publishing online. It is easy to start podcasting with the microphone built into your laptop or with an inexpensive microphone from the computer store. You don't have to spend big bucks to get going. Don't forget that I started off using a cheap MP3 player with a built-in voice recorder!

Record your first bits of audio, start editing them with your sound/audio editor of choice (which will be Audacity or GarageBand), and then publish as an MP3 file.

Finding a home for your new podcast is as easy as signing up for WordPress.com or buying a domain name and setting up hosting on your own. In the end, I think you'll be happier with the DIY option, because you'll have a lot more flexibility to grow your podcast.

Once you have completed some shows and look at your blog, think of how cool you'll feel! Finally, don't forget to submit your podcast to iTunes when you have some episodes done, and you're off to the races!

Hey, is this thing still on?

PROMOTING YOUR PODCAST ON ITUNES

To get more listeners, use buttons provided by iTunes on the sidebar of your blog to point people to subscribe to your podcast. By pushing them through iTunes, you make it easier for them to download and carry it on their MP3 players, plus increasing your ranking within iTunes. The more listeners you have, the closer to the top of the list you are within your genre.

When you write the post for the episode, make sure there is a link to subscribe in iTunes and remind people to subscribe in iTunes as well.

Finally, ask listeners to rate your podcast in iTunes. Apple selects highly rated podcasts from each genre to promote on the main page. If you get on there, you will get a sudden increase in listeners.

You can even go a step further and *charge* for episodes of your podcast. While not promoting *per se,* having a $2.00 an episode show does add a bit of exclusivity to your show. It's interesting to note that you can sell episodes of *audio* podcasts on iTunes, but not *videos*. Only studios and networks can sell video on iTunes.

CHAPTER 8

Video Blogging

At the first Northern Voice in February 2005, there was a great session on podcasting and video blogging (or vlogging as it was called a lot back then). I sat in the audience and thought that I could do a podcast without too much trouble, but a video blog, no way. Back then nothing about doing a vlog was easy. Editing software, bandwidth, and storage space weren't cheap (or free). The consensus was that vlogging was only for the hardcore sorts who also had access to their own servers (or friends who had their own servers).

Just four years later and it's a different story. Vlogging is as simple as buying a $150 hand-held video camera, recording, connecting it to a computer, tweaking it a little (maybe), and uploading. Done. There are at least a half a dozen free services where you can upload your video and have them host it. Creating your video blog is a two-part process because you'll have your "real" blog but also the "homepage" on whichever video-hosting service you choose. Both are going to be crucial to your success as a video blogger. So, lights, camera, action!

Content

If there is any question in your mind what the content of a video blog should be, I think you need to be reading a different book. So, let's march forward. You've figured out that you want to record and post videos by this point, which is good, and I applaud you because I find doing video blog posts a real challenge. Oh, not because they are technically hard or particularly challenging, I'm just not a fan of being on camera. A lot of people aren't, and if that's you, that's okay. Creating quality video content can also be a challenge. I easily get distracted and stray off topic with solo videos.

Interviews (where I'm the interviewee) are great, but monologues are the death of me—and my audience.

Right now, most vlog posts are ten minutes or less in length. Why? Oddly enough, it is because YouTube and other free video hosts cap video uploads to ten minutes (or 2 GB). It's a fair thing, I think, to cap the size and length of videos, not to mention it matches people's attention spans pretty well. Frankly, shorter videos of five minutes or less are better, the exception being if you are going to do paid tutorials or seminars. Even then, however, I'd chunk the sessions into five- to ten-minute segments.

> *Right now, most vlog posts are ten minutes or less in length. Why? Oddly enough, it is because YouTube and other free video hosts cap video uploads to ten minutes (or 2 GB).*

Picking your video "genre" is an important step here. Are you going to do some kind of monologue or news program or many interviews? No, you don't have to decide now, nor are you stuck to just one style, but it's a good idea to have something in mind. Having a plan can help the creative spark that guides your decisions.

Next, you need to decide where you want your audience to watch these videos. Sure a laptop or desktop PC is a no-brainer, but what about iPods, iPhones, or cell phones? This won't effect the content of your videos as much as what you'll do in post-processing.

Enough about content, let's get to recording some videos.

Recording Your Video Blog Posts

Whether you start with a built-in webcam or a hand-held camera, a vlog starts with hitting Record. This is the easy part. It's after you've hit stop that the fun really starts: editing. Let's not get ahead of ourselves here though; let's start with recording.

There are books that go into far more depth than I will on the art and science of recording good video, but this is a book about blogging, so I'm just going to give you the highlights that can get you started.

When you're sitting down (or standing up) to record your video, you need to have a good idea of what you want it to look like in the end. Yes, you're a director now (put the beret down), so figuring out how it will all look is important. If you're filming yourself with a webcam (like the iSight built into my MacBook Pro), you'll be able to see yourself as you film. For something where you are going to use a stand-alone camera, either a friend is going to have to frame it for you or you'll need a video camera where the view screen can be turned towards you. I've done a far number of the "just turn the camera on myself" videos and without being able to see the framing on the screen, I just had to guess that I was actually on camera. Sometimes the effect was pretty funny, too.

Once you say, "Cut! Print!" and you're ready to put it all together, you'll need software to edit (if you want) and compress (you want this) the video before you can post it online. This section explores the mechanics of recording, the basics of editing, file formats, and video compression.

THE RULE OF THIRDS

There is a photographic rule called "The Rule of Thirds" that dictates how to frame a subject in a camera shot. It means taking your view finder and dividing it into thirds horizontally and vertically, which is sort of like a big tic-tac-toe box (see figure).

Where the lines cross are the places the eye tends to look. Putting the focus of your subject (say, the eyes) at the top left or right intersection of the grid instead of at the center makes the video look better. It's an odd thing because you know when a video or picture follows the rule of thirds; it just looks right.

Be sure to have Google handy for looking up details on all of these topics. You'll run into issues not covered here, not to mention that if you don't already have a camera you're going to be shopping for gear as you read.

The Camera

I'm going to venture that if you're interested in creating a video blog, you're probably interested in video already. You might already have a video camera and have been doing home movies or been playing around with your webcam. If you've been experimenting with video, you know that it all comes down to the camera. Cheap cameras result in cheap-looking video.

Recording video with your cell phone sounds like a simple idea, but the quality of those videos is poor. Hey, that's okay for some things and there is nothing wrong with using different cameras in your vlog, not to mention videos posted from cell phones that capture spur-of-the-moment action. However, unless you're going to use that gritty, bouncy, poor audio quality as your shtick, you're going to need a dedicated video camera.

Until recently, the next step up from cell phone cameras was a full-on camcorder, but when Pure Digital Technologies (now part of Cisco Systems) launched the Flip camera in 2007 everything changed (see Figure 8.1). The Flip is built for one thing: recording video and uploading it to the Internet. It essentially has one button, start/stop recording, and when you connect it to your computer, not only is there basic editing software already there but also tools to upload the video to YouTube. You might think it is odd to talk about a specific

product like this, but the Flip was so revolutionary that other companies rushed to copy it. Now pocket-sized, HD-quality cameras are affordable for almost everyone, and they are the logical choice for a budding video blogger.

FIGURE 8.1
The Flip Camera® from Pure Digital Technologies.

These devices do have their limitations, of course. Often they can't record more than a couple hours of video, the microphones are not the best, and they usually don't have a ton of additional settings for capturing video. Shortcomings aside, the sub-$150 price tag for non-HD versions, makes these pocket-sized recorders something to really consider for the casual or novice video blogger.

Stepping up into the world of "real" camcorders brings up the price considerably, but that added cost does bring benefits. Larger camcorders usually offer better quality video, more complexity, more features, and more settings. These devices are for people who are going to shoot a lot of video and want to shoot video that looks a bit more professional.

Think of these as the step up once you get going. A newcomer to the video world is the DSLR camera. *DSLR* still cameras have been around for years and are known for their capability to capture professional quality shots. Recently Nikon, Sony, and others have come out with DSLR cameras that also shoot HD video. This goes beyond the standard movie setting on a point-and-shoot camera (which is often a great option for fast video), because you can use the high-quality lenses you take still pictures with video. Having tested a few of these cameras, I can say that these devices are ones to watch. Certainly, they're not the first choice for a new vlogger, but if you're a photographer who is upgrading your camera body and want to get into video, these are worth serious consideration.

All decent video cameras (and still cameras) have a tripod mount on the bottom of the

device. Although you might not think you'll want to mount the camera on a tripod, even if you are just shooting yourself, having the camera steady on a tripod adds a lot to the end result.

All camcorders, or any device that records video, have a built-in microphone to record audio. The quality of these mics varies widely, but seldom are they capable of delivering more than rudimentary quality. If you're buying a camera and plan to use its built-in mic, it's worth doing a few in-store tests first. With the exception of a few lower-end devices, most video cameras have a line-in or external microphone port. If you're buying your first camera, think of this as a "nice to have" not a "need to have" feature.

TIPS FOR SHOOTING BETTER VIDEOS

Shooting a video is easy; shooting a good video is a different matter. Like photography, there are do's and don'ts to keep in mind when shooting.

▸ **Frame the subject correctly.** Refer to the rule of thirds sidebar earlier in the chapter. Also, watch the backgrounds. People don't have trees sprouting from their heads, so make sure that what's *behind* the subject is okay.

▸ **Use good lighting.** Let's face it, fluorescent lighting makes even a supermodel look like the undead, so try to avoid it if at all possible. Natural light is best, but when you can't use it, use other lamps to light the subject *evenly*. Watch for shadows that make the subject look off. I have a set of lights with daylight bulbs, which are very easy to pick up. Pick up the daylight bulbs at any hardware store and you can turn just about any light fixture into studio lighting.

▸ **Do test shoots.** If you're using a new system or not shooting where you usually do, it never hurts to do a few test records to see how things come out.

▸ **Use a tripod.** Hand-held video is great when on the go, but when you want to shoot something that looks professional, put the camera on a tripod.

▸ **Use an external microphone, if possible.** If your camera doesn't have an input for an external mic, you can record the audio portion like a podcaster would and then match the two up.

▸ **Use the Internet for hints and tricks.** I know that there are a ton more tricks to learn—I don't even pretend to know them all, which is why you have the Internet. Search for the questions you have, even "shooting better videos," and I'll bet you'll find some great tips.

All set? Have that camera all ready? Cool, let's start recording. No, please don't record your dog/cat/pet skateboarding or waterskiing. It was cute the first time we saw it. 1,000,000 repeats later, not so much.

Your First Recording

Recording a vlog post is very much like recording a podcast from Chapter 7, "Creating a Podcast Blog." The main difference is that people can *see* you in the vlog post and not the podcast (hand away from your nose, thank you). This is no small thing. It's much easier to control your voice for the purposes of a podcast than it is to control both your delivery and your mannerisms. Many people have no idea what they look like when they talk and are often surprised at the result when they see themselves monologing on video for the first time.

Like the previous chapter, I'm putting recording before talking about posting video to your blog because it's a good idea to have several episodes of your show "in the can" (complete) before you launch your site to the world. Set a target of 3–5 completed videos before you launch to the whole world (and iTunes). If you already have a blog and want to add video to the mix, you have other content there already. After recording an episode, post it, but put off your big announcement (and submissions to iTunes) until you have completed a few more.

Part of the recording process, and developing your style, is figuring out if you want to have titles, graphics, or music in your posts. Personally, I don't. I do more "talking head" style or interviews. Adding music and titles gives your video all the more punch when it's done. Just like with podcasting, if you're doing a show with a guest or more than one person, make sure they know how you are doing the intro so they don't think something is wrong or they are supposed to say something. While it might be just awkward silence on a podcast, it *looks* like an awkward silence on video (read: makes the person look like a doofus).

Like podcasting, I don't usually have show notes for video, because it doesn't serves me well. Off the cuff might work for audio, but when I *look* like I'm grasping for the next thought, well, it isn't so cool. There is nothing wrong with having show notes to help you to keep on track. (Note to self: Use show notes.)

As discussed, the length of your video depends on two key factors: who you're hosting with and what the end result size/quality will be. For the sake of argument, use ten minutes as the longest you can record, but file size restrictions add a whole new wrinkle to this process. Remember YouTube, for example, limits the file size of your uploaded video to 2 GB. Honestly, 2 GB is a lot of video. To get ten minutes of video to measure out to more than 2 GB, you're going to be recording and processing at near broadcast quality levels. Not to mention the time needed to upload 2 GB of video (let's say hours just to be safe) isn't something that you want to get into.

Because you're just recording video right now, let's skip file size and compression until later and focus on time. Although you might record more video than you need, the final product should be ten minutes or less. Hold the phone. If I don't want to host my videos on YouTube or wherever, can't my videos be longer and higher quality? Yes, they certainly can and you can certainly host the videos yourself, but here's why this isn't always the best idea. Bandwidth and server storage space cost

money. Google is willing to give it to you free—let them. Unless you are going to be selling your videos as part of a class, having YouTube (or viddler, or Vimeo, or whomever) host the videos gives you not only storage space and bandwidth, but also another place and touch point for promotion. Be concise or at least know you're going to edit the video down to ten minutes or less. Got it. What's next? Audio, you can't forget the audio portion of the video.

I'm going to repeat myself here from Chapter 7—always do a mic check. Always. Maybe the batteries are dead (I've had to *run* out and grab batteries before a shoot) or the audio settings were left over from a shoot outside where there was a lot of background noise to overcome or the mic isn't on or plugged in. You just don't know, so check. Trust me…recording a great interview only to find there is no audio (and no backup audio recording) leads to fits of uncontrollable swearing.

Getting the mic positioned for the best recording isn't an easy task. A built-in mic can't really be positioned. You can only be so close to the mic and be framed correctly for video. This is the point where you do the best you can and try to improve the audio in editing. You can use an external mic to record the audio separately, and then match it back up to the video in editing. Although this might be a little tricky at first, detaching the recorded audio from the video and adding another piece is a lot easier with tools like Windows Live Movie Maker or Apple's iMovie.

Ready to record? Okay, take a sip of water, swallow, take a breath, hit record, and pause for about 2 seconds. Regardless if you're using tape or some digital recording media, it takes a couple seconds for the recording to really start.

If you get right into your intro, you'll most likely be clipped off at the beginning. The wee bit of extra silence can be trimmed in editing, or left if the timing works out right.

Ready, set, … oh wait, I wasn't ready. Can I start over? Be ready to flub. We all do. Professionals flub up all the time (and it's always funny) and you know from watching blooper reels on DVDs that actors do it all the time, which makes it even more amazing that movies actually get finished!

The first few times you record, you'll probably need some time to warm up before you can relax. I generally do a first take that I discard, and then record a second (or third or fourth) for real. In the first take, I often haven't quite got my point condensed or solidified in my mind. Because I fly without a net, sometimes I need a little practice first. When I'm podcasting, a little flub isn't a big deal, but with video it seems that the flubs are always worse. Chances are, and this is absolutely okay, that you're going to either have to reshoot or edit out the flub. Unless you're going for the unscripted feel, in

which case, make as many mistakes as you want. Now that you have an episode recorded (may I suggest doing several test videos to experiment on), let's get to editing.

Editing Basics

One of the good things about video blogging is that you have free options when it comes to having access to basic video-editing software. On Windows, the program is called Movie Maker (see Figure 8.2), and on Macs it's iMovie (see Figure 8.3), which is part of iLife. Both of these applications are designed to be drag-and-drop editing tools where a lot of the work is done automatically for you.

NOTE

There are a few different versions of Movie Maker out there. Outdated versions of the software are included with Windows XP and Windows Vista, but you should make a point to download the most up-to-date, and best, version: Windows Live Movie Maker.

FIGURE 8.2

iMovie with events below and active project above.

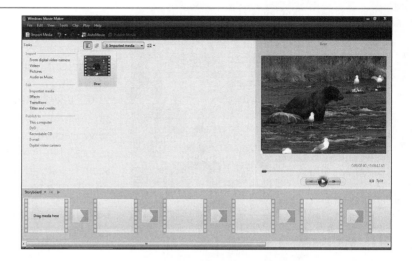

As with audio editing, with video editing you're still dealing with timelines, but now you see frames of the video instead of a waveform of audio. It should be easier for you to find the right spots in the video to cut, jump, or add titles because you can see where it should go.

Every video editor has its own tricks up its sleeve, but don't worry about that too much. Programs like iMovie and Movie Maker are relatively simple to use and there's a lot of help available online.

Once you get your video imported into the application, your next step is cutting out the parts you don't want. Generally, this means splitting the video at certain points and deleting what is in between. Simple, right? Sure, mostly. It will take practice, for sure. Just like editing audio, editing video takes time. Once you get going, you'll probably see why I don't like to edit video and would rather keep the mistakes.

After you complete the edits, you could just jump to the export process or you can gussy the video up with some music, titles, and effects. It's up to you. I've seen a lot of popular vlogs with very little to no editing, no titles, and no music. Then there are some that I wonder how they keep a day job because of their amazing production value. Striking the right balance is up to you.

TIP

It might seem overly geeky, but it's worth your time to mess around with the video (and audio) editors when you're not actually producing an episode. Taking time to just experiment and goof around can lead to amazing discoveries, which is highly recommended.

Like editing audio for podcasts, video editing is pretty straight forward, in theory, but in practice it is something that takes, well, practice to get right. The following are some basic video edits:

- ▶ Opening and closing titles. The trick is to keep titles onscreen long enough to be read, but not so long that people wonder if the video will ever start. It's good to go from a title to the video with a fade. If you just switch (a hard cut), I think it looks jarring.

- ▶ Fades. Both iMovie and Movie Maker have lots of fade styles to choose from, but the style of the fade isn't as important as the duration. Play and replay the fades so it doesn't look like the screen just blinks or the screen flows like molasses.

- ▶ Music. If you want to have a soundtrack playing under your vocal track, great, but make sure that you can hear the voices and music at the right level.

- ▶ Audio track. Listen to your audio track. Listen carefully. Even close your eyes so the video doesn't interfere with what you're hearing. There might be parts where the audio level needs to increase or decrease. Often you can just use a built-in audio leveling or normalizing tool to clean up the audio. Just remember to listen, edit, listen. Only save when you're sure the edit is right.

If you are going to do a regular show, I think the time spent on learning how to put in titles and transitions is well worth the time. For example, if you're talking about sites or products, using a standard "lower third" title (text in the lower third of the screen) for the URL, product name, or other details is very helpful to viewers. Also, using transitions between places where you made edits makes the edits seem less drastic (if it looks right; cutting in the middle of a scene might look strange).

Music can add just the right touch to a video. You see and feel this in movies. The question isn't "How do I insert a music track?" because that would be the easy part; the question is "Do I have the rights to include the music in my video?"

Using Copyrighted Works in Your Videos

Chapter 7 explored podsafe music in depth, so I won't belabor the point here. For video, you still have to consider copyrighted music, but what if you want to make a parody music video? How about do a parody of another copyrighted work (let's say a *Star Wars* themed video)? What you have to consider is the intent and whether you are making money from the video. Satire is one of the rare exceptions where you don't have to ask an artist's permission first, but it's still a nice thing to do.

NOTE

"Weird Al" Yankovic is famous for his parodies of pop songs. He is so famous that many artists consider it a badge of honor to have Weird Al parody one of their songs. The only Weird Al song to come from a fan suggestion was "Like a Surgeon," which reportedly came from Madonna herself (for "Like a Virgin").

Doing comedic remixes and mashups in video (like doing a fake interview with a celebrity using existing material) can be fun and would likely fall under fair use, but remember you have to *defend* fair use—it isn't a right. If pulling in parts of songs or videos used only for short portions, get permission from the copyright holder.

CAUTION

Keep in mind that using an entire song as the backdrop for a video and claiming it's a satire probably won't fly. Just because you're being funny, doesn't mean you can use copyrighted material!

I know this sounds like a huge downer, and I don't mean to stifle your creativity, but you also don't want to find yourself getting a nasty cease-and-desist (CAD) letter.

TIP

Since the DMCA (Digital Millennium Copyright Act) was passed in 1998, rights holders can very easily ask to have an infringing work removed from circulation by sending a DMCA notice. It is common for a DMCA notice to be sent to the offender (you) *and* your web host. Most web hosts will pull your site and ask questions later because the penalties are stiff for violations, and web hosts are liable as well. If you are sent a DMCA notice, deal with it…fast.

To sum up, let's just put it this way. I'm not going to tell you, "Oh, go ahead, everybody is doing it…" because while lots of people *are* doing it (and infringing on copyright) it doesn't make it *right*. Short excerpts for reviews are fine. Parodies *should be* fine, but you might have to defend yourself. And a DMCA notice can really ruin your day.

Mixing in Music, Titles, and Extras

In both Movie Maker and iMovie, adding music is just a drag and drop away. Once you have the podsafe music in (virtual) hand, you can import it into your video. Like with a podcast, drag the music into the spot where you want it to be and adjust it from there. Where the music starts and ends, how it fades in and out, and its relative volume is all up to you. Each program handles it a little differently. Because all of the software makers say that a child can do it, I think it's safe to say that you're pretty likely to be able to figure it out. (Don't forget the help files—I use them, too!) Adding titles and screen credits are easy, too, with the current crop of video editors (you don't want to know how hard it was not that long ago). Again, this is a click, drag, type, and adjust process (see Figure 8.4).

FIGURE 8.4
Additional audio and title tracks in iMovie.

You might be wondering how much I do when I edit videos. Not a lot. Like my podcasts, I keep video posts off the cuff and rough. I try not to do a lot with them. I've found that if I get too caught up in getting the right title or the music in the right place, I lose sight of what I was trying to do in the first place. This, however, is just my own thing. So although I do add music to my podcasts (because I like radio as a genre), I keep my videos more talking head type. I do the same things in interviews. So editing and tweaking is up to you.

Exporting, Compression, and Video Formats

The easy part is done. Now it's time to get that video out there and online. Wait, how can this be the hard part? I thought editing was going to be the hardest? Sorry, no. You can record a video and skip the whole editing part, but what about exporting and compression? Nope,

you have to do that and unlike audio where MP3 is the file format of choice, for video there are several potential formats to choose from, each with their own special pluses and minuses. Remember when I brought up the whole question about where you wanted people to see your video? Yeah, this is where these decisions come in. Let's get to it then.

What Does YouTube Say?

Because Google-owned YouTube is the 300-pound gorilla of the video world, looking at what they recommend for export settings is a great place to start. If you think I'm just cheating, you're missing the point. When Pure Digital first introduced the Flip camera, they made sure that their export settings for YouTube would make anyone's videos look great (and Pure Digital did a fantastic job of this). If you're going to make a drop-dead easy video product and you want to make exporting painless, YouTube's recommendations are a good place to start.

YouTube recommends the following:

- Dimensions 1280 × 720 (16 × 9 HD) or 640 × 480 (4:3 SD)

- Codec (the compression algorithm) H.264, MPEG-2 or MPEG-4

- Audio MP3 or AAC, 44.1kHz, 2 channel stereo

No, these recommendations don't make much sense on their own. It means scale the video to either high definition (HD) or standard definition (SD) size, use the H.264 compression scheme (this gives the best balance of quality and file size), and keep the audio stereo with standard settings.

What if you want to make the video smaller? What if you produce a great video, export it like that, and it's 3 or 4 GB? That's when you need a little help from software.

When you export from iMovie, you're presented with choices from Tiny to HD, each with dots showing what platforms the size/format is best for (see Figure 8.5). To illustrate how size and compression work hand in hand, I shot a 2-minute, 40-second video with my iSight (so for exporting, I couldn't go to full HD), and added a title to the entire length of the video, a fade in and out, plus about 30 seconds of music at the beginning. This is what I got:

- Tiny (176 × 144, iPod format, mono) 1.6 MB

- Mobile (480 × 360, mpeg-4, stereo) 19.3 MB

- Medium (640 × 480, mpeg-4, stereo) 31.9 MB

- Larger (720 × 540, mpeg-4, stereo) 56.5 MB

POPULAR VIDEO FORMATS

Do you ever wish that the world of computers and the Internet *wasn't* awash in an alphabet soup of acronyms and terms? Me, too. Anyway, it is, and video is no different. There are lots of video formats you might run into or export files to, but the following are some common ones:

- **MOV (QuickTime):** QuickTime was first developed by Apple Computer in 1991 and served as the basis for the MPEG-4 video standard. MOVs can be very high quality files (and therefore very large).

- **WMV (Windows Media Video):** The (current) default Windows video format and the format for HD discs (HD DVD and Blu-ray). Developed by Microsoft, it has wide appeal for its capability to have digital rights (DRM) assigned to it for copy protection.

- **AVI (Audio Video Interleave):** Once the default video format for Windows, it is often still used for sharing movies online.

- **FLV (Flash video)** Flash video using Adobe's Flash encoders. FLVs can be very high quality and size. They need a player to be played within a blog post or on a page.

- **MPEG-4/M4V:** This is the current standard for high-quality audio/video with the best balance of compression to quality. QuickTime and H.264 are all part of the MPEG-4 family of video codecs.

- **H.264:** Part of the MPEG-4 video format and now the standard for video compression. If a video looks good on YouTube, it was probably encoded using H.264.

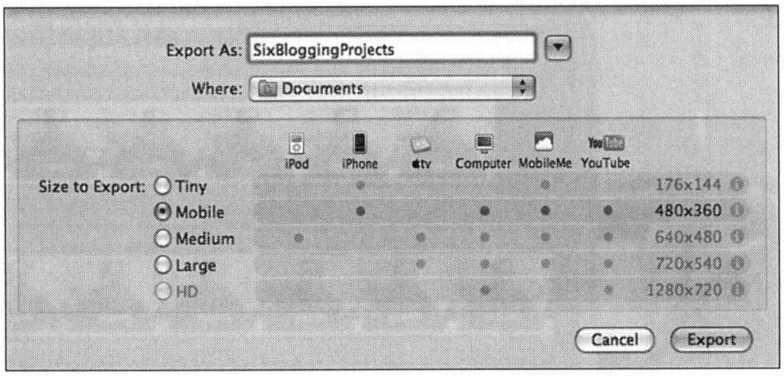

FIGURE 8.5

Export dialog in iMovie showing the options for size and compression.

Wow, huh? That was for less than three minutes of video! Using iMovie, the largest size took about 6–10 minutes to render and export. The bigger the dimensions, the longer it will take. In the end, you're looking at 15 MB (ish) per minute of video at these settings. Can you do better? Can you use different codecs? Certainly, and experimenting is an important part of getting the right look, but there is the gotcha. If you're trying to reach the widest possible audience, keeping the videos in standard sizes (as per YouTube recommendations) enables you to take advantage of re-rendering that hosts will do for you.

The greatest challenge you will face is mobile video. Unfortunately (at the time of writing this book), good solutions and answers allude me. In my day job, I try to make a video available for people using computers, iPhones, BlackBerrys, and other mobile devices and I'm stymied to reach everyone. You haven't yet reached the magic point where things just work. My best advice, and what I do myself, is to keep up on what video hosts suggest for file formats, follow those recommendations, and be patient. Or you could just forget video and just do audio, and life is easy (insert sarcasm here).

Hosting and Promoting Your Video Podcast

Now that you have exported your video (and the headache it gave you has subsided), it's time to upload that baby somewhere. Unlike audio podcasts, your options for video are numerous. Yes, in terms of traffic, YouTube is the giant, but there is also viddler, Vimeo, and Blip.tv to name just three of the best I know. If you want your video to be just "found," YouTube is a great place for that to potentially happen. What Viddler, Vimeo, and Blip.tv lack in traffic, they make up for in additional features. All three offer premium services that give you faster uploads, shorter (prioritized) rendering times, more space, and other goodies like revenue sharing.

Choose a host based on your intended audience and the features that appeal to you at each host. YouTube gives you the largest audience, but they are lagging behind to some extent with their Flash-based player and mobile support beyond the iPhone (that is changing and could be completely different by the time this book is on the shelves). Many of my colleagues who are posting videos promote primarily through their own sites like Vimeo.

If you want a mass-market kind of show, choose YouTube. If you are going to be more of your own promotional force, try one of the other services. The bottom line is that all of them are solid services and the choice is going to be based on the different features offered and how you like the embedded player.

Submitting Your Show to iTunes

Just like in the online music world, iTunes is the 300-pound gorilla for distributing your video. At first the idea of subscribing to a video blog through iTunes seemed ironic, at best, especially when video blogs existed in a strange sort of nether world between "true blogs" and podcasts. Then came iTunes tuning into podcasting, and the distinction between audio and video podcasts was eliminated. With iTunes on the scene, regardless of whether your video is hosted with YouTube or Vimeo, the best thing to do is to submit it to iTunes.

Although your videos can be found on YouTube, there is a lot of chatter on there because it is a catchall for online video. Video blogs stand out a little better on the other video hosts, but still iTunes is the connector to iPods, iPhones, laptops, AppleTV... well, you get the idea. The process for submitting a podcast to iTunes is simple: Make sure you have iTunes downloaded and installed on your computer. Launch iTunes, click iTunes Store, and click the Podcasts link on the left side of the store window. (I know you're not producing a podcast, but iTunes doesn't care; audio or video, it's a podcast) After clicking the link, you should see something like Figure 8.6.

Click the Submit a Podcast button to see a screen like Figure 8.6

FIGURE 8.6
Submit a podcast screen within iTunes where you paste your blog's RSS feed.

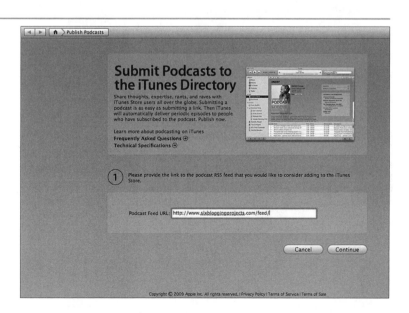

Insert your URL and include the "http" portion, which is either the URL of your blog where you are posting the videos or your video host. Both have feeds, but choose your host as the primary one. You can update the feed address if you need to later. Paste this into the submission box.

The next screen gives you the option to set the topics areas, but you'll get an error if you haven't created at least one episode (two or three is better). The number of topics that you can set is limited. I hope Apple updates at some point to give more choices or even a better tagging system. Until then you just have to make the best of it. That's all you need to get the process started for your video to be available through iTunes. Note the word "started" here, because someone from Apple reviews each submission to iTunes to determine whether it is worthy of inclusion. Yes, most submissions are accepted, and the process generally takes only a week or two, but you can see that Apple can (and does) decide what is allowed on iTunes. If you are involved in several podcast projects, the process can be accelerated. Once you have an approved podcast in iTunes, getting a second one is much easier.

> **NOTE**
>
> Unlike audio podcasts, you can't sell video podcasts on iTunes. If you want to sell videos, you can only list free videos on iTunes. Those will have to be the lure for your paid content.

Once you receive approval for your vlog, you can add categories and keywords. Apple, unfortunately, doesn't give you a lot of options for primary and secondary categories. If you want to update or augment your iTunes keywords, you can do it here or from the link that Apple sent you. For audio podcasts, you have more granular control because most people host their own podcasts now. For video, you're just going to have to manage with what Apple provides. Your best bets will be to keep your iTunes keywords updated and make sure your tags/keywords on both your video host and blog are descriptive.

Posts with Your Episodes

When you post a new episode, make sure you give as much information as you can on YouTube (or wherever you're hosting). This shouldn't be all though—you need to tie a blog post to the episode as well that gives more detail than you can on the video page. Figure 8.7 shows an example from my friend Shane's Closing Bigger podcast.

Shane does both audio and video segments on his site (which also makes it a great example). You can see that the video is hosted on YouTube and that Shane gives some context to the interview in his post. Remember how I talked earlier about making sure you have your blog and your video host page set up? Figure 8.8 shows Shane's page on YouTube.

This chapter and Chapter 7 both show my friend Shane Gibson's blog as examples. Why? Shane uses both media (audio and video) really well. Notice the following characteristics about his content:

▶ The posts around the audio or video are descriptive and even offer more information than is in the segment. He offers links to relevant sites and whatever he thinks would add more value to the viewer.

▶ The posts are tagged and categorized well so that you can find related videos easily.

▶ It is easy to share the posts with others.

▶ When you visit his YouTube page, there is consistent branding between it and the main site. You know that you are looking at the videos from the same person.

▶ Shane gives you a clear understanding about what he is going to talk about or show early in the episode.

▶ Shane sums up his podcasts at the end with the key points. Although this applies to more educational podcasts, having a summary of what you talked about is great even for more informational or news podcasts.

If you want to start video blogging, you probably have seen enough videos and posts to know what you like and don't. Follow the examples of others. If you like one style versus another, go for it! There is a huge diversity out there; just dip in and pull out something cool.

You can see that if you happened upon Shane's videos either through YouTube or through his blog, you'd be able to find all his videos in one place. Right, all his videos. Unfortunately, there isn't a really good host for both your audio and video episodes. Some people use YouTube and other sites to host audio, but I don't recommend it. Putting your video episode into a blog post is easier than putting a podcast in, actually. Just copy the video's embed URL from YouTube and paste it to your post just like any other video. All of the blog engines make submitting videos pretty painless. I guess everyone really likes to see waterskiing squirrels.

For step-by-step directions on embedding videos see Chapter 5, "Creating a Personal Blog."

Hosting Your Blog

Video bloggers are in a unique position, because the most important part of your content is hosted elsewhere (YouTube, Viddler, Vimeo, and so on). You can choose from the gamut of hosting options outlined in Chapter 2, Installing and Setting Up Your Blog." Remember that you are starting to *build a brand* so you need to act like it. Even if you go with WordPress.com, buy a good domain. Even if it's just your name, buy it. Should you pay extra to map it to WordPress.com? That's up to you, but if you're planning on sticking with WP.com for at least a little while, you should. On the other hand if you just want to experiment for awhile, and then move to a "real" host later, that's okay too.

My experience is colored by having changed domain names so many times and moving blog platforms even more often. Having a single, solid domain name to hang your hat on can be the one thing that keeps you from losing links, readers, and search engine rankings.

If I were starting out on WordPress.com today, I'd buy a domain and map it right away. If you don't want to mess with a web host, but want WordPress' power and flexibility, this is the route to go. Yes, buying a domain and getting a web host is how I set up most of my own and client projects, but I'm also willing to spend time with the upkeep that is required. I know not everyone is, so that's why I think WordPress.com is so great.

Now, as for plug-ins, should you go the self-hosted route? I'd look to Viper's Quick Tags for WordPress. WordPress does a great job of embedding video out of the box (see Chapter 5 for examples), but Viper has some nice tweaks to make things a little more customizable.

What? You were expecting this to be harder?

Summary

Being admittedly camera shy, video blogging hasn't been something that I've really enjoyed doing, but you might want to be a TV star with your own channel. If you have a webcam built into your laptop, you can start right away! YouTube and many other hosts enable you to record straight from your webcam to video. Sure, you only get one take, but if you want easy video posting, it doesn't get much easier. If you don't think you can create video in one take (I know that I can't), both PCs and Macs come with video-editing software that will let you record the clip straight from your webcam, insert some music and titles, and export to be uploaded.

On the subject of exporting, file size is going to be your biggest challenge. Start at 640×480 using the H.264 codec in stereo (two channels). If that is larger than the 2 GB limit, try reducing the audio to mono before making the video smaller. After that, it's just a matter of trial and error. Video isn't like audio where the compression tools are dead simple. There is an art and science to it that has a lot of trial and even more error.

Unlike the podcasting set, video bloggers have it pretty easy, otherwise. There are an easy half dozen sites that will host your videos free (including YouTube, of course), so all you need to do is put together a small site to promote yourself with a little more flair than a YouTube profile page. For video bloggers, WordPress.com is a great start, but don't forget to buy that cool domain name, just to be safe. Like the podcasting set, you can submit your show to iTunes; go ahead... you could become Internet famous overnight!

CHAPTER 9

Creating a Portfolio Blog

When I was first working on the outline for this book, I put the various chapters in place to (somewhat) build upon each other. As a photographer and occasional poet (don't ask, I'm not telling where that stuff is hidden online), using the Internet to showcase my work is fulfilling. It's like being able to have a whole section of a gallery, or a whole gallery, to myself. Not only that, I get to design every inch of the gallery to suit me, and my art.

You can have that feeling, too. This chapter is written with a bias towards showcasing the visual arts (photography, sculpture, paintings, jewelry, and so on), but it could very easily be applied to speaking, acting, or music. Run with your creativity! The whole idea and philosophy is to design a site/blog that showcases you. You know you're worth it, so let's do a good job of it. If you're a graphic designer or write code or programs or design websites, I'm not leaving you out here. I consider all those to be creative arts. If you go to WordPress.org, you'll see at the bottom of every page is "Code Is Poetry," so I'm not the only one who feels this way about coding.

Roll out a canvas, because you're going to paint your work, writ large, across the Internet.

What Makes for Good Content on a Portfolio Blog

Very much like the personal blog of Chapter 5, "Creating a Personal Blog," a portfolio blog is all about you. Your art and creative works might be taking center stage, but if you're like me, your creativity and art is as much a part of you as your hair or skin. The goal of a portfolio blog is not only to showcase your works in the best light possible, but also to have it reflect you and the art itself.

Let's take photography, for example. Having a blog with a black background, a scrolling slide show of your pictures, and shadow boxes to look at a particular picture makes each image stand out. The colors and contrasts can easily be seen and appreciated. For an actor, having a selection of video clips or audio segments that when clicked zoom to focus on that example and blur out the rest of the site makes that performance stand out front and center.

Now, imagine being a writer and the contrast between the background and text is poor and there is no way to find out how to contact you—not very effective. How about a graphic designer who has made such an elaborate site that it takes forever to load and once it does, you can't figure out how to navigate the site? My philosophy is pretty simple: If you want to show off your works, visitors should be able to immediately see how to get to them. Maybe (I think this is cool myself) front and center on your homepage is a slide show of your latest works. As each slide comes in and out of view, information about it appears near it. Perhaps even a link to buy it online, something like "Love this picture? You can buy a print of it online right now!"

The important thing to keep in mind is to treat a portfolio blog like any other portfolio. What do you want to show and how do you want to show it to cast your work in the best light possible. Start there and work outward. That's the foundation of everything we're going to talk about in this chapter, which is written from one artist to another; written to help you create an online showcase and portfolio.

Because you already know how to create your works, let's look at how to best showcase them online.

Picking the Right Tool for the Job

Showcasing your work online is just like how you set about creating it in the first place—you pick the right tools for the job. If your work is written, well you have it pretty easy, because the Internet is made for text...unless you illuminate manuscripts, then you need to take pictures of your work. When I showcase my work, or the work of friends and colleagues, I look at what the art form is and how would that best express what they do. Sometimes, sadly all too often, artists get stuck with a "typical" website for their works. Frankly "typical websites" are terrible for artists. Sure the Web might be made for multimedia, but a lot of web designers aren't familiar with it. Even more problematic is that many web designers don't really *get* artists. Let's put an end to that right now. You, maker of creative works, need to just make the site yourself.

Okay, but what *is* the right tool for the job? If a website isn't right, then what is? The answer should be obvious by now that blogs are by their nature multimedia aware. This makes showcasing your works *a lot* easier than is was even a short while ago.

For the photographer, you are going to want to have the ability to have sets and slide shows, allowing people to browse through your pictures. For a singer, you need samples of your work as MP3s and pictures of you in performance. A crafts person needs to photograph her work, and then set up a site that, like a photographer, allows people to browse what she's made. Writers, videographers, everyone...all forms of media are welcome within a

IDEA GALLERY

http://www.studiopress.com/themes/blackcanvas

SIMPLE OR COMPLEX, A PORTFOLIO BLOG IS ALWAYS COOL

Later, this chapter shows you examples of portfolio sites that should inspire you, the sort of sites that would challenge all but the most talented of web geeks to design. This is why, to start things off, I'm showing you sites that we mere mortals could pull off.

The blog shown here isn't really a blog at all, rather it's a demo of the StudioPress (www.studiopress.com) theme Black Canvas, which Brian Gardner designed for portfolio blogs. This theme is simple, clean, and extremely easy to set up. The only thing fancy about it is how it looks (and how Brian built it).

This simple black-and-white theme isn't boring in the least. I'd be willing to bet that when you looked at this theme you knew exactly what to do. Remember, often the people you want to be looking at your portfolio aren't other artists as much as potential clients. You don't want them thinking that all you want to do is something that pushes the boundaries of design. Those are great, too—don't get me wrong— but you also want visitors to be able to see and appreciate your works without frustration.

blog. I hope that by this point you've discovered that setting up a blog isn't rocket science. You don't have to be a computer geek, or have a bevy of them on standby, to put a great looking blog together. Just dispel the notion right now that you *can't* do it, because you can and will.

WordPress.com

If you're not a geek (or wannbe geek), using WordPress.com to set up your portfolio is the *easiest* way to go about things. You won't have to worry about updating WordPress or plug-ins. It's all handled for you, behind the scenes. For many artists starting out with the basic, free WordPress.com blog (which would end in .wordpress.com) is going to be just fine. Keep on your radar, however, buying that domain name. Review Chapter 2, "Installing and Setting Up Your First Blog," to refresh your memory on this topic.

If you have a blog on WordPress.com, you are given 2 GB to store pictures and other files—but *not* audio files (for example, MP3s). In the great scheme of things, two GB of web space is actually *a lot* of space to have at your disposal, but you might use it up quickly if you're storing high-quality images. To solve this problem, store your high-resolution pictures on sites like Flickr, SmugMug, YouTube, and other media-sharing sites. Doing this not only reduces the space you need at WordPress.com (or any other host for that matter), but you'll also get a nice boost in search engine rankings as well.

At the risk of sounding like a broken record, I want to emphasize the importance of buying a domain name for yourself and using it on

WordPress.com. As discussed in Chapter 2, using your own domain makes you look more serious and professional about what you're doing than someone who hasn't taken the time to do this. I think many people, especially those who don't think of themselves as particularly techie, are under the misconception that buying a domain and connecting to a host is a difficult task. Honestly, it isn't. Even the least techie Internet user can search for a good domain, buy it, and follow the directions to be able to use it on WordPress.com or any other host for that matter.

Not to mention how cool will it sound when you can say at a cocktail party, "Oh yes, I bought another domain today and mapped it to my portfolio blog with a CNAME?" Yeah, see?

DIY or Self-Hosted Blogs

The step up from WordPress.com, as you know from Chapter 2, is the self-hosted blog. The big benefit to you, as a portfolio blogger, is more flexibility with using themes, and you'll be able to add plug-ins to your blog. The drawback is that you also have something to maintain and keep track of. This isn't hard, nor is it time consuming, but there is a bit of a learning curve (I stress the *bit* part). Which is right for you? Let's tackle that next.

How Do I Choose Between WordPress.com and DIY?

Your decision is going to come down to two factors: your time and your money. WordPress.com saves you time and money because for many people free is just fine. If you buy a domain through WordPress.com, mapping it to your blog is a paltry $15/year (that includes registering the domain!), and if you already have a domain, it's only $10/year. DIY costs you money for a domain (about $10 a year) and hosting fee (about $10–15 a month), and you have to invest a little more time getting things going. The trade-off is control. On WordPress.com, or any hosted service for that matter, you are limited to which theme you can use, and you can't use additional plug-ins. You don't have these restrictions with DIY. For my time and money, I choose DIY most of the time. I do set up blogs on WordPress.com to use as examples, but I don't actively use one. I have many friends, though, who are happy using WordPress.com and other hosted services. WordPress.com makes using a domain so affordable that, frankly, *not* trying that option is pretty silly. If you later decide to switch to a self-hosted blog, the folks at WordPress.com will help you make the transition.

Making a Site a Site

You saw what a default WordPress blog looked like already. You don't want that, do you? Of course not. You want something with style, panache, and edge. You want a cool theme. Lucky for you there are thousands, maybe even hundreds of thousands of free themes to preview and try. A theme is just the first step because the cool stuff are the add-ons that give your blog some flare. Maybe a nice photo gallery that runs itself and has nice shadow-box features? Maybe some widgets to let people *buy* your works? These are all within the realm of the possible, so let's start making some decisions.

Picking a Good Theme for a Portfolio Blog

Themes (or templates) are what give a blog its look. They are very much like paper dolls or thin bits that you put on and around your content to give it a "look." Sporty, cool, hip, edgy, elegant looks are available to you, no matter what blog engine you use. Personally I prefer WordPress' theme-template system, but that is also because I am knee deep in it almost every day.

All themes are set up as a group of files, images, and a style sheet that the blog engine uses to render the blog for people to use. In the case of WordPress, the themes just call the content from within the theme files. Some themes have special features and layouts that might need a little configuring. Themes for portfolio blogs generally just need simple things like defining how big you want the images to be on screen and where the high-res versions are located. Portfolio themes, like most themes you run into, either on hosted services like WordPress.com or DIY are pretty simple and easy to configure. Remember, this *isn't* rocket science!

> **TIP**
>
> Don't be too cool for school. Although having a cutting-edge, innovative theme is cool, it can also hinder people from actually enjoying your content.

When you're picking a theme, keep in mind a couple of things. One is how flexible the theme is for making changes. If you wanted to edit the theme itself, could you do it easily? Two, and most important, is how *readable* the theme is in a range of web browsers. If you want people to visit your site and look at your portfolio, you *must* make it a pleasant experience. Don't make people guess how to navigate through the site or make them squint to read your text. Figure 9.1 offers a good example of a site that is both elegant and easy on the eye.

When you're looking for great theme ideas and inspiration, visit *Smashing Magazine* (smashingmagazine.com). The round ups of great themes and sites you'll see there are nothing short of brilliant. If their examples don't inspire you, well I don't know what will. For the geekier set, their examples for coding and editing themes are fantastic. I bookmark them all the time for reference. Figure 9.2 shows just the first two of many free portfolio themes for WordPress. (See the whole post at

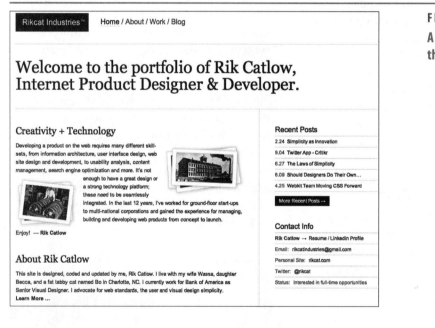

FIGURE 9.1

A simple black-and-white theme can be effective.

http://www.smashingmagazine.com/2008/01/
08/100-excellent-free-high-quality-wordpress-
themes/. Scroll nearly to the end for the portfolio themes.)

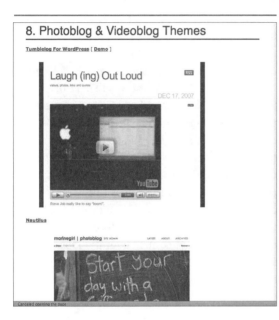

FIGURE 9.2

**Part of Smashing Magazine's "100 Excellent Free
WordPress Themes" post from January, 2008.**

Regardless if this is a photography portfolio,
video portfolio, or something a little more
edgy, there is a template out there for you. The
key is looking, previewing, and testing any
theme before you decide.

GAINING INSPIRATION FROM THE OUTSTANDING AND OUTLANDISH

I love, and eagerly anticipate, when *Smashing Magazine* does their "...for your inspiration" posts. It doesn't matter if it's fonts, logos, websites, themes, even *buttons*—those posts charge my imagination. Probably not for the reasons you think though.

Sure there are lot of themes and site designs that inspire me. Not to mention trying to discern if the "new" design was derived from another template (you can pick up clues pretty easily after looking at as many themes as I have). What really inspires me are the "Wow, that's, umm, well, interesting...." These are the sites that are so on the bleeding edge that you're not quite sure what you're supposed to do if you found yourself at the page.

I look at the range of sites (the ones that I just look at and think, "Cool!" and the others where I think, "Huh?") and use them to try something new. I've applied magazine themes to corporate blogs to give them a range of post options from featured posts to small excerpts in a column and photo blog themes for stores. The key for me is seeking out the places where you can get lots of inspiration. If you read *Smashing Magazine* online on a regular basis, you'll get that jolt. I promise.

Plug-Ins for Portfolio Blogs

Out of the box, WordPress is a great tool for publishing any kind of content, but you're not publishing just any kind of content, are you? Like having a sunroof or new stereo put into your car, a WordPress plugin adds a little refinement, tweak, or enhancement to your site/blog. For the portfolio blog, beyond the core plugins covered in Chapter 2 you will be looking for and adding plugins that enhance the already impressive multimedia capabilities of WordPress. I'll also get into some additional plugins that can help you make a private client-only area and how to sell your works online through your blog. Let's get started with slideshow plugins.

Slideshows

Players and plug-ins for slide shows are common. The leader in the WordPress world is NextGen Gallery (and related sibling plug-ins),

but I have also used one called Featured Content Gallery with great success. The upside to these plug-ins is that they aren't too hard to implement, but the downside is that it can be time consuming to configure one to test, and then configure another to test. Look at portfolio sites you like and try to determine what plug-ins they are using. An alternative to using a plug-in for your portfolio of images is to use the code from the slide show on Flickr or SmugMug. If you use either of these services, you can create sets and collections of works, and then have slide shows for just those images. Putting the slideshow code in is as easy as copying and pasting into a new page or post. As you add more images to the set or collection, they will be added automatically to the slide show. The downside to this is that you don't have a lot of control over the look of the slide show. Figure 9.3 shows an example of an embedded slide show from my own blog.

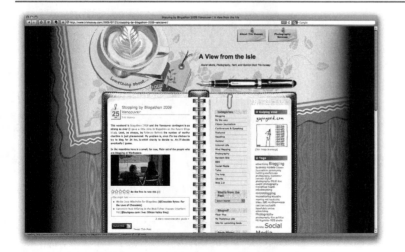

FIGURE 9.3

Example of a Flickr-based slideshow from my own blog

As you can see, it looks nice, but it isn't awesome. Awesome is shadowboxed images that float above the site and make your image pop off the screen. Awesome isn't difficult; awesome just requires plug-ins.

Audio-Video Players

Finding a good audio-video player is no mean feat. I go through several and am always looking for easier to use, faster to render, and more flexible for multimedia types. That said, there are two WordPress plug-ins that are certainly worth your time to try. PB-embed flash and Viper's Quick Tags are two nice plug-ins that I use often. WordPress has a video embed tool, but it is limited in what files can be used with it and the kinds of options for tweaking the look and feel. All blog engines *can* support multimedia, but they differ in how *well* they do the job. Remember, there are two things at play here. One is the theme (was it designed for text or images or video) and the other is the plug-ins that help you display the content. There is no doubt that tweaking and tuning is required to get things just right, but the payoff is worth it.

Shopping Carts

If you want to sell your works online, you will be looking at a shopping cart system to use. Honestly, the kind of plug-in you should look for, and the kind I look for, is one that makes it easier to connect to a PayPal, Etsy (for handicrafts), or eBay storefront.

When it comes to shopping carts, the most important thing is security. You have probably heard of using a "secure transaction" when you do online banking or buy something online. If you run an online store, you need to *provide* that to your customers as well.

Here's the rub. There are good plug-ins for shopping carts for all blog engines, but Movable Type or WordPress plug-ins take configuration. Configuring a plug-in isn't hard; it's just time consuming. Unless you have a lot of things to sell, skip shopping carts and just use services like PayPal or Etsy. Yes, I'm cheating a bit here. I have set up WP e-commerce on a few blogs and am happy to suggest it, but also being the pragmatic sort, I know that many of you don't have the time or patience to get it working (shopping cart setup tries both my time and patience).

You will be happy to know that PayPal, Etsy, and other storefronts make it very easy for you to integrate their systems into your blog. Why? Because then you'll *use* their service to stuff your things (and they take a small cut of that sale). It's in their best interest to make the whole process painless for you.

> **NOTE**
>
> Do you need to have mobile support? One of my core plug-ins is WPTouch for instant iPhone and mobile support. Why? Is mobile browsing that important? Because it only takes one free plug-in, one that you don't even have to configure to be effective, why take the chance? To plan for the broadest possible audience, make sure that people can check out your portfolio while on the go.

Members Only and Private Files

Making a private site or parts of your site private isn't hard. Built into WordPress and Movable Type are ways to password protect a post or hide it as private. Going to the next level are plug-ins that block off the entire site to prying eyes. I combine Registered Users Only and Private Files plug-ins on my WordPress blogs to make things extra specially locked down. Using both of these plug-ins makes sure that only people who you have given access to the site will see it. Even search engines are blocked! I think photographers especially should take advantage of this to give clients a private place to review photoshoots and pick the pictures they want. Although there might be lots of other uses (maybe a private auction), I think the clients-only portfolio site is one of the best.

Pulling It All Together

I bet you're feeling like you just dumped a jigsaw puzzle on the floor and looking at the box top thinking, "Okay, I know I have all the pieces and I know what it's going to look like, but where do I start?"

Nearly all the preceding chapters are going to give you the tools you need to put this all together, from writing to posting to YouTube and even iPhoto. For a portfolio blog, the key is to pull all your material together. I don't mean the blog or picking a theme; I mean choosing what you're going to show and how it will exist online.

When showcasing *anything* visual (graphic designs, photography, and photographs of your works), you want to have at least two versions of each image: a full high-resolution glory (suitable for printing and the media) and a scaled-down version or versions that is better suited to posting online.

For other kinds of works going into your portfolio, make sure you have an online version and possibly an offline version. If you're a writer, think virtual newsroom. Have current works online (and searchable), but have at the ready PDF versions that can be distributed.

*When showcasing **anything** visual (graphic designs, photography, and photographs of your works), you want to have at least two versions of each image: a full high-resolution glory (suitable for printing and the media) and a scaled-down version or versions that is better suited to posting online.*

The same goes for your contact information and other biographical information. Have good headshots, bios, and other materials available either on your site or by request. Your portfolio is your calling card. It's your business card. It's how you get to show off.

This chapter discusses managing images and documents. I know there are a tremendous number of other art forms (again I consider coding and website building to be a creative work), but I think from these two examples you can get a good sense of the options and possibilities.

Gathering, Exporting, and Presenting Pictures

How many digital pictures do you have on your computer (or on backup drives close by)? Hundreds? Thousands? Tens of thousands? More? If you're not one of those latter groups right now, odds are you will be eventually. Regardless, the question here is really two-fold—first, how to gather all these pictures together and organize them into some semblance of order, and second then how to export them so they are web-ready.

Chapter 5 talked a little about iPhoto and Windows Live Photo Gallery and how you use them to save and export files. Here, you explore a completely different scale. There are lots of professional photo-management apps, but Apple's Aperture for OS X and Adobe's Lightroom for PCs and Macs are among the leaders in this area. Because I started out on a PC when I became serious about my photography, I have Lightroom. A view of my current catalogue (just the pictures from 2009) is shown in Figure 9.4.

FIGURE 9.4

A view of just a few of the thousands of pictures I've taken in 2009 alone.

SHOULD YOU WATERMARK YOUR IMAGES?

As a photographer, I don't really want people to use my pictures without asking, but it happens. So, I watermark my pictures. A watermark is a slightly visible mark that is pretty much impossible to remove without damaging the picture. For my watermark, I use my name and URL with the copyright date. No, it's not perfect and can be circumvented, but by making the effort you're making it clear that the images are yours. My watermarks are added automatically when I export from Lightroom; you can do the same with many other tools available online or to download. There are other programs that can add a watermark for you after you export, and some online services will add one for you.

There is a balance, as well, with watermarks between obscuring the image that you want to present, and making it hard to remove the watermark.

My watermarks tend to be more in the smaller type that doesn't obscure the picture. It's clear, however, from all the data around and even embedded into the picture's metadata that the image is mine and I retain copyright ownership of it.

This might not be perfect, but for me it's the right balance.

These pictures are all organized by date, but I could just as easily look at them by keyword (when I import a batch of pictures, I add keywords to them), or flag (good, discard, or none), or other parameters. When you're pulling a portfolio together, you could use keywords (or tags if you like) to pull out portraits, headshots, or events, and then have those as a set for people to view. The next step is to take those groups and export them to be uploaded.

Exporting images is an interesting topic. There are two schools of thought. One is to export as high-res as you can so when uploaded to Flickr, you have a backup of a "master" picture. The other is to reduce the resolution so that people are *less* likely to try to use your works without your permission. I'm in the middle of those two points. I reduce the size to about 2500 pixels on the longest side, use 80% compression quality as a JPEG, make the resolution 72 DPI (screen resolution), and put a watermark on the picture. For a portfolio blog, you're likely to only use an image that is 800, maybe 1000, pixels wide and maybe 600 pixels high. This is because your visitors are going to be looking at the pictures on their computers, which right now is often still a paltry 1024 × 768 monitor (about 17"). A picture about 800 × 600 (ish) pixels fits nicely on that size screen.

Once you export the pictures, and these are going to be close to a megabyte each (maybe larger depending on how you export them), what's next? The answer *isn't* upload them to your blog; it's to upload them to a professional photo-sharing site like Flickr or SmugMug (see Figure 9.5).

FIGURE 9.5

My Flickr page with some of my pictures that I share online.

Why do you want to do this? First, both these sites, and Flickr especially, make it easier for people to find you and your work through search engines. If you're an artist, and you want your works to be seen by a wider audience, having a blog is great, and having a blog *and* your pictures on a photo site is better.

Flickr is owned by Yahoo! (it was born in Vancouver, though). Although there is a free account, I recommend paying for Flickr Pro, which right now is $25/year. Flickr Pro gives you unlimited storage and uploads, not to mention the capability to upload HD videos up to 90 seconds long! SmugMug doesn't have a free option and their plans run from about $40–$150/year. SmugMug is oriented more towards the professional photographer and offers a tremendous number of services for professionals (like being able to offer prints for sale through them), while Flickr is for hobbyists and pros who don't need all the features that SmugMug has to offer.

If you have a ton of pictures (like I do), SmugMug has an arrangement with Amazon's S3 storage service to allow you to back up your full-resolution originals (RAW, DMG, and so on). If you need some additional piece of mind backup and storage for your works, this is a good option to consider.

You might be wondering about the whole "finding pictures through search engine thing," which is good, because it doesn't seem like it would make sense. It does make sense because Google indexes millions and millions of images constantly. People search those images for a variety of reasons, but one of the most common is to find photographs to use in projects. So that people can find your pictures more easily, tag your pictures with good, detailed information. Just like tagging a blog post, you can tag a picture. Figure 9.6 shows an example of one of my pictures with a *few* tags.

FIGURE 9.6

A picture with tags entered to describe it more for search engines.

With all these great pictures online, they also now need to be posted onto your blog. From Figure 9.6, you'll notice a button called All Sizes, which leads you to a page like the one shown in Figure 9.7 (I've already chosen the Medium size as you can see).

FIGURE 9.7

The All Sizes page for the picture from the previous figure (note the HTML code in the lower half of the page).

Copy the URL from the bottom, skinnier box with code and paste into a box to insert into your post. This is actually a two-step process, but let's look at what inserting an image from a URL looks like on a WordPress blog (see Figure 9.8):

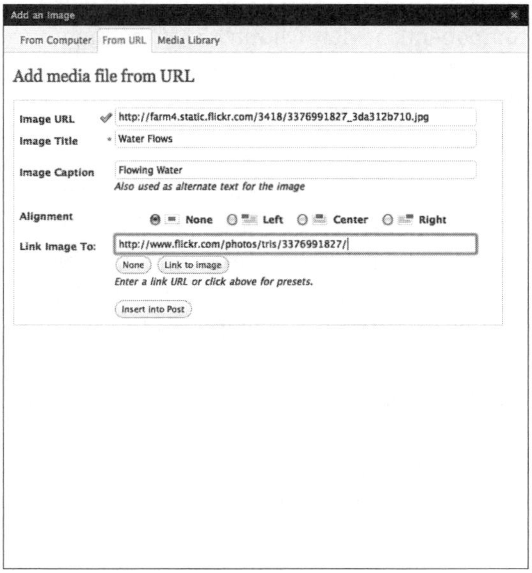

FIGURE 9.8
Insert images from URL window in WordPress.

The second step is to go back to that photo page and copy the link to that page to paste into the space labeled Link Image To:. This ensures that you follow the terms of service for Flickr, which requires you link back to the original photo page. This is the "easy way" where there is an image in the post, just like any other blog post. If you have a slide show like the one used in the Black Canvas theme from earlier in the chapter, then you will likely need to paste the URL of the image into a Custom field, something like in Figure 9.9. (I happen to know that particular slide show needs the field to be called "articleimg" because I use the Featured Posts plug-in often in my work.

FIGURE 9.9

An example blog post with a custom field set for a slide show (this only applies to how the Featured Posts plug-in works).

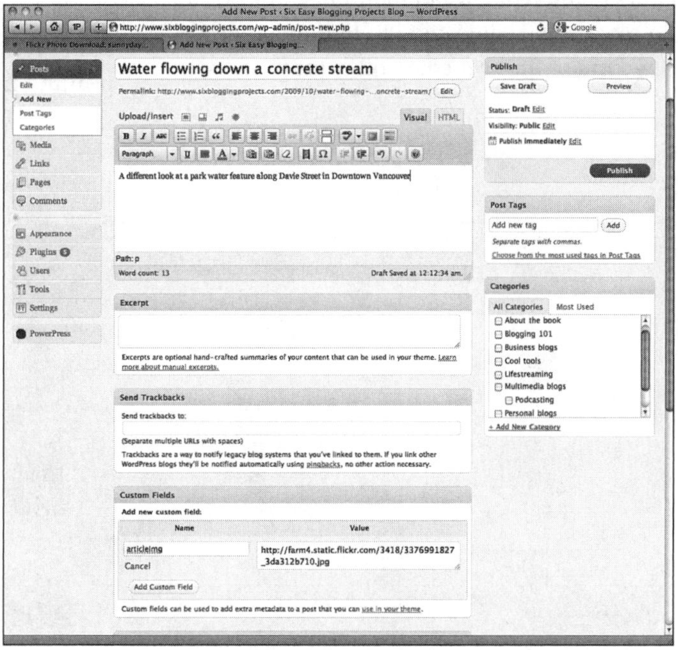

As you develop and enhance your portfolio blog, you will likely come across several different ways to do a slide show. Usually slide shows require a plug-in or two to work, or sometimes you can use Flickr's own Flash-based slide show that you can paste into a post. (I do this to highlight a particular set of pictures.) I can't begin to cover the range of different tools to build online slide shows for your pictures, but when you're looking at trying different ones, look for something that says that it works with the blog engine you are using. It is a royal pain to have set up a slide show only to learn that you can't use it on your blog for one reason or another (speaking from experience here).

Adding Documents of All Shapes and Sizes

Portfolios aren't just made up of photos, especially if you're not a photographer, but portfolio blogs are flexible enough to handle almost any kind of file or media you want to show to the world. If you'd like to add audio or video components, review Chapter 7, "Creating a Podcast Blog," and Chapter 8, "Video Blogging," for more details on those particular media.

What about "regular" documents? You might have a résumé, bio, or *Curriculum Vitae* that you'd like to include as part of your portfolio. Although you can convert these files to HTML, I don't recommend it. A better, and easier, option is to work on your About Me page (see Chapter 2 for more information). This page is where you should add the shows you've done, awards, and other information. Then for the "full" documents, provide a PDF (Portable Document Format) version to download.

If you use a Mac, then making a PDF file is as easy as printing. For whatever document you want as a PDF, go to the File menu and choose Print from the Print dialog box. Click the PDF button located in the lower left corner, select Save to PDF, give it a filename, and click Okay. That's it. Figure 9.10 shows an example of printing from Safari.

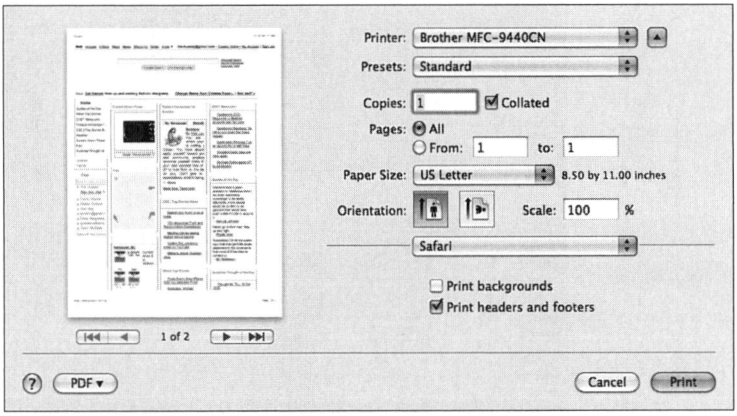

FIGURE 9.10
Print dialog box showing the PDF button in the lower left corner.

Windows users will have to either use the latest version of Microsoft Office 2007, which has a downloadable add-on to print to PDF, or invest in software to create PDFs (Adobe Creative Suite includes Adobe Acrobat for PDFs).

PDF documents, PowerPoint slides, and Word documents are all uploaded to WordPress blogs and other blogs through the media uploader, just like images. It seems counter-intuitive to do it this way, but that is the right way.

Final Word on Content

I've covered all sorts of components and content for your portfolio blog, but before I wrap up this chapter I want to remind you to make sure you flesh out your blog with other types of content. Include pages about shows and awards. Write blog posts about how you make your art and what inspires you. Although your art is going to take center stage, you also want visitors to learn about you, the artist, as well.

You'll probably find it easier to just put up your pictures or videos or what have you, but the additional background about you is just as important. If I'm visiting your portfolio blog, I am certainly going to want to learn about you as an artist and person. So take this time to tell me! For tips on writing and building a community around your blog, review Chapter 3, "Writing and Creating a Conversation," and Chapter 4, "Building Community."

Summary

A portfolio blog is an expression of your art, yourself, and your work. It is more personal than a personal blog. When you're setting up a portfolio blog, the primary consideration is going to be how it is going to look. Although choosing a blog platform, hosted or DIY, is important, all of these choices pale in comparison to presenting your work in the best light possible. To that end, look for themes that are designed to present your type of work specifically. Like all the chapters in this book, my recommendation is to buy a domain, get a web host, and set up a WordPress blog. WordPress, unlike many other blog platforms, remains flexible, easy to use, and fully capable of hosting a range of media. Make your portfolio blog something that you are not only proud of, but something that will grow with you as well.

As you build out your blog, remember to include the range of content that visitors will be interested in. Biography, résumé, and influences and insight into your creative process are all things visitors and readers will be very interested to learn and know.

Of course, throughout all of this, remember that this is supposed to be a fun exercise, not dreary drudgery that seems endless. Have fun and express yourself—just do it online!

CHAPTER 10

Creating Your Online Lifestream

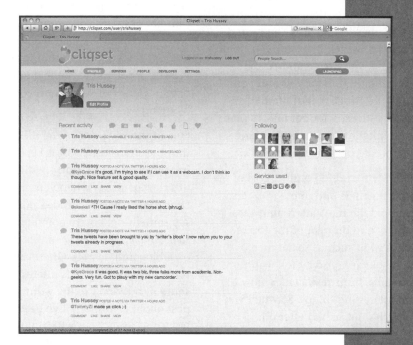

Want to talk about being on the cutting edge of online media? Lifestreaming is the latest facet of social media and blogging. It is so "latest" that I've changed how I've approached the topic a couple times *just in the month this chapter was in development*. Once you discard the hyperbole and buzzwords, the idea of a lifestream is really simple: It is the sum total of all the content that you produce online. Your blog(s), pictures, podcasts, bookmarks from social bookmarking sites, favorite songs, and even updates from Twitter. By creating a home for your lifestream, you are creating a place that becomes a digital hub for you and your readers. I think the criticism that lifestreams are pretty narcissistic isn't too far off; it's pretty egotistical to think that anyone really cares about all the things you produce, except...

I do care what my friends do online. Lots of my friends are gifted writers and photographers. Some of them find the most interesting sites and posts online, and on a lot of the topics that I'm interested in such as social media technology and blogging. So by following my friends' lifestreams, I am *crowdsourcing* how I find new and interesting things. So when you put it that way, it's not so bad after all.

NEW TERM

Crowdsourcing is when you use your network of friends and followers online to help you with a project. It includes finding pictures, brainstorming, and feedback on an article (or book). It has also been called tapping into the wisdom of crowds. In the case of a business blog (for example, in Chapter 6, "Creating a Business Blog"), it can be for a business need. In this case, it's your personal need for information.

What Goes into a Lifestream Blog?

Of all the different types of blogs I've written, the idea of creating a lifestreaming blog is best left for last. Why? A lifestreaming blog aggregates or pulls together *everything* you do online into one place. This is also the most advanced type of blog because it assumes from the outset that not only are you producing content, but you're producing *so much* content and so many *different kinds of content* that for people to keep up with what you're doing you need a special blog just for that. Wow, and you thought just blogging was egotistical!

One of the key parts of the lifestreaming idea is that the short-form post is becoming the rule instead of the exception. Twitter was part of this new genesis—when you only have 140 characters (spaces included, just like SMS) to say something, you're going to make that *something* count. I've seen this transition in my own blogging as well. Often I see a post or some news that I feel is interesting and want to share it, but don't really want to write a whole post about it. Initially I've been tweeting these links out, sometimes with a little comment—often very little because of character constraints. Recently (during the time I've been writing this book), I've been experimenting with a service called Posterous to share posts and thoughts, but do not feel compelled to write a lot about the link.

Posterous is a new microblogging/blogging hosted service that was built so that you could post to it just by emailing things to it. I can email a picture, YouTube video, podcast, or whatever else I found online, and then

Posterous creates a post from that email. It also can republish posts to a number of other places. Like pictures to my Flickr stream and videos to YouTube, Posterous is essentially a hub where things emanate. Posterous is becoming a popular way to *push* things into your lifestream, whereas Facebook and FriendFeed are designed to *pull* information in to create your lifestream. I think this is an interesting paradox in blogging. Blogs started as a way to share links and bits of minutiae and later morphed into long form writing, and now we're coming full circle I guess.

This chapter looks at the two types of lifestreaming blogs, the short-form collectors (Tumblr and Posterous being the two most important), the aggregators (FriendFeed/Facebook being the leaders here), and the ways you can build your own with a few plug-ins and a little work. Because this is a new kind of blog, by the time this is in your hands you might read this and think "oh how quaint, he has a Posterous/Tumblr/FriendFeed blog." This is an area that's evolving quickly. The good news is that even if some of the tools I discuss here have become outdated, the methods behind them should carry on. So quickly in fact, that a new aggregator like FriendFeed ("new" as in launched to the public around Oct 13, 2009, just three days ago as I'm writing this sentence!) called Cliqset has emerged on the scene and is trying to tackle the information fire hose issue in a pretty unique way (more on that shortly).

Why Lifestreams? Wasn't Blogging Enough?

You'd think having your own soapbox on the net would be enough for most people, wouldn't you? Well, I'm talking about bloggers here, and not just any group of bloggers, but *early adopter* bloggers. Yes, these bloggers have to try the latest shiny new thing in order to be happy. They live to test, discover, and then tell people about it. The other side of that coin is that many early adopters, myself included, tend to generate tons of content. For example, as I'm writing this chapter, I have

- ▶ 14,250 pictures on Flickr
- ▶ 21,330 messages (tweets) on Twitter
- ▶ 2,190 posts on my personal blog with 1,409 approved comments
- ▶ 1,202 favorites on StumbleUpon

Yes, "wow" is an apt response (pretty much what I said putting these numbers together) to this kind of content generation—and pretty much all since mid-2004. These numbers don't take into account guest posts I've written on other blogs, blogs I was paid to blog on (don't ask, I've lost count), or blogs from companies I used to work for. The birth of the lifestream came out of the need for people like me to have one place that their subscribers/fans/friends could go to catch up on *everything* they produced.

As bloggers became frustrated with trying to keep up with everything (remember most bloggers are also information junkies, too), the idea emerged: What if you published *everything* to one location? At first people did things like have all their posted pictures from Flickr also appear on their blogs and have a day's worth of tweets as a post every night. These were a good start, but created their own problem: Blogs became choked with so much content that people couldn't find the posts that they *wanted* to read! Back to the drawing board.

It was during this time that bloggers figured out something: There were two different kinds of information sharing they wanted to do. There was aggregation of content and then there was the "I see something really cool and want to share it, but don't want to write much about it." And these don't even factor in the notion of writing long form content. Both content aggregation and link sharing are types of lifestreams and both are equally powerful to use. What I think is curious is that early adopters instead of picking one or the other, picked *both* kinds. In some ways, they are the ones who gave life to these new forms all at once. Ultimately, the lifestream blogs grew out of

- ▶ Bloggers generating lots of content
- ▶ Bloggers creating myriad kinds of content
- ▶ Bloggers creating content on more than one service
- ▶ High-speed mobile data networks enabling people to send more pictures and movies faster than before

Bloggers wanted a solution, and we got it. We got lifestreaming.

Starting Your Lifestream Blog: Inputs

For the most part, lifestreaming blogs are built on services. There is very little DIY going on in this area (for the moment, that is). The reason for this is the complexity of what lifestreaming means (or does). Quick posting isn't hard, but blog posts have grown to desire more metadata than the typical quick post. Aggregating content from various services, again, isn't hard, but in this case you have to ask yourself, "Isn't it nice to have a place to look at a condensed view of what people post and create instead of having a massive load of content?" For example, during a busy conference time, I could post 200 pictures to Flickr in one night, send out a dozen tweets (many of which are fragments of conversations), and maybe write a couple of long-form blog posts. If I put that all into my blog, I don't think you'd get to the posts at all! After the third page of pictures, you'd give up and go home (I would, too).

For this reason, services rose up to allow us to both segment our content (quick posts, pictures, tweets, and links) and aggregate the content into digestible lumps. FriendFeed, shown in Figure 10.1, was the first of the stable and consistent aggregators, with Facebook playing catch up.

FIGURE 10.1

A look at FriendFeed (only the people I follow) as an example of how I read other people's lifestreams.

Newcomer Cliqset could be the next Internet darling or just another good idea that didn't work out. That said, Cliqset is taking the main complaint about FriendFeed and Facebook, the deluge and hard to filter stream of information, head on. Instead of having you group *friends* into segments, it instead groups *content* into segments. For example, it organizes all the videos and pictures together, or all shared links together, which lets you look at content in context. Cliqset is in the early stages, but even if it doesn't take off I think they are on the right track with the idea to segment content types.

Tumblr and Posterous are the leading quick-posting lifestream sites, with Posterous receiving a lot of attention right now because of a few high-profile users switching to their service for all their "blogging." Because you can't ever have too much content, let's start with the quick-posting lifestreaming blogs first.

Quick Posts

At first, when people wanted to write a quick blog post, they used one of the quick-posting *bookmarklets* from their blog engine of choice and fired the post off. That was so 2005. Now bloggers want to create more than just blog posts quickly; they want to post to Twitter, share bookmarks, and so on. They want to put out there a dash-off post that is more than just sharing a link, but less than writing out 200 or so words on a topic (the long-form blog post).

NEW TERM

A bookmarlet is like a regular bookmark, but it contains a little Javascript instead of a link to a website. This Javascript tells your browser to go to a certain site and perform some action. In the case of Posterous or WordPress, these bookmarlets help you quickly create new posts.

By 2007 the blogosphere/social media/web 2.0 had started to mature and people were looking for other ways to share information. Tumblr (www.tumblr.com) was one of the first quick-posting (you could also call them "light") blogging engines to come on the scene and might be considered the benchmark for other services that have come later.

The idea of a quick-posting blog is simple: You're setting up a blog without frills, with very little to configure, and pretty much the dead easiest blog to run. Once you have it set up with a free account (requires less than a minute), posting can be as simple as an email to the service or a bookmarklet to click in your browser (I prefer the latter).

Although this sounds very bloggy (it is really), the extras come in with quick connectors to other services. Tumblr, for example, let's you post to Twitter and import RSS feeds from other places (like Flickr, FriendFeed, and other blogs) as links. Posterous (www.posterous.com), the service I've been using lately, enables you to post not only to Posterous, but your other configured services as well. For example, you are able to simultaneously email a picture straight to Flickr and Twitter via Posterous.

Quick-posting services give you an alternative to the long-form blog post, but what if you want to pull more information into one place—not just those quick posts, but tweets, new images on Flickr, videos on YouTube, or Google Docs? This is when you get into the world of aggregation. But before you get into that, let's continue with the other facets of the quick-posting blog.

Like most social media and blogging, Posterous and Tumblr have a component that allows you to follow and subscribe to other people's Tumblogs (as they are called) or Posterous updates (see Figure 10.2). In turn, people subscribe to yours as well. Together these form something like a multimedia news stream to read and follow each day. As you build up content, you gain followers. As you follow in turn, then you are exposed to more content, and you post more content, and so on.

IDEA GALLERY
www.twitter.com/trishussey

FOLLOWING MY LIFESTREAM ONLINE

Unlike giving you links to my blogs, pictures on Flickr.com, or other places where my original content originates online, these are the places where my content gathers. Each of these sites is a little different from each other. Twitter is mostly tweets, but interspersed in there are links to posts that I share and posts that I've written (short or long). Tumblr is all original content (and there isn't a lot there at the moment) as is Posterous (which has a lot more content). If you want a look at the sum total of the stuff I post, FriendFeed and Cliqset are the places to go.

Feel free to follow me on any or all of these services and leave a comment to say, "Hi!" You can visit my lifestream sites on

Twitter: twitter.trishussey.com

Friendfeed: www.friendfeed.com/trishussey/

Tumblr: trishussey.tumblr.com

Posterous: lifestream.trishussey.com

Cliqset: cliqset.com/user/trishussey

As you look through all of these, you will certainly see duplicate content. That's not an error; it is the result of cross-posting content to various services (like Posterous to Twitter and both to FriendFeed).

FIGURE 10.2
A sample of Posterous one Sunday morning—the list of people I follow on Posterous is in the right column.

Like traditional blogging, the key to being successful at it is to only write and share things you are actually interested in, while at the same time constantly seek out new sources of information and inspiration. As I said earlier, I'm using Posterous to share posts, articles, and links that I think are interesting, pertinent, or important. By the same token, I don't want to post stale content, and because I don't always have time to write a whole post, I usually am able to jot down at least a sentence or two about the item. These Posterous posts then go to my Tumblr blog and Twitter. I could also have them go to my personal blog, but that would send off a cascade of duplicate tweets because of how I've configured that blog, and no one wants that.

Like traditional blogging, the key to being successful at it is to only write and share things you are actually interested in, while at the same time constantly seek out new sources of information and inspiration.

One of my long-time blogging colleagues Steve Rubel of Edelman publicly gave up on blogging and switched his posting to Posterous (see Figure 10.3). Steve felt that his blogging was suffering because of the pressure to write more and better posts. When in reality often what his readers are interested in is what *he's* interested in. I've known Steve for a long time; he and I have (good naturedly and with great mutual respect) disagreed on character blogs in the past, and I think his move has resonated with many of his long-time bloggers. Frankly, it's hard work generating content. Writing great posts and keeping up with the happenings *du jour* can be a full-time job. Unfortunately very few people are employed to do just that.

With the quick-post blog, folks like Steve Rubel and I can share a quick opinion with you, but not feel compelled to write a longer post about it. Now, what if you want to catch up on what I've been saying on Twitter, Posterous, my blog(s), posted on Flickr, and so on? This is when you visit my aggregated feed on a site like FriendFeed or Cliqset.

FIGURE 10.3

Adding an item from Steve Rubel's Posterous using the Posterous quick post bookmarklet—my mouse point is hovering over the bookmarklet in my bookmarks bar.

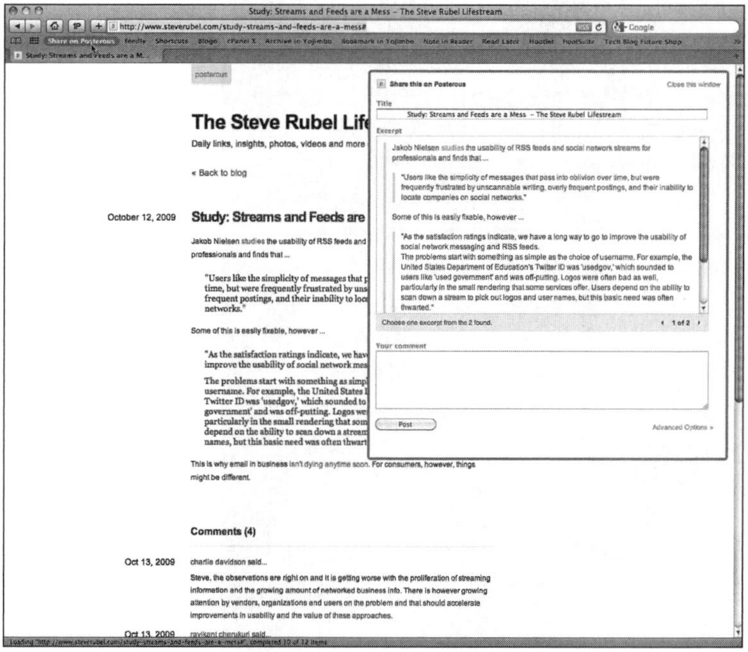

IS THE SHORT-FORM POST KILLING LONG BLOG POSTS AND QUALITY CONTENT?

There has been a recent trend of prominent bloggers (and pundits) saying that with the advent of Twitter and sites like Posterous, blogging is dead. What they are referring to is the "traditional" long-form blog post (roughly 200–300 words) as something that people aren't interested in either writing *or* reading any longer.

My feeling is that the capability to quickly post links you find to Twitter (I use a web-based service called Hootsuite, www.hootsuite.com, to do this) or shorter thoughts and comments through Posterous is making for *better* blog content, not worse.

The content that I'm not putting on my blogs now, while less frequent, is more thought out and I think better written than my earlier posts. I find that because I can quickly share items that interest me with less pressure to write sage commentary about them, I post those more frequently so I'm sharing more *content* (which helps people find more interesting content). When I find a couple things that interest me, I have time to write about them. Previously I would have a backlog of content that I felt I *had* to comment on. Now a lot of that content is shared with less commentary, and I only concentrate on the topics that really interest me.

What is happening is that people are adapting to the deluge of content that they're trying to manage by segmenting it into groups that are easier to manage. The latest tools and services, like Twitter and Posterous, make it easier to segment and share content in these manageable chunks.

Twitter

A friend of mine described Twitter as Facebook with all the good stuff taken away and only the annoying parts (status messages) left behind. As far as a lifestream blog goes, Twitter (like a lot of these inputs) is both an input (your updates/tweets going in) and a destination (posts, pictures, and comments) for your lifestream (see Figure 10.4). This dual purpose is one of those things that you just have to manage as you put your lifestream together. When Twitter is used as an input, it is taking your tweets and having them appear somewhere else as well. Most often this has been Facebook, but later FriendFeed became a destination of choice.

FIGURE 10.4

My "Twitter stream" of the tweets from the people I follow on Twitter.

Here's the rub...sending *all* your tweets somewhere gives the readers no sense of context. If you are sending a lot of "@ replies," then readers outside of twitter only get one half of the conversation.

> **NOTE**
>
> An @ reply is Twitter parlance for tweets that respond to those of another Twitterer. My editor, for example, might see me tweet about a movie I just saw and reply, "@trishussey I assume you're also working hard on your book." These people never let up.

Within your Twitter stream, this can be solved by following all the people your friends generally talk with, but you can't always do that. Facebook has recently tried to connect wall posts and Tweets using @ replies to a person's Twitter or Facebook profile. I don't know if this is going to reduce or increase confusion, but it is surely another sign of how users would like to connect as many services together into a web of information as possible.

Often I get comments on my Facebook wall about something I tweeted. This has both a positive and negative side. The positive side is the conversation there is easy to keep up with and understand; the negative is that it's only happening in Facebook so my Twitter-only followers have no idea it's taking place.

FriendFeed is one of the interesting places for Twitter inputs. Because FriendFeed can fully connect to other services, a comment left on a tweet in FriendFeed can also be posted to Twitter. It's the best of both worlds because you expand your conversation and additional readership of your tweets, but also the conversation doesn't just end there. In the reverse, Twitter is often my destination of choice for *sending* additional updates to. Each blog post I write is automatically posted to Twitter, as are my Posterous updates and my Blip.fm songs. Which then begs the question, as I hope you're asking yourself right now: Isn't Twitter enough? No, and here's why: Twitter archives stink.

Unfortunately, you have no idea how long any particular piece of information will stay in the Twitter archive and no idea how long a reference to you or one of your own tweets will stay. The reason, and double-edged sword that is Twitter, is that Twitter is growing so rapidly with new users and content being added at an astronomical rate, that the space to store it all runs out just as fast. At the time of writing, there is no fixed length of time Twitter archives go back to. I could say six months now, but, literally, tomorrow it could be four or five months. For this reason, Twitter is a great place for conversation, as great input for my lifestream and destination for my content, but I'm not counting on it as an archive of my content or conversations.

NOTE

I say this even though the founders of Twitter have assured users that Twitter is actually *keeping an archive of all tweets*, but what I still don't know is how I'll get to actually *use* that data in the future. Twitter has become a tool of historical record. The campaign and election of President Barack Obama, fires in Los Angeles, and both the Iranian and Afghan elections of 2009 are only recent examples of how world events were tracked, discussed, and shared around the world using Twitter. These are things we should preserve for future generations as part of history.

Flickr and Other Photo-Sharing Sites

I love taking pictures. In the 30 plus years I've been taking pictures (my first camera was a Polaroid One Step at age 9), I've taken tens, if not hundreds, of thousands of pictures. About 14,000 of those pictures over the past five years are on Flickr, and that number is constantly growing. I'm not alone in this kind of photo sharing, nor is Flickr alone in being a photo-sharing site. There are at least a half dozen that come to mind from SmugMug to Google's Picasa to Facebook itself, and those are only the relatively large ones. I post all my (public) pictures on Flickr to FriendFeed with additional viewing spaces on my blog as well.

Although looking at the pictures my friends share in shear awe and amazement is something I enjoy doing, it's when these pictures tie into an *event* that photo sharing really shines. You can't be at every conference and event, and even when you're there you miss things or just want to remember them. Browsing through the sum total of pictures with tweets, blog posts, and so on, gives context and the vibe of an event. When a major event occurs, like a moment of global history, it is often photo sites like Flickr and sites like TwitPic (where people post photos through Twitter) that bring these moments to the world. On January 15, 2009, U.S. Airways flight 1549 crashed into the icy Hudson River in New York City, and the first pictures and video of the miraculous landing and rescue came through Twitter and other social networks.

Although few, if any, of the pictures will ever have this impact on the world stage, pushing pictures (and video from YouTube) into your lifestream is one of those inputs that are universally enjoyed by all readers.

Harkening back to Chapter 5, "Creating a Personal Blog," I don't make *all* the pictures I post on Flickr public. Some are only for friends and family. These pictures are not in the stream that FriendFeed or my Blog pick up. Those are set to only pull from *public* pictures.

Your Blog(s)

This should be a no-brainer, right? Of course, your blog should be an input into your lifestream, right? I would say, yes. Your blog posts should be a part of your lifestream, but you might start contributing posts on other blogs or have more than one blog and start to wonder whether you might be clogging your lifestream with too much stuff.

Here's a good example of this from my own blogging. I contribute to the blog for a large Canadian electronics store. I'm one of a half dozen or so bloggers, so adding that entire blog to my lifestream, isn't really appropriate. Most

people feel that your lifestream should be limited to content that *you* create or share. Then there are two blogs of my own, plus ones that I contribute to for clients. Where's the right balance?

When you add a blog to a lifestream, you have all of its posts pushed in carte blanche. This is great when you are the only author, but a little confusing when you aren't. There is a great way to handle multi-author blogs and other blogs you contribute to: link sharing. When I write a post for a client's blog, I want to share not only my post, but also drive more traffic to my client's site, so I share the link through Twitter or Google Reader. Sharing a link through Twitter is as easy as copying the URL of the post and pasting it into the Twitter post area. Twitter automagically shortens the link for you, so you get more space for your actual Tweet. If the blog already tweets out new posts to a Twitter account, then I share (or re-tweet) it to my followers as well.

The other part of this is a situation where you can over share a post by linking too many services together. The following is an example:

- ▶ I post a link and short missive to Posterous.
- ▶ I have Posterous set to post to Twitter, one of my blogs, Tumblr, and FriendFeed.
- ▶ My blog also posts that item to Twitter and FriendFeed.
- ▶ FriendFeed picks up my Twitter feed as well.
- ▶ The end result is that the post shows up twice on Twitter, three times on FriendFeed, and on three blogs (Posterous, Tumblr, and my other blog)—all within moments of each other.

This is confusing, redundant, and probably annoying to my readers as well. This is why it's best to try to keep a handle on what service is posting and where. I have my blogs post to Twitter (personal and this book's blog) and Posterous to Twitter. FriendFeed picks up the two blogs, Posterous, and Twitter. The entire content of the post is only in one location, the spread through Twitter helps build traffic and interest in my blogs, and the consolidation through FriendFeed gives people an entire look of my total published blogs. Yes, there is duplication through Twitter, but because I still want my Twitter updates on FriendFeed, this small overlap is something I can live with.

There are ways to only share posts from a particular category or author, but I haven't had consistent success with doing that. The easiest course to follow is to just map out (draw if you have to) where content goes and keep only two duplicate posts on any one service.

YouTube and Other Videos

Like your pictures on Flickr, your videos on YouTube, viddler, and Vimeo should also be in your lifestream. Just as with a video blog, don't forget that having your videos in more than one place isn't a bad thing. Although you might think this is just for the video blogging set, all of us might put a video up from time to time. I suggest having your videos pulled into FriendFeed, and then include your video in a post to share on Twitter and elsewhere. As discussed in Chapter 8, "Video Blogging," your video posts have more weight if they are supported by a little text and explanation.

Videos (and podcasts, for that matter) are an interesting part of your lifestream because unlike other types of content, they almost demand attention right away. Videos just seem to call out, "Play me now—I'm really cool…," whereas posts, links, and pictures can be put off until later.

Hmm, maybe this means that if I want more attention, I should shoot more video.

Sharing from Your Feeds

Google Reader has long had a function where you can share items that you find interesting. It was this function, in my opinion, above all else that vaulted Google Reader into the lead of RSS readers. In fact you might argue that the post/item sharing in Google Reader was the first lifestreaming tool. By sharing your interests, the items that you find interesting, your friends can enhance their own feed reading— the wisdom of the crowd brought to information gathering.

As Google Reader has evolved, it has even expanded its Send to… options to include Twitter, Posterous, Tumblr, as well as that old favorite— email. One of the reasons I stick with using Google Reader as a solid RSS reader is the sharing features. It's like having my own set of minions finding cool stuff for me. Come on…who doesn't want minions?

More than minions, the more and more diverse the people you follow on Google Reader (like all of these services there is the following-follow model at play here), the more interesting things you are exposed to. You might learn and find out about people around the world as well as around the corner. It is this kind of richness that makes sharing and building a lifestream worthwhile.

If you'd like to subscribe to what I'm sharing through Google Reader, visit www.google.com/reader/shared/tris.hussey. I guarantee that it's a pretty eclectic mix of things from around the Internet, so you never know what you might happen upon.

Pulling It All Together

It started with Facebook. When you could add your pictures from Flickr then add your blog posts, Twitter updates to your Facebook status, then… You get the idea. Bloggers got to the point where trying to keep up with all the cool stuff their friends do online became a chore of its own. With so many services (social bookmarks, online photo albums, blogs, and shared items) your friends might participate in, it gets *intense* to say the least. This is where Facebook got the idea of *aggregating* the information together, and it was pretty popular. Soon after this, FriendFeed came onto the scene and offered a lot of the same things as Facebook, but with more services (and fewer of the Facebook annoyances). FriendFeed became the darling of the digirati, but didn't catch on with "mainstream" people like Twitter did. I think it was because FriendFeed could easily become a fire hose of information that blew away all but the more hard-core info warriors. Recently a newcomer, Cliqset, came onto the scene as an alternative to FriendFeed, but still based on its strengths as an aggregator. Undaunted, people are also creating WordPress plug-ins to give individual bloggers the capability to pull in their own lifestreamed content into their blogs. What is the best way for you? That's what this section is all about.

THE DUPLICATE CONTENT CONUNDRUM

My Posterous content is also on my blog and links to the Posterous posts on Delicious (a bookmark-sharing site), Identica (a microblogging site), and Twitter. What will search engines like Google do with all this duplicate content and isn't that bad for search engine optimization (SEO)?

Well it certainly isn't great, but if it's being accused of spamming that you're worried about, I think Google can see that if the content originates somewhere else and is just reposted, you're not trying to spam.

In truth it's going to depend on how much content and where it's going. A regular blogger like me has content everywhere, but Google knows that the central source is on my primary domain. This is also why I use subdomains when possible for this content. The caution here is not to use lifestreaming tools to spam the Internet with your content, but just make it more widely available (linking back to a central source).

NOTE

On Aug 10, 2009, Facebook bought FriendFeed. It was so sudden that it came as a complete surprise to the entire tech community. How this will all fall out is still up in the air, including how Facebook will or won't absorb FriendFeed. The upside has been a reemergence of discussion on the topic of lifestreams in general.

FriendFeed

When FriendFeed (www.friendfeed.com) came onto the scene, they offered a single, simple service: Tell us where you post all your stuff online and we'll create links to it all in one place for people to read (see Figure 10.5). Once

you have all *your* stuff here, go and check out the stuff from all your friends, too, and follow their lifestream as well. At first there was some resistance to the idea of pulling all your content together (even if it was just links to the content), but among the digirati the idea took off.

Setting up a FriendFeed account is very simple and a good example of how similar services work (I'll get there—I promise). When creating an account, and after the standard username (or Open ID) email confirmation routine, you start adding services. Because FriendFeed is only *pulling* existing content from services, you only have to give it your username (or URL) to get access to that content (sometimes you have to provide log-in credentials, too).

FIGURE 10.5

My inputs into FriendFeed aggregated.

Again, like the quick-posting blogs, Twitter and Facebook, to get something out of FriendFeed and other aggregators you need to find people to follow (see Figure 10.6). Like all social media, you can start with your email address book and find friends already there. From there, doing topic searches is a great way to find people with similar interests. As you follow people, they form your stream. The stream is the real-time flow of information from the people you follow. As the people you follow post to Twitter, Facebook, their blogs, and Flickr, those posts appear for you to like, comment, or spread around.

Sound overwhelming? Yes, it certainly can be. FriendFeed took the idea of aggregation and blurred it (a little) with quick-posting blogs but also adding the concept of groups or "rooms" that could be public or private and define affinities with the community. These rooms let you add content specifically to them, and it didn't even have to be your content (just like sharing from an RSS feed).

FriendFeed isn't the only aggregator out there, but it was the first one to get a real hold of the geekerati. Unfortunately for FriendFeed, mainstream users didn't take to it like Facebook or even Twitter. The end result was that FriendFeed became one of the playgrounds of the geekerati/digirati, which while not a bad thing, did result in a lot of FriendFeed comments (on items from popular people) getting way out of control. I think this intensity scared a lot of people off. Not to worry, with FriendFeed as a part of Facebook, I have a feeling things will be changing.

Conventional wisdom is that Facebook is going to use the best of FriendFeed (easily adding content without having to add a Facebook app to your profile) to make Facebook like a FriendFeed for everyone. The downside is that Facebook is still a "walled garden" where information goes *in*, but doesn't easily get back *out* to other places on the Internet, which has made room for newcomers like Cliqset to emerge.

FIGURE 10.6

The best of the day from the people I follow on FriendFeed.

Cliqset: The New Kid in Town

Just as nature abhors a vacuum, the innovators of the Internet adapt quickly to come out with new services and tools that build on what has come before. Cliqset, first made available in October 2009, is a brand-new player in the aggregator market (see Figure 10.7). It works and acts very much like FriendFeed with the idea of pulling your content into an aggregated lifestream for people to read. It does have a new twist that I think could give it some serious potential: You can choose to see or hide types of content with just the click of a mouse.

Looking at my Cliqset page, as in Figure 10.7, it looks pretty similar to FriendFeed. This makes those who use(d) FriendFeed and like(d) it comfortable with the interface and how it works.

The major complaint about FriendFeed was that it quickly became an information fire hose and it was pretty hard to slice the content into groups. For example, what if you only wanted to see the pictures that your friends were sharing or just links and Google Reader shared items? Cliqset saw this as their opportunity to differentiate themselves from other aggregators (see Figure 10.8).

FIGURE 10.7

My Cliqset profile page with some of my streams in view.

FIGURE 10.8

The people I follow on Cliqset, but only showing Google Reader shares and favorited tweets on Twitter.

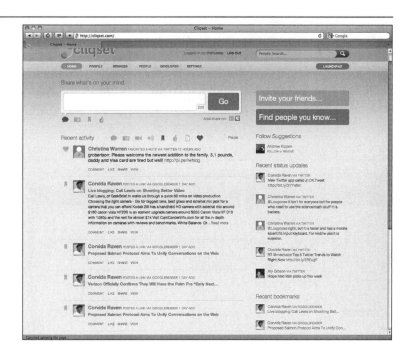

This is the kind of innovation that is going to be needed for lifestream aggregators to get any traction among mainstream users. Cliqset is too new to know if it will stand the test of time and beta testers, but as a refinement of lifestream aggregators, I think it is already a winner.

NOTE

You can follow me on Cliqset by creating an account, going to my profile page (cliqset.com/user/trishussey), and clicking Follow.

DIY Lifestreams

For the DIY set you might say, "Hey, FriendFeed was cool, but they were just scooped up by Facebook! I want my own setup!" Sure, no problem. The best option right now is to first set up a WordPress-based blog and use the Lifestream plug-in to add your content streams to it. Chapter 2, "Installing and Setting Up Your First Blog," examined how to buy a domain and set up a basic WordPress blog. The next step is to download and install the Lifestream plug-in from WordPress.org (http://wordpress.org/extend/plugins/lifestream/).

The Lifestream plug-in is simple to configure. Just click a service, enter the feed information, and save (see Figure 10.9).

Figure 10.10 shows the configuration needed to add Twitter to your new personal lifestream. Unless you have protected your Twitter updates, you won't need to enter your Twitter password. Clicking Add Feed is all it takes to add the feed into the stream.

The final step is to create a blog post or page (I suggest a page), give it a title, and insert *[lifestream]* in the body of the post. When you click publish, you have your own personal lifestream (see Figure 10.11).

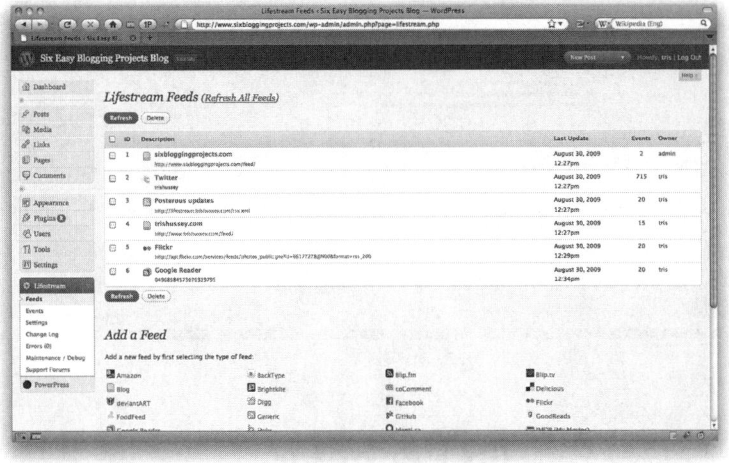

FIGURE 10.9
In the Lifestream plug-in configuration screen, click its icon to add a new service.

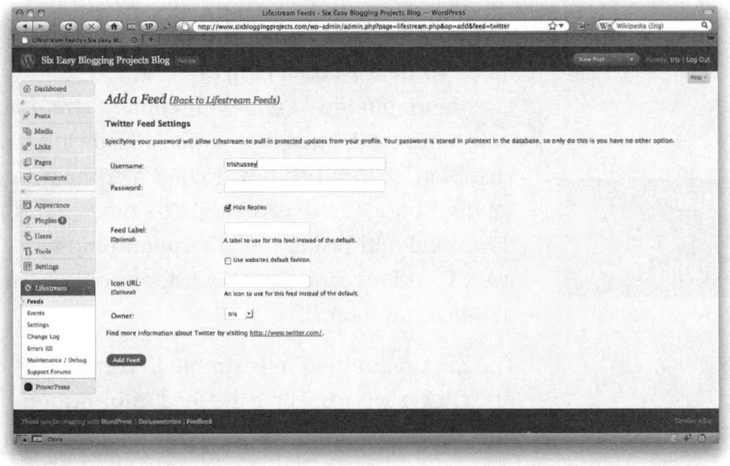

FIGURE 10.10
Adding my Twitter feed to the Lifestream plug-in.

FIGURE 10.11

Final product: my
lifestream on my
WordPress-based blog.

Is this as good as FriendFeed, and so on? Not really. These plug-ins make a nice list of things, but don't provide for comments, sharing, or "likes." However, if you're just looking for a list all the stuff you post, this should work just fine. Also, don't worry about replicated content here; these are just links to the originals (which is better for SEO).

If you're going to go hard core and install a whole stand-alone system, check out two open-source, free options: AmpliFeeder (Windows servers) and SweetCron (LAMP servers). Both of these servers are complete in terms of features, but you *do* have to set it up yourself, a topic that runs outside the scope of this book. Like

taking on a Drupal or WordPress MU install, this isn't something for the casual blogger. This is cranking the geek-o-meter to an eight, maybe nine.

All this begs the question, how much DIY is worth it in a niche dominated by services? Not much. If you want a great place to gather all your content, FriendFeed and Tumblr are excellent choices. If you would like a nice way to publish to several services at once, I think Posterous is a winner. I would reserve DIY options as an add-on to the lifestreams you are already doing. Although this is ironic for the chapter, it's certainly how most people are doing it right now.

The power of lifestreaming sites and applications are the connections to other sites and other users. Creating these yourself just isn't practical or feasible. You would end up, essentially, connecting to a *service* that connects you to other people using their own servers to set up lifestreaming. The bottom line for DIY is that it's great to add your stream to your site, but don't expect to have the full range of features you might have if you chose to use FriendFeed or Tumblr.

> **CAUTION**
>
> Once online, and made public, it's out there…forever. Even if you think you have deleted something, say a picture from Flickr or blog post, you haven't—there are copies made in caches around the Internet. This might not seem like a big deal, but when it comes to that "oops" moment (when the picture you wish you hadn't posted or the post you hadn't written), you have to remember that once something is on the Internet, it is always there somewhere.

The Comment Conundrum

Generating lots of great content is one thing, but what about when people have something to say about your content? They might leave a comment, favorite/like it, share it, or any other of the myriad ways content is built on and shared. Although this is great, it also presents a problem—how do you keep up with all the conversations about your content online? This is the problem that people started to face once updates and posts started posting on Twitter and Facebook and blogs. The systems didn't connect, so readers and authors alike weren't getting the breadth of the conversation going

on about the topic at hand. Something just had to be done. Of course, when something is in the hands of geeks, you know a solution can't be far off.

The Problem: Comments, Comments Everywhere!

Twitter replies, comments on FriendFeed, posts on your Facebook wall, comments on your original post are valuable and interesting, but they're also all over the place. This became the biggest challenge in trying to use and manage lifestreams. For example, my Twitter updates (tweets) are cross-posted to Facebook as my status updates. Not a big deal, right? The problem arises when the conversation is mostly on Twitter—people on Facebook can't see the whole conversation. Likewise if people comment on my status update on my Facebook wall, those comments aren't reflected in my Twitter stream. In fact, the systems are so disparate, I often have no idea what a Facebook wall comment is referring to until I go onto Facebook and look at my wall.

Similarly, comments on FriendFeedeed weren't reflected on my blog (or wherever the original source was) and vice versa. FriendFeed and other services tried to build some connectors so that comments on a Tweet would be cross-posted from FriendFeed to Twitter and comments on the original blog post would appear on FriendFeed (and vice versa). The gap there is that for these to work 100%, the commenters have to have Twitter and FriendFeed accounts (and myriad others) for everything to come together. That's not particularly realistic. Managing all these posts/comments and different plug-ins to connect your blog to all these comment systems was starting to get a little out of hand. So as FriendFeed started to take off with the early adopter crowd, a solution had to be found. We didn't have to wait very long.

The Solution: More Services!

What do you do when comments are seemingly everywhere and there is no connection among them? You build a system to connect them. At first FriendFeed let you post your comments there to be cross-posted on Twitter. This was especially important and helpful with Tweets posted on FriendFeed. Then Disqus (pronounced like "discuss") came into being. It was intended to connect all your comments into one place or system (see Figure 10.12).

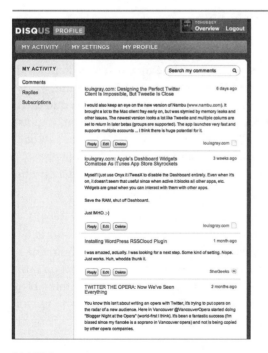

FIGURE 10.12
A few of my comments on other blogs picked up by Disqus.

Although Disqus has been successful at solving the problem of comments everywhere, it hasn't been perfect. To take advantage of Disqus, you have to sign up for it. Then you need to have it find all the places you comment, and so on. This, I've found, is hardly a foolproof or painless process. Of course that said, you should connect your comments to Disqus, FriendFeed, and all the other places you can. It is a truism of lifestreams and Web 2.0 (maybe 2.5 now) that there is rarely harm in making sure you connect up services together.

There is also a similar service called IntenseDebate from Automattic (the company behind WordPress.com), shown in Figure 10.13. I've found this service makes it easier to connect to various profiles, but I've also found that it is not as well supported beyond WordPress blogs.

The perfect solution for comment proliferation hasn't been created yet. Both Disqus and IntenseDebate have helped to pull comments together in their own ways, but they also divided the comment pools into two competing groups. I'm not sure if this is going to help or hurt in the long run, but for the moment, it's the best we have.

FIGURE 10.13
Recent comments gathered by IntenseDebate across several different blogs.

Summary

Lifestreaming is "the new black" online. The unbelievable amount of content people are generating, not just the geeks like me, is pretty amazing. To help bloggers keep up with people and topics they're interested in, the concept of "lifestreaming" was born.

Lifestreaming is connecting in one location all the various places you do things like write, post photos, save bookmarks, pick songs, and other social media activities.

Lifestreaming, for the time being, is dominated by services where you create an account, connect to the other services you use, and then choose if you are going to post to them (inputs) or pull them in (aggregation). Like the rest of social media, lifestreaming is all about sharing, connecting with friends, and following people who you find interesting.

There is a huge aspect of having followers, following, liking, and resharing as a part of lifestreams. For better or for worse, lifestreaming has started to make a huge impact on how bloggers consume content. A lifestreaming blog is really just finding the right services to use for inputs and aggregators.

CHAPTER 11

Making Money Through Your Blog

As a professional blogger, I'm often asked how I make money through my blogs. The answer, truthfully, has always been very simple: People pay me to write for them. This doesn't mean that I don't know about banner ads, Google Adsense, affiliate links, or optimizing my pages for them; it's just that I've always chosen not to use them too often. As the bonus chapter for this book, this is intended to be the capper; the final piece that you might want or need to give your blog an extra something. Okay fine—it also helps to pay the bills.

Where do you go from here? It's pretty simple. Money made through your blog comes from one of two places: Either selling space on your blog or selling your words to other people or blogs. As simplistic or crass as it might sound, that's what it all boils down to. Myself, I've chosen the latter. Lots of my friends have chosen the former. Some of my friends have chosen the former and have been very successful at it (*very* successful).

The easiest way to think of earning money from your blog is to break the ways into two areas: direct and indirect. The direct approach encompasses things like getting sponsorships, various writing gigs, syndication, and selling goods or services through your blog. Direct ways focus on you leveraging your talents to generate additional income. Indirect is selling or placing ads on your site. Indirect includes ads, affiliate links, and the sorts of things where you are supplying space on your site for someone else's ad, and taking a cut. This binary (and maybe arbitrary) way of organizing puts the focus on who is doing most of the work: you or someone else.

Nuts and Bolts of Making Money from Blogs

Whether you opt for the direct or indirect route, in general, attempting to make money from your blog isn't a terribly geeky exercise. However, there might be a little code pasting, plug-in installing, and maybe some theme tweaking to get it all together.

Now, if you're just going to be a professional blogger and get paid to write posts, the biggest thing to learn is how to write great content and deal with other blogging engines (than the one you are partial to). Although the idea of making money online is nothing new, the idea of making money through or by *blogging* is rather new. The reason isn't that blogs are some kind of magic website through which it takes a special set of skills to make money. It's because the ethos of blogging was supposed to be above the pettiness of "making money." Long-time blogger and social media maven, B. L. Ochman, (www.whatsnextblog.com) told me once, "Purists are rarely realists." Her advice then was in regards to character blogs, but it rings just as true for making money online as well. The bottom line is if you want to spend your time writing online all day, you either have to be independently wealthy, have a job where this is tolerated, have no job, or earn some kind of money from it. I chose the last option.

Making Money Directly

Because you know already that this route has been my bias for making money through my blog, I'm not going to pretend that I'm not biased in favor of this mode of income generation. That said, it isn't the most lucrative way to make money through your blog. These are active income streams, meaning you have to do something to get something. No do, no get. There are four basic ways to make money directly from your blog:

▸ Getting sponsors for your blog

▸ Syndicating your posts to other blogs

▸ Writing posts on other blogs

▸ Selling things directly on your blog

Each of these, of course, has their own pluses and minuses, but they each have one thing in common: You're in control. Let's start off with getting sponsorships.

Blog Sponsors

Sponsorships for blogs generally take a few forms. Often a hosting company gives a blogger free hosting in exchange for having a banner or mention like "Server space and bandwidth graciously provided by…." This is a passive sponsorship in that the hosting company isn't paying the blogger, rather the blogger just isn't paying for the hosting account either. Another example of this kind of passive sponsorship is a company covering a blogger's travel expenses to attend a conference. What I'd call "active" sponsorships are much less common because bloggers don't often just receive money like a grant. If a

blogger receives money from a company, it has been in exchange for advertising space on their blog or to write for the company's blog. Neither of these are really "sponsorships" then, are they?

Getting people to sponsor you or your blog often isn't as much something that directly brings money into your blog as it is a means to not have to pay for something you otherwise would. For example, soon after I started blogging, I started using the (now defunct) blogging platform Blogware, which was offered through resellers by Tucows.

Blogware was a great system, but it had a couple interesting quirks. One was the amount of disk space you were allocated (which wasn't much even for the time) and the other was that you had tightly controlled amounts of bandwidth allotted to your blog per month. This was how Tucows/Blogware allowed their resellers to make more money: selling their customers more disk space and bandwidth on demand. Hitting your disk space cap wasn't too big a problem. Sure it was inconvenient when it happened, but it generally wasn't a showstopper. Now running out of bandwidth? Yeah, that was a much bigger deal. When you ran out of bandwidth, your blog was turned off. Yes, rather inconvenient when you just wrote a killer post and it got some serious link love.

As I started to get more than a little attention on my blog, my friend who was a Tucows reseller had been kindly just giving me disk space and bandwidth as I needed it. However, this was costing him real money at the same time. I had an idea—why not ask Blogware/Tucows to sponsor my blog?

So I asked.

And they said yes.

This was the first big thing I "earned" as a blogger. I received access to software and such before, but this was something that I needed and wanted, something that was going to start costing me serious bucks in the near future. So I got unlimited bandwidth and disk space in exchange for mentioning Blogware and Tucows in the footer of my blog and talking about Blogware on my blog. It wasn't difficult to talk about Blogware because I was a big proponent of it back then (it was ahead of its time in many ways). There are two things to take away from this example: First, you don't know until you ask, and second, there are win-wins in business blogging.

TIP

Asking someone to sponsor you can be an intimidating thing to do. Get over it. Although you might run into a lot of rejections, you will *never* get a "yes" if you don't ask. At the end of the day, if the worst thing a person can tell you is "no," then you really haven't lost anything.

Nowadays, I tend to seek sponsorships to cover the costs of going to conferences. If I want to attend a conference where I'm not speaking, I offer a company to blog the sessions for them, giving them the always nice "My attendance and these posts are sponsored by…" line at the end of my posts. The direct win for the sponsor is more along the lines of being associated with a prominent blogger and "getting the scoop" at a conference.

There is a concern about sponsorships, however, which is that you as the blogger could be tainted by the sponsorship. The fear is that you won't say something bad about the sponsor or their product because they have sponsored you. This is a real, legitimate concern and something that all of us who have accepted sponsorship money or support have faced. The best way to handle this is to make it very clear who is backing you, so if there is any accusation of bias at least it's out in the open. In terms of conflicts of interest, the biggest problems between a blogger and her readers occur when it looks like the blogger has something to hide.

Additionally, there's a trust element between you and your readers that takes time to build. I've built up a reputation through many years of blogging that even if I'm given a free product or access to a product to try (like testing computers, laptops, phones, or printers), I'm going to give the straight story. I might love or hate the product. I might even pan it (politely), but privately give the company detailed feedback on the product so they can improve it. You can be honest without being hurtful. Sponsors appreciate this because they don't want tainted bloggers writing about their products. A blogger who is not trusted by his readers is useless to a sponsor because if people think a review is biased then it's a worthless review, no matter how glowing the praise. You can't *always love* the products you try. I don't love all the software or hardware I own. Ultimately, it's about balance. Few things are all good or all bad. I love my Mac, but sometimes it drives me nuts. I have received lots of free useful apps, but that doesn't mean I don't have constructive criticism about them.

The key to getting sponsorships is to be real, honest, valuable, and helpful to the sponsors. Along the way, you're going to have to prove to others that you can be unbiased, and if you receive sponsorship for something you disclose it. Beyond that there is only one other thing to remember: You don't know until you ask.

Writing Posts on Other Blogs

You might already have guessed that this is my preferred method for making money from my blogs. Before I had my first sponsorship, I was writing posts for other blogs. I was one of the first "professional bloggers," hired to contribute nothing but blog posts. My job was simple: Here is a blog on Topic A, write a post a day on it and we'll pay you x dollars. At the peak of my pro blogging I was *trying* to maintain close to twenty blogs. That meant reading hundreds, thousands maybe, of other people's blog posts to get source information, then write something interesting given the news of the day. If there was no news of the day I had to find a new angle on the topic that I thought might be interesting. This was hard work.

To give you an idea of what sorts of direct hire opportunities are out there, during my career as a professional blogger I've been part of the third largest blog network (b5media), been a partner in one of the first professional blogging agencies (Bloggers for Hire), and...completely burned out on blogging.

WHAT IF YOU REALLY DON'T LIKE IT? HANDLING PR PITCHES AND REVIEWS

Although bloggers often receive things to test, contrary to popular belief bloggers aren't showered with freebies galore (sorry). When you do receive something and are asked to review it, what do you do if you don't like it? What if you are getting email after email from a PR person asking you to review something that you aren't interested in?

Honesty and open communication are the best policies. If a PR company is dying for a stellar review and you just can't give it, be honest about it. If I've received something to test, and I know that I'm not going to give the most glowing review, I give my PR contact a little heads up and also additional feedback about my experience. Nine times out of ten, the PR people I've worked with, and developers themselves have appreciated my honest (and polite) feedback. Building a good rapport with companies is key to both their and your success. You can be both a critic and supporter of a company at the same time, and still be an asset to the company.

However, being bullied to write a great review or fearing to be cut off from early access is something that many bloggers will make public. PR companies are under unprecedented scrutiny, and potential clients don't want to see that a PR firm has been blackballed by bloggers for being unprofessional. Often overzealous PR people will try to get you to write *anything* about their client's product. If I'm not interested, I tell the person straight away. If I am interested, but it's a PC application (I have a Mac), I say that I have a Mac and if they offer a Mac version in the future I'd be happy to look at it.

PR people have a tough job and are under tremendous pressure to perform for their clients. Although this is no excuse for unprofessional behavior, a little communication goes a long way to keeping everyone happy.

FINDING BLOGGING GIGS

Although the notion of being a professional blogger isn't making headlines any more, that doesn't mean that you can't still become one. Keep an eye on the Problogger Job Board and Bloggers for Hire for potential gigs.

When you apply to blog for others, they are going to ask to see examples of your work. Don't worry if you haven't blogged on a particular topic before; the important thing is to have an established blog with a good track record of posts and using all the current social media tools. It's most important to show that you "get" the medium, not as much that you're an expert in a particular topic.

The key to getting a job writing for other people is showing that you not only can write well, but that you understand how blogging/social media works and how to research information on topics quickly. Really good professional bloggers don't have to be subject matter experts on everything, they just need to be able to find what the hot topics are, analyze what others are saying, and write some good commentary about it. Being able to quickly understand a topic enough to comment on it is one of the things that separates great pro-bloggers from just okay ones—that and being able to type at preternatural speeds.

Sure it was a lot of fun and I wouldn't be where I am now if I hadn't gone pro, but I also remember trying to get a day's quota in the meager 30 minutes I had left in the day (that set my 12 posts in 20 minutes record). Would I do it all over again? Totally. In fact, I still am. I still maintain my personal blog, company blog, and contribute 3–5 posts a week for a large Canadian consumer electronics chain's blog. That doesn't mean, though, that it's not a constant grind. It's important to keep a sense of balance in your life. I know, for example, that I can really only handle three blogs and still have a day job. For me, trying to do more leads to burnout. You might be able to do more. You might find you need to do less. It's all about figuring out what works for you.

If you want to make the jump to professional blogging full time (most pro-bloggers are part-time folks writing for a little extra spending money), you have to know how much you can write during a given day. Not just *write* but write good posts of about 200 words each, with links to sources and good tags for SEO. Believe me, the people who I know that do it full time work hard (and type fast).

If you want to make the jump to professional blogging full time (most pro-bloggers are part-time folks writing for a little extra spending money), you have to know how much you can write during a given day.

The first step to going pro is to write and maintain a blog for several months and show that you have solid knowledge *and* passion for your topic. It doesn't matter if your blog is on computers or coin collecting, you have to write good, smart stuff to go pro.

Think you're up for the challenge? Start writing.

Selling Things Online

This is the most obvious way for you to make money from your blog, if you already have a business or hobby where you sell things. You can sell e-books, music, jewelry, cards, clothing—whatever it is that you want or can sell. The most interesting part of these blogs is that they span almost all the kinds of blogs in this book. They are personal, business, and portfolio blogs all at once. If you're thinking about selling things online and you haven't done this already, read through those chapters as well as this one. Selling things that you have made or created yourself are so tied to you that you have to be passionate about them. You must present them in the best light possible and you have a big challenge.

If you're selling something physical or at least semi-tangible (like e-books or downloads or music), you're going to need an eCommerce/shopping cart system to make this happen. If you've gone the DIY route already, you could install an eCommerce engine via Fantastico or install one of the several WordPress plug-ins for eCommerce (or whatever blog engine you chose—if you chose to ignore my advice completely and chose something *other than* WordPress), but frankly there are times when it's best to leave things to the pros. This is one of those times.

Whether you use eBay (www.ebay.com), Etsy (www.etsy.com) (for arts and crafts—see Figure 11.1), or PayPal (www.paypal.com) to sell, let them do the heavy lifting. They have made setting up an online store drop-dead simple. I've gone both routes and would much rather spend my time doing almost anything than trying to configure and get a shopping cart working on my own. Etsy and eBay have all the hard stuff worked out. They accept payments, they can handle downloads, they handle receipts, and they take a cut. I think the cut is worth it (usually just a few percent of the purchase price) given how unfun it is to set up a cart, get transactions working (and secured), and handle all the other easily forgotten details.

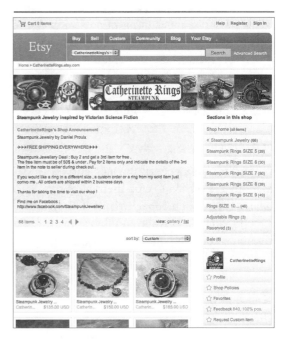

FIGURE 11.1

Etsy storefront for Canadian jewelry maker Catherinette Rings.

Earning money directly from your blog is very satisfying. You've worked hard, you've created something that other people value, and you've earned something for it. It gives me a thrill to see the check or deposit as payment for something I've written. On the other hand, it is nice to earn money just by having my site or blog *be there* and not have to do anything day to day with it. That's the world of *indirect* earning.

Making Money Indirectly

As mentioned earlier in the chapter, "indirect" means that once a particular system is set up, it runs itself. It doesn't mean that there isn't work to be done to optimize or tweak; just that left to their own devices, the money comes in from your blog. If you frequent the Internet, which is 40 years old in 2009, you've seen one of the most dominant forms of passive income generation: Google Adsense. There is, however, more to life than Adsense or simple banner ads. You can make money by suggesting products and services to people (affiliate programs) or you can sell space on your blog directly or many other schemes for leveraging the traffic and audience of your blog for monetary gain.

When sites like Geocites, Blogger, and other free services started to crop up (ones that offered a "free homepage/website"), they were supported by the ads surrounding your content. People, by and large, accepted this because they were getting a free website and the ads surrounding their content were paying for this privilege. Once people started having their own sites, sites they built and controlled themselves, they wanted to earn their own money from their content. And thus, the ad network was born.

> **CAUTION**
>
> There is a really big "but…" in this discussion of ads and ad networks. If you use WordPress.com, you cannot put ads on your site. That is a violation of the Terms Of Service (TOS), and it will get your blog deleted with little or no warning. The folks at Automattic (the company that runs WordPress.com) are very firm on this. They do not want WP.com to become like other services infested with spam blogs. So, no ads. You've been warned.

Let's get back to AdSense. Google didn't invent the ad network, nor did they really invent a new idea with text-based contextual ads; they just found a way to do it really well. Because Google Adsense is one of the drop-dead easiest ways to make money from your blog, let's cover it first. I am, however, convinced that making money with Adsense is somewhat of a dark art. Some people manage to make *lots and lots* of money with Adsense and others, pretty much nothing. With that caveat in place, let's continue…

Google Adsense

If you pick nearly any random scattering of blogs, you will see ads on them and chances are those ads are Google Adsense. The reason for this is simple: Putting Adsense ads on your site or blog is easy. The amount of configuring you have to do for just a basic set of ads to show up is pretty minimal. The payouts on Adsense, well, they can be great or they can be non-existent. The key with Adsense is putting the ads in the right place *and* writing good content that triggers good ads. Adsense ads are *contextual* ads. If you have ever used Google to search the Web (and, who hasn't?), you've seen this in action. For example, a search on google.ca for "Vancouver tours" yields the results shown in Figure 11.2 (at the time I wrote this).

FIGURE 11.2

Example Google.ca search showing the Adsense ads.

HOW TO WRITE FOR CONTEXTUAL ADS

In addition to some template tricks that I discuss later, the following are some tips for how to write for contextual ads:

▶ Use descriptive titles like "Best MP3 player for joggers and runners." Titles with strong keywords not only help Google index your post better, but help to match the content to appropriate ads as well.

▶ Break out the thesaurus. There is more than one way to skin a cat and there is more than one way to describe a product, idea, or service. Within the framework of your natural writing style, work in as many variations of the idea as you can.

▶ Use descriptive tags and categories. Using categories like "News" or "Products" are as good as "Music News" or "Audio recording products." Don't make readers, search engines, or Adsense guess what the topic is about.

Companies pay (bid, actually) to have their ads appear on pages like this one. The companies at the top, just above the search results, paid the most to have their ad there. For a time, it was a little hard to see on Google where the "sponsored links" stopped and the results started because the ads didn't look much different from the regular search results. They were relevant to what you were looking for, right? Sure, but people *paid* to have them there, on top, for you to see and hopefully click on *before* you saw the actual search results. That's the power of textual ads, which is the same as you might see in Gmail and the same as you *want* to appear on your blog. If you're writing about fly fishing in Idaho, then having ads for crocheted tea cozy patterns isn't going to match your audience.

Getting started with Adsense is just a form field away.

1. Go to www.google.com/adsense and log in with your Google ID (see Figure 11.3).

2. If your account *doesn't* have an Adsense account associated with it, you'll see a page like the one shown in Figure 11.4.

3. Fill out the required information and click the Submit Information button at the bottom of the page.

FIGURE 11.3

Logging into Adsense.

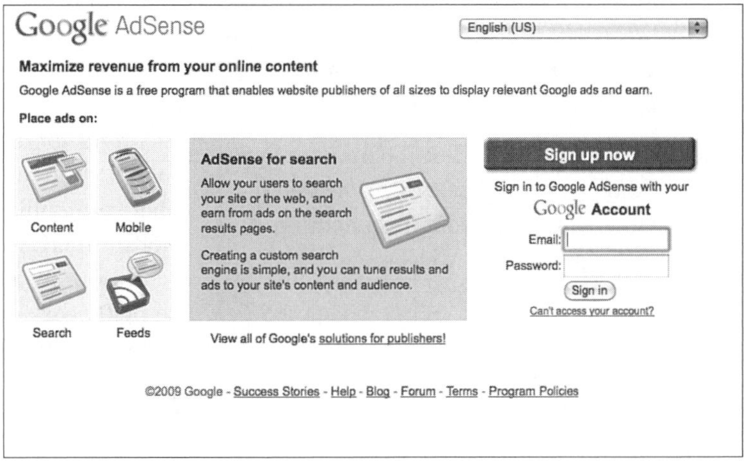

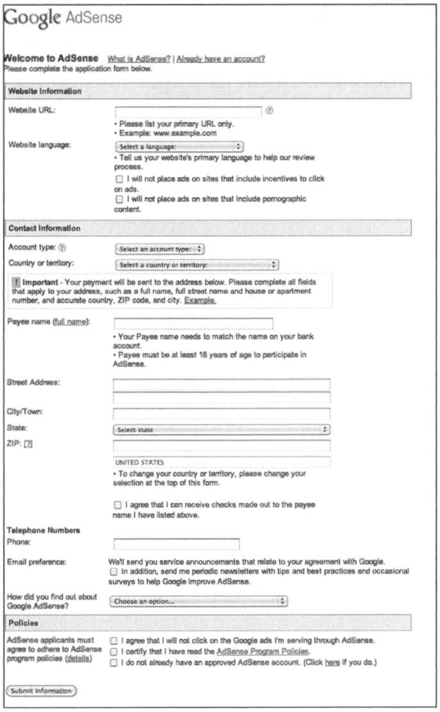

FIGURE 11.4

Application for Adsense.

After your account is approved (essentially, everyone is), you'll be in a position to start adding code to your blog and tweaking the ads. I'll save that for more of a nuts-and-bolts part of the chapter (just a few more pages, I promise). The important thing to keep in mind is that Adsense isn't the be all and end all of ad networks/ad programs. Sure, Google is proud of the system they built (and rightfully so, in my opinion), but it is neither perfect nor the best solution for everyone.

How much can you earn from AdSense? Essentially, it can range from nothing to thousands of dollars a month. You earn money from AdSense when someone clicks on an ad on your site. Generally that single click pays you a few cents. No, that's not very much, but AdSense is a game of scale and numbers. To make money with AdSense, you need enough people to click on the ads to earn money. To do this, you also have to *attract* a lot of people to your site to click on the ads in the first place. Generally, people put AdSense on their blogs when they reach a certain level of traffic per day (between 400 to 1,000 page views a day), a level that represents a sort of critical mass of potential people to click on the ads.

What else is there? Okay, how about if you got a 5% kickback from a store every time you sent someone there and they bought something? Sounds pretty good, huh? Welcome to the world of affiliate programs.

Affiliate Programs

You like to recommend products to your friends, right? Generally when you tell a friend to go to a certain store or buy a brand of detergent, you don't get anything out of it (maybe the thanks of your friend). So, what if your recommendations earned you 5% of what your friends spent? Yeah, that's cool, eh? That is how affiliate programs work.

You sign up for a program, often a service you use already, and they give you a special link or coupon code that you give to friends. It doesn't stop there—you can sign up for affiliate programs for all sorts of products and services. In fact, affiliate marketing is big business. There are millions of affiliate marketers in North America bringing in billions of dollars a year. How do you get started? That happens to be pretty easy—you start out at affiliate marketing how to blogs, of course!

The easiest way to start with affiliate programs is to go with the folks you know. Let's use Amazon as an example (see Figure 11.5). The Amazon Associates program has been around for years and it lets you recommend books, movies, music, and other things (depending on where you live) and get a small percentage of any sales made as a result of traffic coming from your site.

FIGURE 11.5
Amazon Associates homepage.

Amazon's program might not be the most lucrative one of its kind, but people certainly trust buying from Amazon and trust is important when you're using affiliate programs on your blog. Part of the hesitation people have with buying things is whether or not it's a good deal. When a friend recommends something to you, you feel more confident in your purchase (unless it's coming from crazy Uncle Louie). Now, if you have an affiliate link or offer on your blog, this is a statement that you recommend this product to your friends. Whether it is buying a domain name or web hosting or premium WordPress themes, your readers are clicking and making a purchasing decision based on *your* recommendation. This brings me to the next important part of affiliate links: disclosure.

What if your friend told you to buy a computer from a particular store and you later learned that your friend got a kickback from the store for every referral? How would that color your perception of your purchase and your friend? Exactly. You might start wondering whether you really got the best deal and what other kickbacks your friend is getting.

Using "kickback" instead of "commission" or "percentage of the sale" colors how you perceived the questions, but the idea is still the same. When you receive a commission from the sale of a product, you are recommending one product over another partially based on money. Sure, you might really love the product and would recommend it regardless. The commission is just a bonus, right? But how do your readers know that? They don't until you tell them.

Using "kick-back" instead of "commission" or "percentage of the sale" colors how you perceived the questions, but the idea is still the same. When you receive a commission from the sale of a product, you are recommending one product over another partially based on money.

Although Amazon links and Google Adsense are clearly ads, other affiliate links might not be so obvious. It's good practice to disclose an affiliate link. Just saying that tells the reader, "I like this product, but you should also know that I'm getting a commission for you buying it."

One of the hallmarks of blogging has been its culture of transparency and openness, which means that it is *expected* that you *will* disclose affiliate links and other similar things (like when I receive a free product for review that I get to keep). Not disclosing this information can get you in hot water. It's happened to even prominent bloggers (who should know better), so don't feel alone, but it's best to just avoid the whole issue and let people know.

How do you choose what to sign on with? Start with the things you already use. For example, I like to use NameCheap.com to register my domains and they recently came out with an affiliate program. Because I like them a lot and have recommended them in the past, I'll probably join the program. Same goes with hosts I use (and like), and the themes from StudioPress and DIY Themes. There are affiliate programs for almost everything. I think there are even affiliate programs for referring affiliate programs!

When you decide to join a program, do a little Google research to see whether complaints or other issues come up. If you know people who are already in the program, ask them about it. After you sign up, you get special codes and links to use and information on how to track your sales. These vary from program to program. It's also important to read the fine print of the program, such as how long after clicking a link (referral) does a purchase count towards your commission. For example, someone might click on a link from your blog so they can get a look at a hard drive on Amazon, but not buy it until a couple days later. Will you still get credit for the sale? In Amazon's case, most likely yes, because it stores a cookie on the person's machine. Other affiliate programs might not work that way so it's important to check. Sometimes the devil is in the details.

All caution aside, I have several friends who earn enough money for "a nice dinner out" to "quit my job and do this full time" in affiliate marketing. The important thing is to do some research, ask around, and try the program for a little while.

Other Ad Networks

There are more than just Google and Amazon out there in the online ad world. There are many other ad networks that you can join. Sometimes they are specific to a niche or product and sometimes they are more general, just like the banners you see all over the Internet.

Like Adsense or affiliate programs, it's important to look into these programs carefully and see what kinds of ads they run. Are there restrictions on how many ads you can have

per page? Are there restrictions on *your* content? Can you put restrictions on *their* ads? (Having an adult-dating site ad appearing on a children's clothing blog isn't really a good thing.) All of these are questions to investigate.

Once you get to the point of signing up, check the sites that also carry the ads. You don't want to fall into "the wrong crowd" on the Internet (spammers and other malcontents). I'm always hesitant to give blanket "Oh, these folks are great…" endorsements because sometimes ad networks have done things like generate codes for you to embed in your site that Google doesn't like (for search indexing). Another thing to keep in mind is that Google in particular doesn't allow competing ad networks on your site. If the ads you're inserting in addition to Google's are also contextual (the ads change to relate to the content on the page), Google will kick you out of Adsense. Believe me, you don't want to be on Google's bad side.

Final Word on Ads

If you've looked at any of my blogs while you've been reading this book, you will notice that I don't have ads on my sites. I debate about putting Google Adsense back on my blogs (they used to be there), but I generally don't bother. Don't take this to mean that I'm anti-ads or anti-affiliate programs. I've tried them and have chosen to earn money through my writing or sponsorships, not through ads. I think this is one of the hallmarks for what blogging is—the freedom and ability to choose how you want to run your blog. Of course, you are able to buy this book through Amazon on my blogs; I think that's a pretty understandable thing, though.

Pulling It Together on Your Blog

Have you picked your ad program of choice yet? Adsense? Amazon Associates or another affiliate program? Regardless of which one you choose, there is one unifying factor among all of them—they require you to paste various HTML codes into your blog to make them work. You also need to make sure that the ads are placed so that people will see *and* click them (an unclicked ad is just a pretty picture, after all). At the same time, they must not be obtrusive and interfere with your readers' ability to digest your content.

Once you have ads on your blog, you need to track how well the ads are doing, which means doing a little more Web stats work than your average blogger. Not to worry, like all the things in this book, none of this is rocket science. If you can copy and paste, you can do all of it with ease and aplomb.

Ad Codes 101

Let's talk ad codes for a second (maybe more than a second). The first thing to know is which ad codes can (or should) go into your posts and which are best kept in the header, footer, and sidebars. (If you're really cool, you might be able to sneak them in between posts, but that's some pretty tricky hand coding.) The second thing to know is that ad code tends to be fragile. Yes, it can break.

Fragile code isn't that different than that antique vase your Aunt Minnie gave you. Jostle it around and the results might be unpleasant. Functionally, what this means is that when you're pasting code, into your posts

especially, you need to do it in HTML mode *not* the visual editor. Visual editors make life *easy* by keeping messy HTML code away from you, but this also means that if you paste HTML code *into* a visual editor it will essentially neuter the code and make it just funny looking text.

Because you might not like working in HTML mode, some kind souls have made plug-ins where you can paste the code into a separate window and let it inject the code into your post without breaking the code or messing up the rest of the editor. For the sake of teaching you, let's pretend you're going to do this the old-fashioned way and just paste things into posts.

In the realm of pasteable ad code, Google Adsense is not one that works very well within posts. In order to get Adsense code *within* your posts, you have to edit your blog's template to have code in by default, not as you write the post. Affiliate links and Amazon code is generally okay to paste into posts as long as you remember to stay in HTML mode once you paste the code in until you hit Publish.

> **NOTE**
>
> I might be considered overly cautious for this approach of staying in HTML mode once I've pasted code into my post (until I publish it), but it's better to be safe than sorry.

HTML mode is important for any ad code that has the magic word "Javascript" in it. I'll caution now, that sometimes Javascript is stripped out when you publish a post. This is a safety and security precaution and doesn't mean that you did anything wrong. If you can see a preview of the ad *before* you copy and paste the code, you can usually tell right away if you're going to need to switch into HTML mode to paste it in.

The biggest clue is if there are images or any kind of dynamic interaction going on. These are codes that have some cool things going on, and cool things often don't like being pasted in visual mode. Affiliate links are often the easiest to handle because often the link is just a normal link with extra codes in it. Even Amazon has basic, simple, boring HTML link URLs that you don't have to switch into HTML mode to use.

Thus far I've been talking about pasting ads into your *posts*, but what if you want to just have them in the header, footer, or sides of your blog? This is a much easier proposition, believe me. Let's start with sidebars. In WordPress and other widgetized blog templates, you can create "text widgets," which are simply containers for HTML code to go into the sidebars of your blog. Yep, they are built to take HTML code and actually use it instead of breaking it. Figure 11.6 shows how pasting some HTML code into a sidebar widget looks.

It probably looks pretty geeky and difficult, but it really isn't. The process goes like the following:

1. Copy the code from Google, Amazon, or whomever your ad provider is.

2. Go to the administration portion of your blog where you are able to add widgets to your theme (for WordPress, it's the Appearance button and the Widgets link).

3. Create a text widget (In WordPress, this means dragging a text widget to one of the sidebar areas) and paste the code into it.

4. Save the widget.

5. Enjoy, because you're done.

In fact, if you've been tricking out your blog already, you already have been playing around with pasting things into sidebar widgets. It doesn't matter if it's a Flickr widget or an Amazon ad for the Deal of the Day, because they all work the same way. This is another nice thing about blogs—nothing is really *that* hard. Mostly it's copying, pasting, pointing, and clicking. You can do a lot with just a few clicks and some practice.

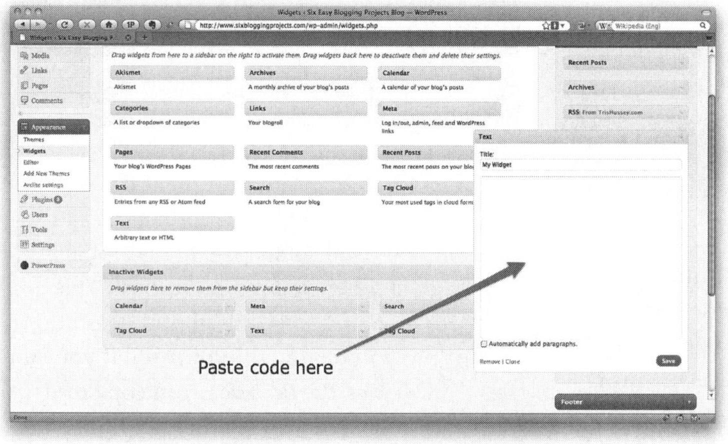

FIGURE 11.6

Pasting code into a WordPress widget.

Paste code here

Putting ads into the header and footer is a little trickier. This usually involves editing your theme's template (the header and footer files, in fact) and understanding a little more about how your blog works. Again, it's not hard, but something about which you should do a little more investigating before trying out. The trickiest part of editing a template file is making sure you don't accidentally delete something important. There are in-depth tutorials on how to do this for all major blog platforms; a little Googling is all it takes to find them. I said "usually" because more and more theme developers are providing header and footer widgets where you can include text widgets for ads. This makes creating dynamic-looking sites very simple and probably reduces the number of email the developers get from people who have broken their themes.

Hopefully when you're done inserting ads into your blog, it doesn't look like a mess, but if it does, let's hit that as the next step—optimizing your template for ad performance and esthetics.

Optimizing Your Blog's Template

You've seen sites and blogs that look so cluttered and chock full of ads that it looks like… well, you know. Let's try to avoid that happening to you, okay? The best way to do this is to be judicious with your ad placements. You don't need to fill every space in your sidebar, in your header, in your footer, within posts, and between posts with ads.

I'm of the "less is more" school of thought when it comes to ads. I might put an Adsense block at the top of the sidebar, and then an Amazon banner in the sidebar (one of the tall ones). If I'm writing about a particular item or book, I will include an affiliate link within the

post. My style is not to beat people over the head with ads, but to offer ads in a way that they seem natural and part of the design.

Design is only part of the optimization strategy here. The other part is bringing visitors to your blog who are *looking* for what you have ads for. Yep, you guessed it; this falls under the wonderful world of Search Engine Optimization (SEO) again. If you've been following along with my SEO recommendations thus far, you're well ahead of the game here. For Adsense in particular, you can add these magic codes around your content (again, this is a template editing thing):

```
<!-- google_ad_section_start -->
<!-- google_ad_section_end -->
```

And then add this variation around the side bar:

```
<!-- google_ad_section_start(weight=ignore)
➡ -->
<!-- google_ad_section_end -->
```

These codes focus the Google Adsense codes so when the magic of Google is picking which ad to display, it only considers content within the first set and *excludes* content within the second set. This helps to make your Adsense ads more relevant to the content you've written on that page. This section and the one following on tracking performance, dovetail into one another.

As you get a solid baseline of data (I suggest a month at least), you can see how well the ads are performing. If something isn't working, then you can adjust your ads. Maybe the colors blend in too much into the page. Maybe they aren't big enough. Maybe they aren't relevant enough. The more you look into the data, the more you can decide whether or not a particular kind of ad or affiliate program is working for you.

Tracking Your Performance

Earlier in the book I touched on web stats or analytics for bloggers. One of the fullest featured ones for seeing how Google Adsense is working on your blog is, yep, Google Analytics, which Chapter 2, "Installing and Setting Up Your First Blog," examines in more depth. Coupled together, you get great insight into how well the ads on your blog are targeted and whether people are clicking on them. Now, for other programs, you'll need to rely on the data you get from Amazon or another ad provider. Look for the following:

▸ Number of impressions (the number of times an ad was displayed on your site over all)

▸ Number of clicks

▸ Number of conversions

From these data, you can discern a lot. For Google Adsense, which are pay-per-click (PPC) ads, you only have to worry about the first two metrics. Look at the ratio of clicks to impressions; this is your click-through rate (CTR). It won't be terribly high—maybe a few percent. That's fine; it's normal. You get paid just for someone clicking on an Adsense ad.

For ads like Amazon, just clicking isn't enough; they have to click *and* buy for you to get paid. These are pay-per-conversion ads. Looking is step one, clicking is step two, and buying is step three. If you aren't offering something that people will be interested in if they do click, then you might think about either offering

something else or picking a different affiliate program. Something that looks good on the ad, but then when people get to the site doesn't seem quite right, isn't going to earn you any money.

If you're selling your posts or syndicating them your metrics are a little different. If you are paid a flat fee regardless of how the post does trafficwise that's easy, but if you have a fee plus performance bonus, you need the metrics on readership, search engine traffic, and referrers to know if you're hitting the mark or not.

If you've gone the route of sponsorships, you might be asked by your sponsor for your monthly traffic, the number of impressions that ad has had, and the number of clicks. These data aren't hard to gather and give, if you plan for them. Before you get into offering banner ads yourself, look into ad management plug-ins for your blog engine. These save you time, energy, and hassle by not only managing your inventory, but also providing you with the metrics you need to gauge ad performance.

Obviously if you're selling goods yourself, you'll have all the data you need. You'll know the traffic on your site and you'll know exactly how much you've sold. You also are keeping everything in-house so there isn't as much pressure to report the data to someone else!

Figure 11.7 shows you what keywords people use to reach one of my blogs. In addition to the traffic data, knowing these keywords helps you determine whether your posts are tuned for search engines correctly. If you are selling things directly, this is critical to you getting customers. If you just have general ads on your site, these data can help you tune your offerings to your visitors better.

FIGURE 11.7

Keywords on Manscaping411.com.

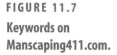

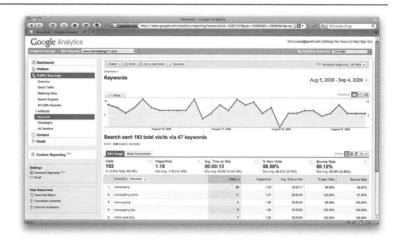

Summary

Making money through your blog is both easy and hard at the same time. It's easy in that there are lots of different ways to do it, and it's hard in that you have to choose which one is right for you and then actually make money utilizing it. You can make money directly by selling your own ad space (sponsorships), writing for other people or syndicating your content, or selling some good or service that you offer (and explain on the blog). You can also make money *indirectly* through various ad networks and programs. Altogether it is possible, but difficult, to earn a nice amount of money from your work. The key for you as a blogger is to offer the right kinds of ads, have the right kinds of metrics, and keep the layout optimized so your readers can enjoy the content *and* have your ads still perform well.

Index

G

FREE Online Edition

Your purchase of **Create Your Own Blog** includes access to a free online edition for 45 days through the Safari Books Online subscription service. Nearly every Sams book is available online through Safari Books Online, along with more than 5,000 other technical books and videos from publishers such as Addison-Wesley Professional, Cisco Press, Exam Cram, IBM Press, O'Reilly, Prentice Hall, and Que.

SAFARI BOOKS ONLINE allows you to search for a specific answer, cut and paste code, download chapters, and stay current with emerging technologies.

Activate your FREE Online Edition at
www.informit.com/safarifree

> **STEP 1:** Enter the coupon code: XWUQFDB.

> **STEP 2:** New Safari users, complete the brief registration form.
> Safari subscribers, just log in.

If you have difficulty registering on Safari or accessing the online edition, please e-mail customer-service@safaribooksonline.com

Safari
Books Online

Addison Wesley • Adobe Press • ALPHA • Cisco Press • FT Press FINANCIAL TIMES • IBM Press • lynda.com • Microsoft Press • New Riders

O'REILLY • Peachpit Press • PRENTICE • QUE • Redbooks • SAS Publishing • Sun microsystems • Wharton School Publishing • WILEY

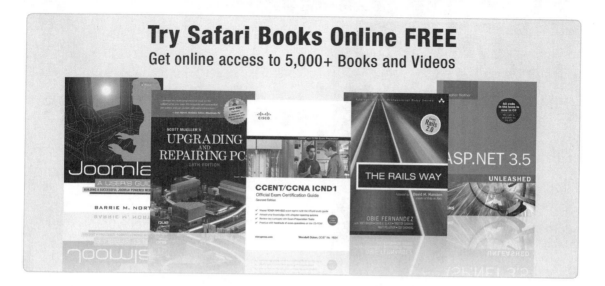